THE PLAN OF NASHVILLE

Avenues to a Great City

The Plan of Nashville.
(Drawing, 2003: NCDC)

THE PLAN OF NASHVILLE

Avenues to a Great City

NASHVILLE CIVIC DESIGN CENTER

Mark Schimmenti • Gary Gaston

Randal Hutcheson • Raven Hardison • Andrea Gaffney

Written and Edited by
Christine Kreyling

NASHVILLE • VANDERBILT UNIVERSITY PRESS • 2005

© 2005 Nashville Civic Design Center
Published by Vanderbilt University Press
All rights reserved
First Edition 2005

This book is printed on acid-free paper.
Manufactured in Manitoba, Canada.
Design by Deborah Hightower Brewington,
Vanderbilt University Creative Services

Library of Congress Cataloging-in-Publication Data

Kreyling, Christine, 1949–
The plan of Nashville : avenues to a great city /
written and edited by Christine Kreyling;
produced by the Nashville Civic Design Center.
        p. cm.
        Includes index.
ISBN 0-8265-1458-8 (cloth : alk. paper)
ISBN 0-8265-1459-6 (pbk. : alk. paper)
        1. City planning—Tennessee—Nashville. 2. Urban
        transportation policy—Tennessee—Nashville.
        3. Nashville (Tenn.)—Social conditions.
I. Nashville Civic Design Center. II. Title.
HT168.N3K74 2004
307.1'216'0976855—dc22
                                        2004022129

To Martin S. Roberts, Jr.

The Nashville Civic Design Center gratefully acknowledges those who have supported the process and the printing of the Plan of Nashville.

The Frist Foundation

The Memorial Foundation

Judy and Steve Turner

Judy and Joe Barker

Vanderbilt University and Vanderbilt University Press

Earl Swensson Associates

Orion Building Corporation

Tuck Hinton Architects

We also wish to acknowledge the following sponsors:

American Constructors, Inc.

Barge Waggoner Sumner & Cannon

BB&T Insurance Services, Inc.

Colliers Turley Martin Tucker

Everton Oglesby Architects

First Tennessee

Giarratana Development, LLC

Gresham Smith & Partners

Hawkins Partners

Samuel H. Howard

Littlejohn Engineering Associates

Marketstreet Equities Company

R. C. Mathews Contractor

I. C. Thomasson Associates

Village Real Estate Services

Waller Lansden Dortch & Davis

Continuing support for the Nashville Civic Design Center is provided by the Metropolitan Government of Nashville and Davidson County, the Metropolitan Development and Housing Agency, and the University of Tennessee College of Architecture and Design.

CONTENTS

FOREWORD

A CITY BEGINS with its people. Usually, there are just a few of them, arriving over the hills or the prairie, or following the circuitous route of a river. Always, they are seeking something that includes the freedom to live the lives of which they dream. If they have made the right choices for the right reasons others follow and then a city grows. Generation after generation, more choices are made and change follows. In all of this we are not all involved or affected. But there is a critical period in the life and ultimate success of a city when an overwhelming majority come to believe that they are the identity of their city; and they define the place in which they live; and the city is their shared responsibility.

I believe this is the beginning of Nashville's Century because the people of Nashville now acknowledge and accept their responsibility, and the Plan of Nashville is important and very tangible proof of this truth. The Plan is the result of two years of committee meetings, discussion groups, and neighborhood forums. Literally hundreds of Nashvillians have participated in the process, sharing their hopes and dreams; their concerns for their city, as it is right now and as it might grow to be; their vision of a future that preserves and perfects the place they have come to call home.

In the Plan of Nashville, the people of Nashville—as they face the new century—have written down their dreams, and even drawn pictures of what their city might be. It is a city that will continue to be a better and brighter place, for the generations that come after us, for our own children and their children, and for families who have yet to know that this is the place they will choose to make their own.

If it is used rightly over the decades, the Plan of Nashville will serve as a point of reference. Sometimes, Nashville will go back to it and discover that goals have been met or dreams have been neglected. At other times, it may serve as an intriguing reminder that, as time passes, the details of the dream may find different directions, even while the ideals remain the same. This Plan, then, is a gift to the people who will build our city's future, but it is also a gift we give to ourselves. I am personally grateful to every Nashvillian who has helped make it happen.

Mayor Bill Purcell

PREFACE

The Plan of Nashville is a vision. It is also a process in which members of the Nashville design community and the community at-large volunteered many hours to collaborate on a vision for their city. This book is the physical manifestation of their ideas and efforts.

The Plan is produced by the Nashville Civic Design Center, a nonprofit organization dedicated to elevating the quality of Nashville's built environment and promoting public participation in the creation of a more beautiful and functional city for all. Working with government officials, regional planning groups, neighborhood organizations, businesses and residents, the Design Center leads community discussions and workshops and conducts research to further understanding of the relationship between a society and its built environment. The Design Center is not a regulatory institution. Rather, it advocates and supports the highest standards for contemporary community design.

A partnership of the University of Tennessee, Vanderbilt University, the Metropolitan Development and Housing Agency (MDHA), the government of Metropolitan Nashville and Davidson County, and the private sector, the Civic Design Center was established in December 2000 and opened its doors in June 2001. The center does not charge for its assistance, nor replicate the work of existing government agencies, nor provide services that compete with design professionals. The Design Center is an outgrowth of the Nashville Urban Design Forum, founded in 1995 to present monthly public discussions of urban design issues. The Design Center's Board of Directors, as well as its sponsors, represent a cross-section of Nashville and Davidson County's professions and perspectives.

While the majority of the Design Center's resources are directed toward working with individuals, neighborhoods, and organizations that apply for its assistance, the Design Center also initiates independent research aimed at developing a collective vision for the city. The center's first design director, Mark Schimmenti, an architecture and planning professor with the University of Tennessee's College of Architecture and Design, urged the Board of Directors to consider a project to bring together many levels of the Nashville community—from design professionals to neighbors—to capture and document their collective vision for downtown and the surrounding neighborhoods. The board agreed, and the project came to be known as the Plan of Nashville.

The Plan was initiated in 2002 under the leadership of Seab Tuck, then president of the Design Center's board. Subsequent board president Jeff Ockerman and the Executive Committee have provided additional leadership and support. Seab has continued to serve as the board's liaison with the Plan, facilitating and coordinating what became a very ambitious and complex effort. Both a cheerleader and a task master, he has been one of the most important driving forces behind this project.

The process for developing the Plan of Nashville was initially sponsored by the Frist and Memorial Foundations. These foundations have been steadfast in their support of the Design Center; without them we could not have conducted the many meetings and community workshops that served to capture and document the collective vision.

Of all the individuals who came together to make the Plan a reality, it is imperative that we acknowledge first the staff of the Nashville Civic Design Center: Design Director Mark Schimmenti; Associate Design Director Gary Gaston; design interns Andrea Gaffney and Raven Hardison; and interns Blythe Bailey, Chris Barber, Brian Bobel, Michelle Bowen, Isabel Call, Matthew T. Champion, Brian Christens, Daniel Cooper, Ellen Dill, Matt Gregg, Jason Hill, Margaret Martin Holleman, Ben Palmquist, Amanda Posch, Astrid Schoonhoven, and Nekya Young. Each faced serious challenges, crushing deadlines, major frustrations, and tedious tasks with diligence and dedication. And although executive director John Houghton departed midway, his initial philosophical and organizational guidance of the Plan had impact throughout the process. Finally, Gary Gaston, in particular, is to be commended for his dedication, discipline, and hard work.

We very much appreciate the role that Mayor Bill Purcell played in establishing the Design Center, and for the continuing support he has provided to the center and the Plan, as well as the emphasis he has placed on the importance of the neighborhood, an emphasis that the Design Center and Plan also endorse. With the mayor's blessing, Metro government staff members Randal Hutcheson, David Koellein, and Judy Steele made major contributions to the process and publication of the Plan. Randy in particular, with his arduous research into the history of planning in Nashville, served as one of the backbones of this book.

The University of Tennessee's College of Architecture and Design, under deans Marleen Davis and Jan Simek, has supplied faculty and students who have served as a major resource for this Plan. Metro government, through MDHA, has provided ongoing support for the Design Center, which has been critical to our success.

Throughout the project, the Design Center engaged many volunteers who gave their time, energy, and professional expertise to develop the Plan. Too numerous to list here, they are all specifically recognized in the section that delineates the process for the Plan of Nashville (see "Citizen Planners: Documenting the Process," pages 229–42).

Upon completion of all the community meetings and the consolidation of historical research, we began preparing to shape the results into a publication. We knew that there was only one person, Christine Kreyling, who had the knowledge and skills to take the mountains of information and opinions, maps and diagrams, and produce a text that would prove valuable to the professional as well as the interested Nashvillian. We thank her for doing a remarkable job.

Many of the ideas presented in this book are supported by statements written by local and national experts in planning and design; we thank them for their willingness to share their words and ideas.

The illustrations in this book were produced in large part by the Design Center staff. But we must also applaud the graphic work of Ken Henley, Corey Little, Frank Orr, Jerry Fawcett, and Susan Barbera for making this a more beautiful and visually compelling Plan. Special thanks also go to Omari Green, a student at the Nashville School of the Arts, who provided graphic assistance at each and every workshop.

Vanderbilt University has supported the Design Center from its inception; the institution's role in the Plan of Nashville book has been equally unfaltering. Vice Chancellor Mike Schoenfeld offered the talents of Vanderbilt Creative Services in the persons of Assistant Vice Chancellor Judy Orr and senior graphic designer Deborah Hightower Brewington, copy editor Donna B. Smith, and photographers Neil Brake and Daniel Dubois. Likewise, our publisher Michael Ames, director of Vanderbilt University Press, along with Dariel Mayer, production manager, guided us through the book process.

When we were ready to print, Steve and Judy Turner, Judy and Joe Barker, Orion Building Corporation, Earl Swensson Architects, and Tuck Hinton Architects generously supplied the funds to assure that the Plan would find its way into the hands of many.

We have tried to acknowledge the broad base of citizen support for the Plan of Nashville by listing participants on the end papers of this book. If a name is missing or misspelled, it is because we were unable to decipher a signature on a sign-in sheet; for this we apologize.

There are a number of organizations and individuals who deserve special mention. The Nashville Downtown Partnership, under Steve Gibson and later Tom Turner, organized and paid for more than one activity that supported the Plan. The Adventure Science Center, Armistead Barkley Inc., Holy Name Church, the Magness Potter Center, MDHA, the Metro Parks and Recreation Department, the Metro Planning Department, the Nashville Convention Center, the Nashville Cultural Arts Project, the State of Tennessee, and the Vanderbilt University Law School all donated space for the community meetings.

Colleagues who assisted with research include Ann Roberts and her staff at the Metro Historical Commission, as well as the staffs of the Nashville Room of the Nashville Public Library, Metro Archives, MDHA, the Tennessee State Library and Archives, and the Tennessee State Museum. Sandra Duncan and the staff of the Metro Arts Commission ensured that public art forms a vital component of the Plan. At an early stage in this publication, Christine Kreyling sought and received editorial advice from Christine Bradley, Don Doyle, John Egerton, and Harvey Sperling. The book's review committee—Rick Bernhardt, Marleen Davis, Kim Hawkins, and Seab Tuck—also provided valuable organizational suggestions. Former Metro planning director Robert Paslay supplied unique historical insights. Keel Hunt advised on implementation. Jeanne Stevens and Bob Murphy were available for consultation on transportation issues. None of these individuals is responsible for the content of this book—nor for any inadvertent errors—but they all helped to deepen the level of knowledge contained within these pages.

In closing, the Plan of Nashville is dedicated to the memory of Martin Roberts. Martin loved the built environment and truly worked for the betterment of our community through that belief. As a founding board member of the Nashville Civic Design Center he was an adamant supporter of the Plan of Nashville and of utilizing a community-based process to arrive at a unified vision.

Unfortunately Martin did not live long enough to hold this book in his hands or to see what the vision would be. But his example gave all involved the strength of mind and love of Nashville to persist in their best work. It is to Martin Roberts that we dedicate this vision.

David Minnigan
President, Board of Directors
Nashville Civic Design Center

Shelby Street Pedestrian
Bridge at night.

(Photograph, 2004: Frederic Schwartz
Architects, Dave Anderson)

"The sustainable
city—a human
event, not a
sculpture."

Hillel Schocken,
"The Sustainable City"
(2003)

INTRODUCTION

CITIES ARE MADE, not born. A metropolis or town doesn't grow spontaneously, like weeds in a lawn. A city is a willed artifact, embodying the evolving intent of the people who live in it as they react to specific conditions: geography and topography, climate and technology, demographics and economics, history and politics.

This evolving intent may be read in three dimensions. A society projects its concept of the good life in the largest of its public works—its metropolitan form, as constituted in its architecture and landscape architecture, streets and boulevards, parks and plazas. And nowhere is it more evident how good —or not so good—is the life of a city than in its urban core. Those of us who admire Boston or San Francisco, Charleston or Savannah—and feel concern about St. Louis or Houston—

have in mind the central city, not the suburbs.

The Plan of Nashville is the latest record of the evolving intent of the citizens of Nashville. The Plan was orchestrated by the Nashville Civic Design Center, founded in 2000 as a non-profit dedicated to the practice of urban design. This design discipline, which integrates streets and buildings, land use and transportation, is a new approach for Nashville.

Also new is the territory encompassed by the Plan and the process that produced it. Since Nashville became Metro in 1963, there have been more than one hundred plans that have dealt with some aspect of the central city. Most of these plans were developed by Metro departments and their consultants—or by private developers hoping for government subsidies—and were constrained by politics and patronage.

We've had plans to take advantage of federal funding, such as windfalls for interstates and urban renewal. We've had plans as prelude to a big development—the Gateway Plan for the city-owned land around the Arena campus—or as a response to disgruntled property owners complaining about struggling businesses—the Downtown Access and Traffic Plan. Some plans came in reaction to specific problems: what to do about a Church Street at rock bottom, or a Fifth Avenue with great buildings and few tenants.

The Plan of Nashville is painted on a broader canvas, and with a broader brush. The canvas is the city center and the first-ring neighborhoods. It is the first plan for downtown that is not bound by the inner loop of the interstate since 1963, when the loop existed only on paper. The Plan departs from the island concept to

From Nowhere to Somewhere

The cultural memory of what many of our cities once were has followed their physical fabric into oblivion. In the 1990s, a downtown with little sign of human presence and endless stretches of blank, lifeless walls once placed Nashville firmly among these lost cities. Everywhere, one could see the signs of Nashville's eroded identity. Urban renewal had converted a whole set of neighborhoods adjoining downtown into an asteroid belt of surface parking. The country-music nightclub district ran barely two blocks on Broadway and the street itself had the unpleasant and desolate character found in many failing "main streets" in the era of American suburbia. Even the Ryman Auditorium was locked up in mothballs.

A walk from the Vanderbilt campus across the river to Five Points in East Nashville is comparable in distance to a stroll in central Paris from Gare St-Lazare to the Luxembourg Gardens. The difference is that the journey in Paris is rewarding to the spirit every step of the way, whereas the journey in Nashville takes you through moonscapes of urban desolation, deserts of parking lots, demoralizing walls of submerged and elevated freeway and past desultory one-story industrial and commercial bunkers—for which there is not enough Prozac in the world to mitigate the psycho-spiritual punishment.

So why shouldn't Nashville want to be as good as Paris? This is a fraught question, especially in Nashville, which as the Country Music Capital of America is held hostage by the crippling popular notion that country life is the only acceptable manner of living and the highest expression of democracy and decency. Hence we get suburbia, which has been the attempt to deliver that idea materially to the masses. The result is a sordid, puerile cartoon of country life, not real places but consumer products devoid of both natural and civic amenities.

However, I returned to Nashville in 2002 and found a city on the brink of a substantial rebirth. After years of civic self-destruction and inertia, Nashvillians saw that the city wasn't growing very well, believed Nashville should be a beautiful city, and were trying to be intelligent about how to make it so.

"Nashville is a city that is no longer afraid to admit it made mistakes," Mark Schimmenti, the design director of the new Nashville Civic Design Center, told me. And, as the conversion of the failing Church Street Mall into a proud, grand library demonstrates, Nashville is a city that's not afraid to begin to correct them either.

This time I got excited about being in Nashville. It has only been in the last fifty years that the idea of the city fell into utter disrepute among the American public. Everywhere I go now I detect a yearning for the kind of urban excitement that the 'burbs just haven't been able to deliver, even in the best malls (if such oxymorons exist). The knowledge for how to accomplish this urban revival is now institutionalized in the civic leadership of Nashville, a city once known as the Athens of the South.

Nashville has begun to make important steps to recover its lost "cultural memory" by turning towards the city again and away from the myths of suburban life.

James Howard Kunstler
Author of The Geography of Nowhere, Home from Nowhere, *and* The City in Mind

Excerpted from an essay that appeared in Metropolis *(February 2003).*

consider more organic and historic boundaries, and emphasizes the links between the surrounding neighborhoods and the core. The time frame is also expansive; this is a fifty-year vision, not a quick fix.

The planning brush was wielded by the more than eight hundred people who participated in the Plan process. Nashville offers many instances of good intentions and tax dollars producing developments that later necessitate even more tax dollars for replanning and reconstruction. The public housing projects that the Nashville Housing Authority built and that the Metro Development and Housing Agency is now demolishing, and the downtown shopping mall that was bulldozed for the public library are but two examples. These are manifestations of top-down planning that have proven, over the long haul, to be unsuccessful in solving the problems they were designed to address.

The staff of the Civic Design Center decided on a grassroots approach because their goal was to enable the citizens of Nashville to realize the choices before us, what directions we want to take and what tools will help us get there. Participants in a series of community workshops set forth the issues, the positives and negatives presented by history and existing conditions, and then described how they wanted the city to look and work in the future. Local planners, architects, landscape architects, preservationists, and public artists took this communal vision and, utilizing basic principles of urban design, turned it into the Plan.

The purpose of the Plan is not to engender massive new public expenditures, but to channel expenditures that are bound to be made anyway by government and private developers. The Plan presents a vision of greatness that can encourage outside interests to invest in the city and enable the local community to measure the worth of individual projects against the collective good.

For example, say someone wants to build a skyscraper on a parking lot that the Plan has designated for a park, or a civic building, or a sightline to a major monument. By comparing proposal with Plan, Nashvillians can see not just the present gain but the future lost. From the published Plan, potential investors are able to see, not just what the city is, but what it wants to be.

Ultimately, the Plan will help Nashville re-imagine itself as an urban entity. As John Houghton, then NCDC executive director, pointed out in a 2002 interview with the *Nashville Scene*, "If you study the rhetoric about Nashville ever since the consolidation of Nashville and Davidson County, we talk about Metro Nashville, about the CBD [central business district], about individual neighborhoods. We seem to have lost the ability to think about the city of Nashville, even though it's still out there." This Plan thinks about the city, within both its regional and local contexts.

Nashville began when land speculators decided that a site that combined river access with game to hunt and a long growing season was a good investment. The founders' intent to rationalize a wilderness is evident in the city's first town plan: a grid of one-acre lots with four acres reserved for a public square on the bluffs overlooking the Cumberland.

From this grid Nashvillians have cultivated a network of spoke and ring roads, lined with neighborhoods and subdivisions, strip malls and big boxes—everything from a Hillsboro Village to a Cool Springs. Today we are sprawling beyond the horizon all the way to the Highland Rim, and the question is whether the center that begot all this will hold.

Downtown Nashville has made great strides since the days of boarded-up storefronts and winos passed out in planters. But land use is still too restricted to 8-to-5 offices and special events. And shaky tourism along with a stagnant office market have made us more conscious of the vulnerability of the central city. A basic tenet of the Plan is that for the central city to hold its place in civic life, we must rebuild it the old-fashioned way, with a mixture of residences and retail, offices and entertainment, schools and civic spaces.

In the two hundred and more years of its existence, Nashville has evolved through many self-proclaimed and actual identities: trading post, Athens of the West-then-South, Union Army supply depot, engine of the New South, Powder City, Minneapolis of the South, Wall Street of the South, Music City USA. In this Plan, Nashville is the City of Neighborhoods. This does not imply, however, a city in pieces. The Plan establishes the neighborhood as the basic building block of the city, but places equal emphasis on the mortar between the blocks— the streets that form a network of connectivity and are the principal public spaces of our community.

Other themes in the Plan:

- Understanding the history of Nashville's built environment is crucial to planning for the future. It is only by knowing the hows and whys of the past that we can build on existing strengths and mitigate weaknesses.
- The Industrial Revolution is long gone; land uses established to feed the revolution are very much outdated. Thus the Cumberland River, no longer a major avenue of commerce, is re-imagined as an amenity for new neighborhoods that grow to public parks along its banks.
- Our current transportation infrastructure is dysfunctional and hostile to urban form. The Plan distinguishes among the purposes of specific street and road types, as well as between modes for trade and personal transportation. The Plan then presents a long-range vision for a more balanced system that serves pedestrians and bicyclists as well as cars, and does not sacrifice the long-term welfare of downtown and the traditional neighborhoods to short-term gains in motoring speed for commuters in the far-flung suburbs and long-distance travelers.

- Even before the automobile enabled us to sprawl, densities in Nashville never reached the degree of compactness of the northeast's urban neighborhoods. The strategy for new infill on the many vacant or underutilized parcels of land, therefore, relies on a low- or mid-rise model rather than high-rise towers.
- The public school is an important component of the successful neighborhood. For downtown to become a viable one, its residents must have access to an elementary school as well as the existing Hume-Fogg High School.
- Nashville's topography offers fine sightlines, but past city planners have done little to protect or enhance them. The Plan maps the best view corridors of the city and presents ways to enhance them.
- The key is remembering people. If what we build connects to human needs—for beauty, for social engagement, for work, for recreation—then we will create a city that is a satisfying experience for all its citizens.

"Design gives form to value," writes architecture critic Robert Campbell.[1] The Plan of Nashville, like the plans before it, explicitly states and implicitly reflects what the makers of plans intend to have worth and meaning. And this Plan, like all plans, is an historical artifact; it does not stand in isolation but is in part a reaction to previous values and intentions that no longer seem germane to current conditions.

But the primary value embedded in the Plan of Nashville is that of urban form itself. The Plan is rooted in the belief that human beings can reach their maximum potential as social animals dwelling in a community. This is a departure for Nashville, which has always vibrated uneasily between the commercial and industrial creed of the North and the agrarian creed of the South, and for America as a whole.

Historically, Americans as a society have distrusted cities. That is in part because of the nature of the continent as "discovered" by white Europeans—what F. Scott Fitzgerald calls the "fresh green breast of the new world"—and in part because of the timing of its colonization, when the Romantic philosophy that contends that a human being is at his or her best when closest to nature dominated Western thought.

The result has been a culture that views the city as a necessary evil. For every Benjamin

Franklin, who saw the interdependence of urban life as the tool of progress, we have had many more Thomas Jeffersons, whose ideal was not the city on the hill but the big house in solitary splendor on its little mountain.

The anti-urban tide, however, is turning in this nation. Perhaps because most of us now live in the metropolis, we recognize the need to make it more livable. Or perhaps we have come to realize, if unconsciously, that the city is not a place of confinement but a locus of liberation.

HISTORY

"The disadvantage of men not knowing the past is that they do not know the present. History is a hill or high point of vantage, from alone which men see the town in which they live or the age in which they are living."

G. K. Chesterton,
"On St. George Revived,"
All I Survey
(1933)

NASHVILLE PAST AND PRESENT

THE FIRST KNOWN photograph of Nashville is of the public square. This is fitting, for it is the public square that is the point of vantage for Nashville's history in three dimensions.

It was with the square that the settlers from North Carolina first began to apply an enduring shape to the land they claimed. That shape was supplied by surveyor Thomas Molloy, who in 1784, before Tennessee was even a state, platted a village of one-acre lots, with four acres reserved for a civic square on the bluffs above the Cumberland River near Fort Nashborough. Molloy laid his lines as a grid running up and down and across hills and valleys with no regard for topography—obvious progenitors of the downtown street pattern of today.

The sole offspring of Fort Nashborough, on the other hand, is a small representation of the 1780 fort that was constructed by the Daughters of the American Revolution in the 1930s and functions as a theater in which pioneer life is reenacted for school children and tourists. The original stockade had no real progeny because it was a defensive gesture, a holding pattern to be used until its inhabitants felt safe to venture out and begin to turn earth into property.

But Molloy's four acres are still where blocks coalesce into town. From them we can look out in space and back in time to see Nashville as it has been formed and re-formed for more than two hundred years.

The Shape of the Land

Nashville is at the center of a web of often-competing influences. The city lies between the Appalachian mountains and the Mississippi River, between the states of the North and the Deep South. This midway geography predicated the contradictory cultural pulls—the Scotch-Irish homogeneity of East Tennessee and the black/white dichotomy of the delta country to the west, the commercial and industrial impulses of the North and the agrarian ethos of the South—to which the region has responded.

Before Nashville began, the land on which the city rests was a hunting ground for Native Americans, who tracked the animals drawn to the salt lick and sulphur spring that lay just east of the site of the Bicentennial Mall near what is now Fourth Avenue North. Today the Lick Branch stream courses twenty-five feet beneath the Mall, flowing into the Cumberland River through a massive, brick-lined culvert.

Nashville lies in the Central Basin of Middle

> "History is all explained by geography."
>
> Robert Penn Warren,
> *Writers at Work: First Series* (1958)

The topography of Nashville, with high points highlighted in orange and floodplains highlighted in green. Note the locations of the historic creeks that once flowed through downtown. (Diagram over map, 2003: NCDC, Andrea Gaffney)

Tennessee, which is inscribed by the Highland Rim, a horseshoe of ridges gouged by narrow river valleys that opens to the south. The watershed within the Rim is what made the Basin a garden. Leaching from crevices, bubbling up from springs and tumbling over limestone shelves, the waters traced a filigree of streams and rivers in the Basin's limestone bed and delivered silt to the depression, in which grew cane and grasses and forests. When a handful of French trappers and traders arrived in the eighteenth century, the Basin was a land traversed by all but owned by none.

Permanent settlement depended on the domestication of the land—the chopping of trees for the building of shelter, the clearing of fields for the grazing of livestock and the raising of crops. And that required the social building blocks of families, families intent on making homesteads and towns, establishing institutions of government and education.

The domesticators set out from the Watauga settlement in North Carolina in 1779. Land speculator Richard Henderson sponsored their expeditions as a means of securing his personal land purchases in what would become Middle Tennessee. Separate parties traveled to the site of what is now Nashville via land and water. James Robertson and his band drove their livestock along a four-hundred-mile overland route and arrived on Christmas Day, walking the final legs of their journey, legend has it, across a frozen Cumberland River. John Donelson led thirty-three boats, ferrying more men, women, children (including his daughter Rachel, the future Mrs. Andrew Jackson), and free Negroes and slaves, as well as household furnishings and seed for crops, in a tortuous thousand-mile journey down the Holston and Tennessee Rivers, then up the Ohio and Cumberland Rivers, to join Robertson's group on April 24, 1780. The settlement they made was Nashborough—changed to Nashville in 1784 to rid the town in the new nation of all taint of England.

Within the Basin, the principal river is the Cumberland, which scours a serpentine path through the city. It was the river that was the initial lifeline to the rest of the world, connecting Nashville to the Ohio, Tennessee, and Mississippi Rivers—and beyond.

The chain of hills or knobs that encircles the city shaped the underlying structure of Nashville's historic pikes and railroad tracks, which follow the paths of least resistance first traveled by bison and the natives who hunted them.

The bed of limestone on which Nashville rests for many years inhibited the development of comprehensive water and sewer lines—the city still had fifty thousand septic tanks in 1963—which precipitated the custom of large lots in much of the city. And the historically swampy areas of town—Sulphur Dell north of the

Capitol and Black Bottom south of Broadway—have traditionally been problematic for development. In Molloy's survey, the acreage around the salt lick and spring was set aside for common use, perhaps because this land had more value as a natural resource than if subdivided.

What the first settlers found to work in the Central Basin was rich agricultural land, where the Highland Rim buffered crops and livestock from the downrush of arctic air from Canada, while catching the surge of warm, moist air from the Gulf to the south. This temperate climate, with its not-too-long hot summers, limited the region's ability to go the way of the Deep South into a one-crop economy, with its vast slave work force—Andrew Jackson himself lost several cotton crops to early frosts—and established a tradition of economic diversity that endures today.

But that diversity would come later. The primary—and most lucrative—economic activity on the frontier was speculation in land.[1]

Using the Land

Platting turns land into real estate. And a grid system is the most practical method of parceling, offering simplicity of surveying and recording and the capability of being repeated and extended indefinitely.[2] The grid as the first step in settlement planning is thus ubiquitous both geographically and chronologically. Orthogonality is also a symbol of human power, freezing spatial structure in an obviously manmade, whether hierarchical or egalitarian, configuration. There are no straight lines in nature.

Nashville's original settlers hazarded the considerable perils of westward migration because they were seeking the wealth to be had from land as real estate. James Robertson, for example, had lived among the Cherokee as agent for North Carolina and Virginia. "He could have claimed land anywhere on this first Indian bor-

der, land sufficient for a farmer or a planter," writes Anita Shafer Goodstein in her history of early Nashville. "Obviously, he sought not just this but rather land in quantities large enough to create capital, to speculate with, lands that could be turned into the basis of position for himself and his children."[3] By 1787 Robertson had title to 33,000 acres, much of it his fee for locating land purchases for absentee speculators.

Many of the original settlers, however, "died without ever gaining title to a piece of ground," historian John Egerton points out. Those who stayed and survived, or the heirs of those killed in the Indian fighting, were guaranteed 640 acres when North Carolina organized Davidson County as a political unit in 1784. Similar grants were made to soldiers for service in the Revolutionary War. But war, whether with the British or the Native Americans, was hazardous duty. "At considerably less risk were the ones who came later," Egerton writes; "they may not have been as diverse or self-sufficient or as courageous a group as their predecessors, but they had more political power, more influence, and more money to begin with—and they got the land."[4]

The parcels they got were delineated by the National Land Survey of 1785, although in North Carolina—from whence Tennessee sprang—the division practiced by the survey was common from the start. An initiative championed by Thomas Jefferson, the National Survey regulated two-thirds of the United States territory and determined the size and placement of many towns. The survey gridded the territory into "townships" of six square miles, and then into thirty-six sections, each measuring one square mile or 640 acres. Some of these sections were then broken into more manageable halves and quarters.

This national open grid, explains urban historian Spiro Kostof, "is predicated on a

1714 Frenchman Charles Charleveille opens a trading post north of French Lick Creek (also called Lick Branch), flowing near a natural salt lick and sulphur spring, near what is now Jefferson Street, to conduct business with Chickasaw, Cherokee, Choctaw, and Creek tribes that use the area as a hunting ground.

1768 First survey of land near Lick Branch by Thomas Hutchins.

1769 Timothy Demonbreun arrives at the French Lick and establishes a trading operation; legend has it that he occasionally took refuge in a cave in a limestone bluff along the Cumberland River that is today visible from Shelby Bottoms.

1779 On Christmas Day, James Robertson crosses the frozen Cumberland River with fellow settlers, pack horses, sheep, and cattle to establish a settlement at the French Lick.

1780 On April 24, the party led by John Donelson—including free Negroes and slaves—concludes its thousand-mile river journey to Fort Nashborough, named after North Carolina Revolutionary War General Francis Nash.

1784 North Carolina legislature creates Davidson County; the name of its largest settlement changes from Nashborough to Nashville.

• Surveyor Thomas Molloy draws original plat for the town: two hundred one-acre lots with four acres reserved for a public square on the bluffs overlooking the river. The square's initial civic architecture is punitive: a one-story log jail with a whipping post and pillory out front, paid for by the sale of the lots.

• Nashville's first physician, Dr. James White, hits town. According to a memoir by Felix Robertson, son of founder James, White was given to "occasional sprees of drinking," when he would dress up in buckskin and march through the streets with a gourd of whiskey, compelling all whom he met to drink with him.

1786 Davidson Academy founded by Reverend Thomas Craighead, a Presbyterian minister, at a site on Gallatin Road that is now the location of Spring Hill Cemetery. The academy is subsequently chartered as Cumberland College in 1806, later becomes the University of Nashville, and eventually fathers Peabody College.

1787 Real estate assessed and taxed at one dollar per acre.

1789 Methodists erect the public square's first architecture in solid masonry, a stone church which also serves as courthouse and public meeting place until the first courthouse is built in 1802.

1794 Wagon road established between Nashville and Knoxville.

• Robert Renfro, an enterprising and quasi-independent slave, receives a license to sell whiskey at "Black Bob's Tavern" on the public square. Andrew Jackson and other men of prominence patronize his tavern and rooming house. In 1813, perhaps because of too much imbibing, Jackson and six other men wielding guns, knives, swords, and sticks engage in a bloody fight in the square; the future president is shot in the shoulder and almost bleeds to death.

1796 Tennessee admitted to the Union.

1804 State authorizes turnpike construction. Like many initiatives of the state legislature, however, the authorization does not include a funding mechanism. It is only in 1834 that bonds are issued for radial turnpikes to Gallatin, Franklin, Columbia, Murfreesboro, and Shelbyville; the turnpikes are completed in 1842.

1806 Nashville incorporated as a town.

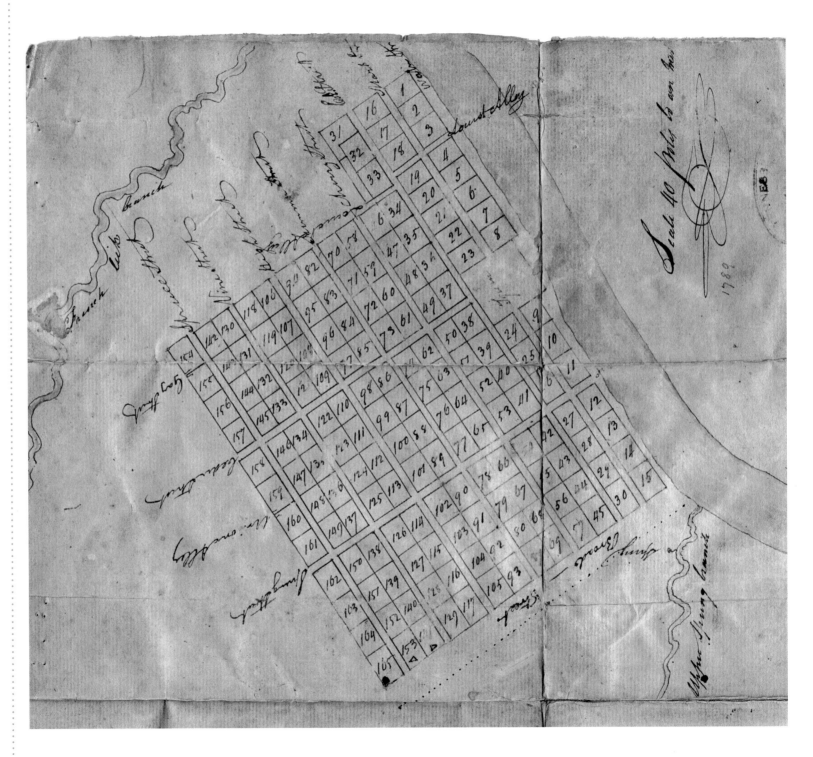

capitalist economy and the conversion of land to a commodity to be bought and sold on the open market. The grid is left unbounded or unlimited so it can be extended whenever there is the promise of fast and substantial profit. In this state of affairs, the grid becomes an easy, swift way to standardize vast land operations by businessmen involved in the purchase and sale of land."[5]

Speculative gridding does not require finesse. The Molloy plat of 1784, as we have already noted, applied a checkerboard to Nashville without regard for the rolling terrain. Proceeds from the sale of the town lots were to provide funds for the necessary civic buildings to be constructed in the square: a courthouse—where the all-important land surveys and titles were secured and recorded—a prison and stocks. But the location of the public square at the edge of the grid, on a high bluff on the west bank of the Cumberland—rather than at the geographical center—acknowledged the primacy of the river to the life of the town.

In the English colonial cities, the omnipresent square or village green tends to be located within the fabric of the town. William Penn, for example, chose a location for Philadelphia's most prominent square almost equidistant from the two rivers. A different method was followed by the Spanish and French in planning New Orleans, whose square is close to the bank of the Mississippi River with the streets platted around it.

Nashville's streets were laid out around the public square in a pattern much like that of the French Quarter of New Orleans, even though the latter is flat and Nashville has a topography that varies abruptly within the small area of the original plat. But the square's relationship to the Cumberland is weaker than that of Jackson Square to the Mississippi. The south edge of Jackson Square was lined with wharves and served as the original port of New Orleans.

The port of Nashville was located at the end of Broad Street (now Lower Broad or Broadway) and connected to the market on the public square via Market Street (now Second Avenue). This correlation between port and market is Nashville's first axial relationship, an urban design technique that was to become a hallmark of the city's urban form.

Another hallmark is how the grid was subdivided so irregularly. Streets vary in width and length, often failing to connect into a coherent network, especially south of Broad Street. Blocks differ in size, and alleys are inserted inconsistently. Plats just prior to the Civil War reveal the apparently arbitrary division of the blocks; the street frontage occupied by individual parcels follows no obvious formula or mathematical increments.

By way of comparison, the grid exercised a ruthless logic on the development of New York City. In 1811, a commission platted the island of Manhattan with identical blocks unrelieved by open space as far north as 155th Street, when the actual city reached only as far as 23rd Street. Nashville's development habits were more *ad hoc*.

Nashville's street system is also distinguished by what Kostof calls "accidental diagonals," which he describes as "the result of trying to accommodate in a regular scheme a prior stretch of road or the coming together of two disparate sections of urban layout."[6] The "prior stretches"

were the historic pikes that were layered on top of the bison trails through the surrounding hills and became the farmer-to-market roads into the city. As streets were laid out adjacent to the pikes, they took their orthogonals from them. The result was a series of colliding and incomplete grids that still give an irregular texture and unpredictability to the street pattern.

The layout of streets was the province of the town. The roads to connect Nashville to other commercial centers in the southwest territory—the historic pikes—were an issue for the state and the county. In 1804 the Tennessee legislature authorized the counties to construct public roads and build bridges. All adult white males under the age of fifty were required to contribute one day per month on road work, or pay seventy-five cents per month instead. This method of funding a labor force proved insufficient. It was only in 1834 that bonds were issued for radial turnpikes to Gallatin, Franklin, Columbia, Murfreesboro, and Shelbyville; these toll roads were completed in 1842.

But the Cumberland River was Nashville's main commercial artery. Barges and flatboats carried materials to the area's major market, New Orleans, with the crews returning overland via the Natchez Trace. Steamboats enabled the river traffic to flow both ways. On March 11, 1819, the *General Jackson* arrived at Nashville's City Wharf from New Orleans, to the cheers of the crowds gathered on the river banks. The Harpeth Shoals, thirty-five miles down river from Nashville, was a hazard to steamboat navigation, sinking the *General Jackson* in 1821. In periods of low water, however, passengers and goods could be transferred to smaller boats and barges for the rest of the journey to Nashville. The contemporary *General Jackson*, which ferries tourists between Riverfront Park in downtown Nashville and the Opryland complex in

---

Map after the original plat of Nashville by Molloy; copy made for John Overton. Note that in the first platting the path of Commerce is not yet present. The public right-of-way is of consistent dimensions: streets are 49.5 feet wide and alleys 33 feet wide; this regularity would be considerably modified as the lots were subdivided and developed.

(Map, 1789: The Tennessee Historical Society, Tennessee State Library and Archives)

"Man walks in a straight line because he has a goal and knows where he's going."

Le Corbusier, *The City of Tomorrow*, translated by F. Etchells (1924)

1807–1825

1807 Bank of Nashville established.

- Nashville's first volunteer fire-fighting force formed; first paid department is organized in 1860.

1809 Tennessee General Assembly authorizes Nashville's mayor and aldermen to raise money through a lottery for the purpose of bringing water to town.

1819 First steamboat docks at the Nashville wharf; the last commercial steamboat is taken out of service in 1933.

1822 City Cemetery dedicated; most of the bodies that had occupied graves in a burying ground near the Sulphur Spring, as well as many from private family graveyards, including that of city founder James Robertson, are moved to the new location.

1823 Nashville's first bridge over the Cumberland River completed in the location of what is now the Victory Memorial Bridge; prior to this, ferries were used to cross the river.

1824 Music publishing begins in Nashville with *Western Harmony*, a hymnbook and instructions for singing.

1825 Philip Lindsley becomes president of the University of Nashville, after turning down the presidency of Princeton University. Some historians credit him with describing Nashville as the "Athens of the West" in speeches as early as 1840. As European settlers drive west across the continent, the term is changed to "Athens of the South," which becomes the city's official moniker when used by Governor Bob Taylor in his speech opening the Tennessee Centennial Exposition in 1897.

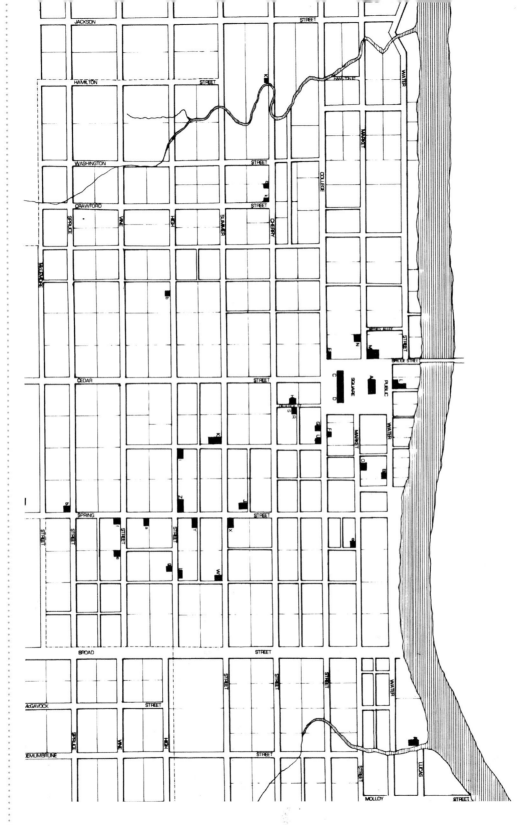

Doolittle and Munson engraving of Nashville in 1831. (Reproduction of original map, 2002: NCDC, Ellen Dill)

Pennington Bend, memorializes the earlier steamboat.

After 1800 the population of Nashville began to climb steadily, at first without the benefit of the roads and steamboats of the transportation revolution. "The major catalyst for growth was the production of tobacco and cotton in sufficient quantities to support a market town," Goodstein writes. "By 1816 the undeveloped lands of Davidson County had disappeared. Farmers and planters rather than speculators had become the favored customers and clients of the town."[7]

The arrival of the steamboat provided further impetus to population growth as well as commercial development of the waterfront. In 1823 the first bridge across the Cumberland was constructed by Irish laborers from Pittsburgh. The location was the path now occupied by the

Riverboats unloading at the city wharf along First Avenue. (Photograph, 1867: Tennessee State Library and Archives)

Victory Memorial Bridge, linking the market square with the East Bank. Despite the clamor for a second bridge at the foot of Broad Street—to give this street the same kind of access to the countryside enjoyed by the square—when a new suspension bridge was finally built in 1853, the site was at the southeast corner of the square, where the Woodland Street Bridge now crosses.[8]

Other municipal improvements included

the city waterworks of 1833, with a reservoir on the river bluffs south of town (now Rolling Mill Hill) and a pumping station on the lower bluff.[9] This water was primarily used for cooking, cleaning streets, and extinguishing fires. Families relied on wells for drinking water, and used outdoor privies, which contaminated the thin soil and the water table in the limestone beneath. Public health was an ongoing problem throughout the nineteenth century. In 1850, for example, 911 people died in a cholera epidemic.

In that same year the first locomotive arrived in Nashville, delivered by one of the steamboats whose commercial viability would ultimately be eroded by the incursion of the railroads. The Nashville & Chattanooga line reached Antioch in 1851, and Chattanooga in 1854 after the construction of a 2,200-foot tunnel through the mountains. In 1859 the Louisville & Nashville (L&N) line chugged into the city across a new bridge over the river three blocks north of the square. The routes the railroads followed into and through the city were predictable: the bottomlands and ravines that were unsuitable for other development. By 1861, when five lines serviced Nashville, the tracks formed a rough circle around the central core, a circle that would be mimicked by the interstates a hundred years later.

From the standpoint of architecture rather than infrastructure, one of the most significant impacts on the central city was the selection of Nashville as the permanent state capital by the General Assembly in 1843. Prior to this date, the capital had migrated from Knoxville to Kingston to Nashville and then to Murfreesboro, before settling back in Nashville. Four acres on what was originally called Cedar Knob were acquired for the capitol building and Philadelphia architect William Strickland was hired to design it. The cornerstone was laid on July 4, 1845, and the building completed

in 1859. This Greek temple of Tennessee democracy was the physical incarnation of Nashville as the Athens of the South, and established the classical vocabulary as the architectural language perennially favored by the city.

The effect on the urban form was also metaphorically Greek: Nashville now had an acropolis, a sacred precinct to look up to, as a complement to its agora or market square. The connection between these two civic spaces established another axial relationship: Cedar Street (later Charlotte Avenue) led directly from the western edge of the square to the southern steps of the Capitol. This link between state and city was later obscured by the construction of James Robertson Parkway and the tall towers on Deaderick Street.

Despite such formal gestures, however, the planning of Nashville during these years was essentially speculative and entrepreneurial, a laissez-faire approach that respected the wishes of individual property owners and was designed to serve the needs of an agrarian economy.

And an agrarian economy had only minimal need for urban development. A Southern port city such as Nashville served primarily as a gathering and shipping depot for raw materials. The transportation lines, river and rail, were simple conveyor belts to larger cities such as New Orleans and Louisville. With a regional population

———

Valley of the Cumberland River from the top of Lindsley Hall on Rolling Mill Hill. Note the State Capitol in the upper left. (Photograph, 1864: Library of Congress)

1828 Andrew Jackson elected seventh president of the United States.

1833 Nashville's waterworks inaugurated with reservoir on Rolling Mill Hill and pumping station on lower river bluff.

1838 Cherokees pass through Nashville on the Trail of Tears.

1843 Tennessee General Assembly names Nashville the permanent state capital; four acres on what was originally called Cedar Knob are acquired for a capitol building.

1844 James K. Polk elected eleventh president of the United States.

1850 Cholera epidemic kills 911 in Nashville.

• First locomotive arrives in Nashville—by boat. The Nashville & Chattanooga's first trip is to Antioch in 1851; three years later the line reaches Chattanooga. The Louisville & Nashville line links those two cities in 1859, just in time for the Union Army to take it over; the 185.5-mile trip takes nine hours. By 1861 five lines enter the city.

1851 Lighting of Nashville's first gas lamp, on Market Street (now Second Avenue North) at the Public Square. Natural gas piped from Texas is first used in Nashville in 1946.

Fort Negley looking northeast. Note the scalped landscape.

(Photograph, 1864: Library of Congress)

"Of all major Southern cities, Nashville emerged from the war with fewer physical and political scars and with advantages gained in the war that prepared it for a formidable role in the new order of things."

Don Doyle,
New Men, New Cities, New South: Atlanta, Nashville, Charleston, Mobile, 1860-1910 (1990)

largely devoted to agriculture, and a labor force of black slaves who were not free to respond to urban opportunities or act as consumers in the marketplace and prompt mercantile activity, Nashville lacked strong stimuli for urban growth. That stimulus would only arrive with the federal forces from the North.

The Business of Making War

For Nashville, the Civil War meant three years of occupation and unwilling collaboration with the Union war effort. But it was the occupiers who laid the groundwork for turning town into city.

Nashville was a strategic prize among the spoils of war, grabbed early—February 1862—by federal troops.[10] The L&N railroad, the only major line linking North and South, was a vital supply route for the invasion. The Nashville & Chattanooga line lay like a dagger, ready to plunge into the heart of Dixie. The town was also the key to usurping Confederate sources of iron and gunpowder. West of the Highland Rim lay an iron belt dotted with furnaces and foundries; along the Cumberland were important gunpowder mills. The iron flowed into Nashville,

where—after Tennessee's secession—factories made cannon, sabers, guns, and ammunition. When the Union army took over, they gained control of these factories and mills, as well as the rail lines that defined the path of penetration.

For the first seven months after federal forces occupied Nashville, a garrison of only two thousand men stood watch as the city was virtually blockaded by Confederate cavalry harassing the inadequate Union defenses. Military governor Andrew Johnson conscripted all the labor he could find, mostly in the form of slaves fleeing from the countryside, and hastily threw up forts on the hills to the south and west. The city was scalped of its trees to build the lines of defense and make it easier to see approaching attackers. Finally, in November, General William S. Rosecrans arrived with fifty thousand troops to shore up the defenses. By the end of the year Nashville was protected by nearly twenty miles of trenches, breastworks, and rifle pits stretching south and west from river bank to river bank, making it the most heavily fortified city in America besides Washington, D.C. The Union army had decided that Nashville was worth keeping.

In the wake of the troops came more African Americans seeking emancipation and other rural refugees, as well as a motley crew of camp followers and prostitutes. The population, which had stood at seventeen thousand in 1860, swelled to more than eighty thousand. After every major battle in the war's western theater, the wounded flooded the town; the occupiers confiscated churches, schools, and abandoned homes to use as hospitals.

This huge influx of people understandably strained the transportation infrastructure and building inventory. Private homes were seized to house officers and their families, hotels and commercial buildings for barracks and jails. The army tore up brick streets for tent foundations and requisitioned fences for firewood. Runaway slaves were settled in makeshift "contraband camps" to the east, west, and south of the city; these camps would become the nuclei of African American neighborhoods after the war. By 1865, eleven thousand blacks lived in Nashville, up from four thousand in 1860.

Business was subordinated to military needs; shipments of food and clothing for the citizens

Nashville & Chattanooga depot and rail yard, which stood in the Gulch north of the current location of Union Station. (Photograph, 1864: Library of Congress)

were of secondary importance and there were chronic shortages. But the Union army's decision to make Nashville the western depot for food, supplies, and ordnance strengthened the city's infrastructure. A new shipyard rose on the East Bank. Government warehouses were constructed near the railway terminals to supplement existing storage that bulged with supplies—$50 to $60 million worth of goods by the end of the war.

The railroads flourished as essentially state-subsidized enterprises. The army took over the Nashville & Chattanooga line and requisitioned more locomotives and freight cars to supply the city. Troops assisted the L&N in rebuilding the river bridge and tracks destroyed by retreating Confederate forces. "Despite constant complaints from L&N officials about financial hardships," Doyle writes, "the company's profits soared during the war, and it emerged from the crisis in a preeminent position among Southern railroads, poised to expand and become the dominant force in the vast territory between

the Ohio River and the Gulf of Mexico."[11]

At war's end, the landscape was denuded and torn up with trenches and fortifications, but the city had suffered no serious physical damage. The downtown needed renovation more than reconstruction. "Nor was the economy significantly disrupted by blockade or destruction," Doyle says. "Nashville's wartime role, on balance, enhanced its power as a regional distribution center."

Reconstruction was also kind to Nashville. By 1870 Tennessee had a new constitution and the state's Confederate veterans had the vote. Northern funds for educational institutions flowed into the city—to establish Fisk University, Central Tennessee College, Roger Williams University, and Meharry Medical College for the freedmen, and to Vanderbilt University and Peabody College for the reconstruction of the white minds of the South. "This was the Nashville," Doyle writes, "in which J. T. Trowbridge, visiting from the North in 1866, 'could feel the influence of Northern ideas and enterprise pulsating through it.' 'It is a nostril,' he

went further, 'through which the State had long breathed the air of free institutions.'"

New South, New Suburbs

In 1881, Union soldier Noble Prentis returned to Nashville to see what had become of the town he had occupied. The picture he painted is of a city that had shifted from defense to offense.

Standing on the high porch of the Capitol, which overlooks the whole city and the valley of the Cumberland until it is shut in by the encircling chains of saw-like hills, I know of few more impressive pictures. Old Nashville lies in a dark mass of roofs, chimneys, spires and treetops, wreathed in a mist of smoke, on the slopes of the capitoline hill. Up and down the river, north and south, stretches the new town, until the houses become scattered and the country begins; but the most impressive feature is the line of public institutions encircling the city like a line of fortifications. First, on the [north], is the great cotton factory; next the massive building of Fisk University; then the three buildings of Vanderbilt University; then the Baptist college for colored people [Roger Williams University]; and thence, on a line drawn toward the river, are Central Tennessee College, a Methodist institution for colored people; the University of Nashville, and the various State asylums. Instead of warlike defenses…the city is surrounded by a cordon reared by Business, Education and Charity—good generals they, who march to the rescue of the world.[12]

What Prentis couldn't see from his Capitol perch was how Nashville was evolving into the "commercial emporium to trade between the

1851–1862

1851 First Presbyterian Church, designed in the Egyptian Revival style by William Strickland, completed; in 1955 the congregation moves to a new church in the suburbs and the Downtown Presbyterian congregation is organized.

1853 Governor Andrew Johnson overcomes stiff opposition to pass legislation for direct taxation to support the state's public schools. Nashville's first public school—named for Alfred Hume, who had developed a plan for the school system modeled on that of Boston—opens on February 26, 1855.

1859 Tennessee State Capitol, designed by Philadelphia architect William Strickland, completed; the cornerstone had been laid on July 4, 1845. The labor force included convicts and slaves. Strickland died in 1854 and was buried within the Capitol's walls; his son Francis oversaw completion of the building.

1862 In February the city is occupied by Union forces. The first dress parade of the troops takes place on the public square, where residents watch from windows and balconies as soldiers from Ohio drill. On March 3, Andrew Johnson is named military governor of Tennessee. The Battle of Nashville in December 1864 is the last major conflict of the Civil War.

Aerial view of downtown from the East Bank.
(Etching, 1888: reproduced by Elder's Bookseller, 1971)

1862–1866

1862 Union soldiers bring baseball to Nashville, playing in a field north of the Capitol near the sulphur spring. In 1866 the first game between organized teams is played on the field; the first professional baseball game is played on the same field in 1885. In 1901 Athletic Park (later Sulphur Dell) stadium is constructed next to the sulphur spring (on what is now Fourth Avenue North) as home of the Tennessee Volunteers professional baseball team. The last game is played there in 1963.

1865 Andrew Johnson becomes seventeenth president of the United States upon the assassination of Abraham Lincoln; in 1868 he survives impeachment by one vote.

1866 First mule-drawn streetcar route in Nashville opens between downtown and the University of Nashville to the south; in 1872 the cars reach to the suburb of Edgefield, in 1880 to Vanderbilt University. Electric trolleys begin service in 1888.

- Fisk University founded for the education of emancipated slaves and named for General Clinton B. Fisk, the head of the Freedmen's Bureau. In 1871 the Jubilee Singers begin a national tour to raise money for their school; Jubilee Hall, the first building in the United States erected for the higher education of African Americans, is completed in 1876.

Midwest and the Gulf States of the South" with a "solid base of manufacturing and finance as well." The city served "a growing territory of retailers and consumers as a wholesale distribution center linked by rail and river to its hinterland." The leading commercial line was wholesale groceries, a testament "to the rise of the urban South and to the decline of subsistence agriculture in the rural South." People had to buy food because they no longer grew their own. Industry focused on textiles, tobacco and lumber. A chronically depressed agricultural economy propelled people from the farm into the city's labor force. Money from all this commerce flowed into the banks that formed another block in Nashville's economic foundation.[13]

The L&N railroad dominated commercial transport, offering low freight rates for goods that came to and through Nashville, rates that made the city the major milling and distribu-

tion center—the "Minneapolis of the South"— for wheat and corn flour. The Cumberland River was the primary avenue for lumber. Trees were felled on the Cumberland Plateau and then lashed together to make enormous rafts that floated to the town's mills and factories, most of them located on the East Bank.

This new scale of transportation, industry, and commerce, which required a large labor force living nearby, had decided impacts on the built environment. The business district grew from the public square along the streets to the south and west, making inroads into what had

Broadway in the 1890s. (Postcard, n.d.: www.historicnashville.com)

been residential areas and raising property values. The industrial/transport belt around the city thickened. Local wholesale merchants needed warehouses and offices. Industries set up shop where they would have access to their chosen mode of transport, river or rails. A growing urban population—including the army of "drummers" or traveling sales agents the wholesalers sent to deal directly with the retail store owners in the small towns and rural crossroads—demanded places to live and shop.

The result was the "squeeze play," propelling residents of means out of the city entirely and compressing those without into densely packed slums. Between the expanding business and industrial/transport districts lay old housing that was ripe for real estate speculators, who converted dwellings into tenements for the poor while waiting for more intensive commercial development opportunities. In the lowlands north and west of the Capitol, near the East Bank and south of Broadway emerged the squalid quarters of Hell's Half Acre, Crappy Shoot, and Black

Bottom, where disease and vice were rampant.

The moral and physical climate of the downtown in general deteriorated with the crowded conditions. Along Cherry Street (now Fourth Avenue North), gambling and drinking and prostitution flourished. Soft coal used to heat buildings and power locomotives blackened the air and left a patina of soot. Hogs rooted in the muddy streets and alleys. Outhouses reeked and leached waste directly into streams supplying drinking water; cholera and typhoid were constant threats. In 1877 Dr. John Berrien Lindsley, the city's public health official, reported that Nashville had the highest death rate in the nation and the fifth highest in the world. Even when water and sewer lines were laid throughout the central city in the 1880s, few families could afford the hookup, much less the plumbing and "water closets." According to Doyle, "[b]y 1898 the city's population of over 80,000 could count no more than 682 toilets, 212 bathtubs, and 52 urinals."[14]

The laboring classes, who had to live within walking distance of their work, were tethered to the city. But those with the funds for the fare were free to flee the democracy of filth and disease, riding the streetcars into the suburban fringe.

Of course, there had been suburbs even before there were streetcars. Access was by horse and buggy or by foot. South Nashville was incorporated in 1850; the first mule-drawn streetcar reached there in 1865, the same year that a line was laid north to Germantown. Residential growth in Edgefield was spurred by the opening of the suspension bridge of 1853; the mule cars arrived in 1872. This animal-powered transit provided reliable service up to roughly two miles from the city center.

But the conversion of the public transit system to electricity in 1888 opened up more remote territory. The favored path for residential

Laying the first streetcar tracks in Nashville.
(Photograph, n.d.: www.historicnashville.com)

expansion was where industry wasn't, and where the prevailing west-to-east winds kept city smells and soot at bay. Thus, Doyle writes, "[t]he major thrust of suburban expansion in the electric trolley car era was to the west."[15]

What the suburbs delivered was more than just a city with a larger footprint. Suburbia was an entirely different pattern of living. Its outlines go back to the ancient Roman patricians, who located leisure villas—daytime getaways—outside the city walls. These places of seclusion and relaxation grew out of the belief in the benefits of country life as cultivated by the urban aristocrat, not the farmer. The spatial remove of the Roman suburban villa from the urban masses defined the social distinction central to the suburb from its beginnings. It was only the wealthy who could afford a town house and a suburban estate, and the private transportation to bridge the gap. In nineteenth-century Nashville, many of those who had made fortunes in commerce and industry constructed suburban villas surrounded by pleasure grounds—for example, the Warner family's "Renraw" on Gallatin Pike—as shelters for private family life. But with the development of public transportation, the geographical gap between urban and rural became the ideal place for the middle class to

emerge in the social gap between rich and poor.

The consequence of the migration to the suburbs was a segregation by race and class unknown in the central city. In general, suburban flight was white, leaving the central city to blacks. But the rising African American middle class also journeyed outward on Jefferson Street, clustering in large homes around the Fisk University campus. Fisk was thus the black counterpart to white Vanderbilt University, which drew development out West End Avenue. In both cases, however, it was the people of means who moved and the poor who remained behind.

The separation of work and home also created distinct male and female zones. Of an evening, men of business shook off the urban dust from their boots, hopped on the trolley, and took refuge at the family hearth presided over by the "angel of the house." The commuter was born.

The form these early suburbs took was dominated by single-family homes of various sizes, with the largest usually occupying the corner lots. All the lots were relatively small—50 feet wide by 150 feet deep was typical—and flanked a connected network of streets, alleys, and sidewalks. Corner stores and neighborhood centers such as Five Points and Hillsboro Village supplied the needs of daily life. Schools and churches served each neighborhood. Because men walked to the trolley stop, women to the shops, children to school, and families to church, buildings were clustered closely together and the land uses intermingled.

The architectural styles of the houses were vaguely organic. The irregular profiles and highly textured surfaces—all that gingerbread and other ornament—celebrated the irregular shapes and textures of nature. Later bungalows visually hugged the earth. The signs marking the streets of suburbia often spoke a similarly naturalistic language: Linden and Holly, Ashwood

1869–1880

1869 Mount Ararat Cemetery established for African Americans.

1870 From the 1870s through the 1920s, Nashville is the traveling salesman capital of the South; the numerous wholesale grocery warehouses are a big draw, as are insurance companies and religious publishers.

1871 Tennessee Manufacturing Company built; becomes Werthan Bag in 1928. The building is listed in the National Register of Historic Places in 1999.

1873 Liquor trade is big business— $5 million; four distilleries produce 100,000 barrels of booze and the city has sixty-two saloons and seventeen wholesale dealers in wine and spirits.

• Vanderbilt University established.

1876 Meharry Medical College founded.

• *Nashville Banner* newspaper established; final issue is February 20, 1998.

1877 First telephone call made in Nashville; on the receiving end is the city's *grande dame*, the widow of President James K. Polk.

• Cornerstone for Nashville Customs House laid by President Rutherford B. Hayes; his visit is the first south of the Mason-Dixon line by a U.S. president since Abraham Lincoln went to Richmond after its fall during the Civil War. In 1976 the building is declared surplus by the federal government and given to the city.

1880 Nashville annexes the city of Edgefield, which had been incorporated in 1869.

1880–1889

1880 The highlight of the Nashville Centennial Exposition is the dedication of the equestrian statue of Andrew Jackson by sculptor Clark Mills on the east side of Capitol Hill.

1881 Tennessee legislature passes the South's first Jim Crow law enabling the segregation of passengers in railroad cars.

• Nashville sees its first electric light.

1886 The second Woodland Street Bridge constructed, replacing the suspension bridge of 1853, which was burned by retreating Confederate soldiers in 1862.

1887 Belmont Mansion and Acklen estate, established in 1853, purchased for Belmont Junior College for Girls.

1888 First of fifteen locks and dams constructed on the Cumberland River by the Nashville District of the U.S. Army Corps of Engineers to aid steamboat commerce. The locks are dismantled after construction of the Cheatham and Old Hickory locks and dams.

1889 First poll tax for voting instituted by Tennessee legislature in an attempt to disenfranchise blacks.

• New waterworks for Nashville. Omohundro Pumping Station takes the city's water from the Cumberland; downtown reservoir relocates to former site of Union Fort Casino on Eighth Avenue; capacity is fifty-one million gallons. In 1912 the reservoir ruptures, releasing twenty-five million gallons into surrounding neighborhoods; miraculously, no one is killed.

• The Ladies' Hermitage Association acquires The Hermitage, home of President Andrew Jackson, from the state and begins preserving it as a public shrine.

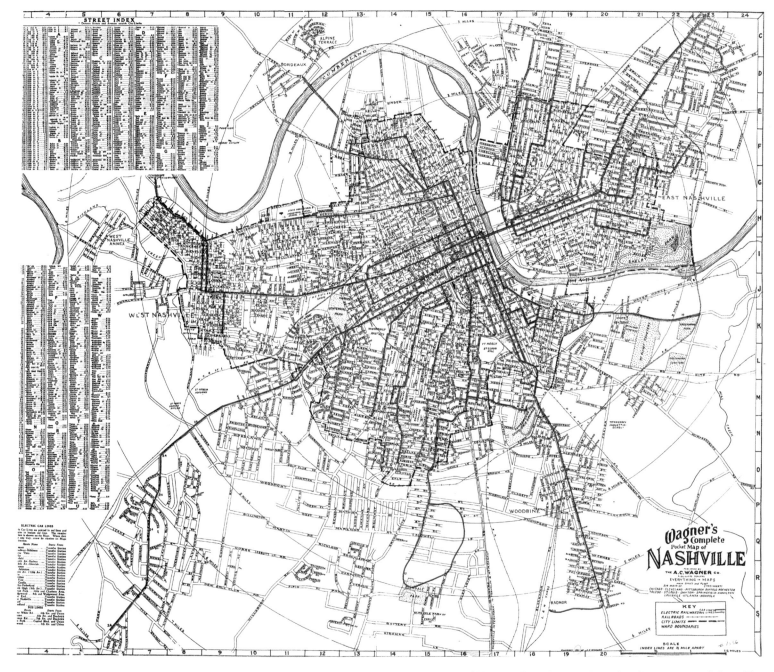

and Cedar. And at the turn of the last century, with the platting of Waverly Place on Eighth Avenue South and Acklen Park on West End Avenue, the street pattern, while still interconnected, relaxed from orthogonals to curves that emphasized the natural topography. All these features were designed to evoke the suburban ideal of buildings in a park, and convey the message that this is the place of green lawns and large trees, the place where the business of Broadway and Market Street is out of place. This is the not-city.

The depression of 1893 temporarily squelched the real estate market. But after the turn of the century the suburban expansion picked up its

Left: The streetcar lines at their peak. Note how fine-grained the routes are within the city and how far the lines reach. (For a map of the lines in 1897, see "Midtown," page 213.)

(Map, 1927: *Wagner's Complete Pocket Map of Nashville*)

Right: West End Park and Acklen Hall; this suburb was one of the first in Nashville to be platted with curving streets that accentuated the topography.

(Photograph, 1894: Nashville Public Library, The Nashville Room)

pace. With the consolidation of the streetcar system in 1902, a consolidation propelled by the high capital costs of generating the electricity, "Nashville experienced a boom on its western frontier," Doyle explains. Aggressive marketing tactics by real estate syndicates included full-page newspaper advertisements, flyers distributed on streetcars and street corners, billboards and posters. In the wake of the streetcar line extensions sprang up Belmont Park, West End or Acklen Park, the Richland-West End neighborhood, and then Belle Meade. The subdivision of the historic plantation of the Harding family into spacious lots for "country homes" on winding roads was the ultimate symbol of the decline of the landed gentry and the rise of the new commercial class.

Common Grounds

Nashville's park system had its origins in the great suburban migration.[16] In the nineteenth century, the city had some open spaces like Watkins Grove (subsequently Watkins Park), which was popular for political barbecues and picnics. And City (1822), Mount Olivet (1856), Mount Ararat (1869), and Greenwood (1888) cemeteries were also shady places for families to stroll on a Sunday afternoon while paying their respects to ancestors.

But real estate developers learned in the 1880s that setting aside part of their subdivision plat for greenspace stimulated sales of the surrounding lots and enhanced overall land values. Because these developers were frequently also principals in the streetcar lines, they located "trolley parks" at the end of the routes to increase traffic on the lines during weekends and to showcase the real estate for sale along them.

The first trolley park was Spring Park, which was laid out in 1885 with a small lake, a bandstand, and a monkey cage at Fatherland and Thirteenth Streets, just when this area of what is now the East End neighborhood was being subdivided. Trolley parks to the west included Richland, Clifton, and Cherokee Parks; the

"In choosing where to live and vacation, we may be setting the stage for the play of ourselves, treating nature as a prop."

Deborah Tall, "Here," *From Where We Stand* (1993)

Centennial Park and the Nashville Parthenon.

(Photograph, 1909: Library of Congress)

"To George F. Babbitt, as to most prosperous citizens of Zenith, his motor car was poetry and tragedy, love and heroism. The office was his pirate ship but the car his perilous excursion ashore."

Sinclair Lewis,
Babbitt
(1922)

latter, eighty-three acres at the end of the street-car line owned by the principals in the West Nashville Development Company, featured sulphur springs, concerts, and dances. All the trolley parks were subsequently subdivided for development after they had served their purpose, which was to convince weekend visitors that if such surroundings were a fine place to spend a Sunday, all week long would be even better.

In their short lives, however, the trolley parks provoked demand for permanent public parks. In 1901 the Parks Board was founded and established a plan for a citywide system of four parks of a minimum of fifty acres each, one for each quadrant of Nashville, as well as smaller neighborhood parks to be equally distributed throughout the city. But the board lacked the money to acquire land for parks. In 1902 Mayor James Head negotiated a complex deal with Percy Warner of the Nashville Railway and Light Company that gave the first seventy-two acres of Centennial Park to the Parks Board as well as a percentage of the gross receipts of streetcar fares. Nashville had its first large park and the promise of funding for more.

The plan for large parks to serve the suburbs in each quadrant was frustrated in South Nashville by the difficulty of finding a site, once the concept of turning the slum of Black Bottom into a park roused objections from the local councilman, who wanted more industry in the area. The Parks Board therefore settled for several smaller parks: South and Howell Parks on Rutledge Hill, Dudley Park at Third Avenue South and Chestnut Street, and a park on Eighth Avenue South adjacent to the city reservoir, which had been constructed as part of Nashville's new waterworks in 1889.

The board had more luck to the east and north. The original 151 acres of Shelby Park were acquired in 1911 from the bankrupt

AMERICAN NATIONAL BANK BUILDING

real estate company that had used part of the grounds for an amusement park in the 1890s. In 1911 President George Gates of Fisk University requested a park near his school that would also serve the new Tennessee Agricultural and Industrial State Normal School (later Tennessee State University), the campus of which had formerly been the Hadley plantation. The following year the Board opened Hadley Park for the black community in North Nashville.

The development of all these parks was an implicit acknowledgement that the open, rural land surrounding Nashville was rapidly vanishing, and that if the citizens were going to have access to nature, the city was going to have to provide it.

Driving on the Wall Street of the South

After World War I, Nashville was poised for a boom, and, like most of the nation's urban centers, boom it did.[17] The industrial giant DuPont had come to town in 1918 to make gunpowder for the war effort. In 1923 the company returned to build a $4-million plant for the manufacture of rayon, warming the hearts of business boosters eager to expand the city's narrow industrial base. General Shoe Company (later Genesco) migrated to Nashville in 1924, leaving the unions of the North for the cheap labor of the South.

Other industries declined. Nashville lost its favored position within the L&N freight rate system, and there was less grain for the roller mills to grind. The timber supply up river from the city was being rapidly exhausted and Birmingham's rise as an iron and steel center eclipsed Nashville's ironworks. Nashville's real economic strength was in the service sector based on Union Street: banking, insurance, and securities. The shifting nature of the economy was reflected in changes in the city's slogan,

from the "Minneapolis of the South" to "Powder City" to the "Wall Street of the South."

The population of Nashville swelled in the 1920s by 30 percent, reaching 153,866 by 1930. The main impetus for the increase was rural-to-urban migration, as depressed prices for their crops led farmers to flee the land. National Life and Accident's WSM ("We Shield Millions") radio station, established in 1925, beamed its Saturday night Barn Dance—dubbed the "Grand Ole Opry" by station manager George Hay—to thousands of good country people come to town but nostalgic for home.

More people earning higher wages meant more disposable income for consumer goods, and merchants were happy to oblige. Nashville's retail district, which had shifted from the public square to the Arcade and Fifth Avenue North before the war, now spread along Church Street. Movie palaces were woven into the retail fabric and increased the synergy of the street; by 1917 downtown Nashville had eight such theaters.

The most significant long-term impact on the built environment, however, was delivered by the rising popularity of the automobile. In 1920 there were 12,000 vehicles registered in Nashville; by 1930 the number had increased to 40,300 and kept climbing. Sales were carefully cultivated by manufacturers and dealers with advertising campaigns designed to persuade consumers that a car was not a luxury for weekend recreation but a necessity of daily life. A 1925 promotion for an auto show declared: "There is no such thing as a 'pleasure automobile.' You might as well talk of 'pleasure fresh air' or of a 'pleasure beef steak'…The Automobile increases length of life, increases happiness, represents above all other achievements the progress and the civilization of our age."[18]

The growth in the number of cars escalated the pressure for better roads on which to drive them. State legislators mounted a campaign for taxes to improve the pikes used to deliver crops to market to "get the farmer out of the mud."

1890 Nashville General Hospital built on river bluffs; the site is selected to take advantage of its proximity to the medical school across the street on Rutledge Hill.

- Bruton & Condon Snuff Company erects a building on Harrison Street, the beginning of the tobacco complex in the area north of the Capitol; the company subsequently becomes American Tobacco in 1900 and then United States Tobacco.

1892 Union Gospel Tabernacle (later renamed Ryman Auditorium) completed.

- Lick Branch Creek disappears from sight, enclosed in brick sewer; the creek had been channelized in 1889 to enable water and sewage to flow more easily into the Cumberland River.

1896 First automobile arrives in Nashville; cars are built in Nashville 1910 to 1914 by Southern Motor Works, later called Marathon Motorworks.

1897 Tennessee Centennial Exposition, with the first Nashville Parthenon as its fine arts pavilion and the site's centerpiece; total attendance: 1,786,711.

1900 Union Station built by L&N line, which dominates Nashville's rail service; 6 percent of the city's work force is employed in the railroad industry. After the decline of travel by rail, the station suffers from neglect and decay; in 1986 the building is renovated into a hotel.

1901 Polk Place, former residence of President and Mrs. James K. Polk, demolished. Polk died in 1849, leaving the estate bounded by Union and Church Streets and Eighth and Ninth Avenues to his widow for her lifetime, then to be offered to the State of Tennessee for the governor's residence. When Mrs. Polk dies in 1891 the State declines to pay the $22,000 asked by the Polk heirs.

• Nashville Mayor James Marshall Head asks the city council to appropriate money to bury utility lines underground; they refuse.

• Watkins Park, the city's first, transferred to the new Parks Board; land was given to the city in 1870 by Samuel Watkins, who had quarried stone for the State Capitol nearby. Centennial Park established in 1902.

1902 Life & Casualty Insurance Company established.

1903 Nashville Arcade opens on May 20.

The Commercial Club's Good Roads Committee and the Nashville Automobile Club (founded in 1915) lobbied for the state to assume some responsibility for road construction, which before 1909 had been strictly a county obligation. In response, Tennessee organized a highway department and in 1924 began a $200-million road building program. Within ten years paved roads connected every county seat and a network of highways fed Nashville. Counties and cities also added their millions to the building fund. The impact on the local and regional economy, Doyle points out, was tremendous. "Nashville's Caldwell and Company, [for example], built a financial empire by selling southern municipal and county bonds, which were required in large part by the surge of road building."[19]

Cars now challenged trolleys for space on downtown streets. A 1928 traffic count taken at Eighth Avenue and Broadway found that twenty-eight thousand cars, as well as six trolley lines, went through the intersection each day. The streetcars could not compete with the comfort and personal freedom of the automobile, and the number of transit passengers gradually declined along with the speed and frequency of service. Downtown merchants, Doyle writes, "at first delighted with this trend, were soon plagued with clogged streets, a severe shortage of parking space, and dangerous traffic that threatened their pedestrian shoppers. New garages were thrown up around the retail district and out lower Broadway, but the number of parking spaces was rapidly outstripped by the rising number of automobiles on the streets."

The automobile's influence on three-dimensional Nashville extended beyond the transportation infrastructure. Cars were not a necessity in the first-ring neighborhoods of Nashville, with their multiple streetcar routes, sidewalks, and compact form, although these neighborhoods could accommodate the vehicles. Residents built garages off the alleys out back or parked next to the curb. Traffic was dispersed through the street network.

New suburbs that were developed beyond or between the trolley lines, however, took a different form because they were organized around the car as the single mode of personal travel. Compact neighborhood form and the weaving of commercial and institutional land uses into the neighborhood fabric gave way to lower densities and compartmentalized land uses. With a car per family and an expanding inventory of roads, distances between destinations became less relevant. Lawns grew larger and sidewalks disappeared. In Nashville the large lot sizes were also the result of all the limestone lying close to the land's surface; water and sewer lines were expensive to install and a half-acre or more was required for a septic system.

The historic pikes became increasingly commercialized with low-density development. Businesses, especially groceries, moved to the periphery to serve the suburbanite with wheels. Auto merchandise shops and service stations also took up positions on the spoke roads into the city. Broadway and West End Avenue to Sixteenth Avenue, in particular, became what Doyle calls "Auto Row," with showrooms, as well as auto parts and tire stores, displacing the mansions that lined the avenue. Signage grew larger as merchants realized that to succeed in a windshield survey they had to send bold messages to slow down, stop, and buy. Customers had to be provided with places to store their cars while they shopped; buildings gradually retreated from the right-of-way and parking moved out front.

During all these developments, downtown merchants looked out their storefronts at the congested streets and saw retail beginning to leach from the central city. The car was evolving into an urban problem, an evolution that would be slowed by the Depression of the 1930s before picking up speed again after World War II.

Government Steps In

The impact of the October 1929 stock market crash was not immediately felt in Nashville. As late as October 1930, visiting officials from the Publix Theater chain were proclaiming that they found no symptoms of business depression in Nashville. The illness arrived on November 14, 1930, with the collapse of Caldwell and Company, the local banking and brokerage firm. In its wake, 120 banks across the South went under. Nashville's unemployment rate shot up to 25 percent by the end of that year.

Many of the unemployed were members of the construction industry. To put them to work, the federal government initiated a massive building program across the country. The result was a New Deal for Nashville's built environment.

Between 1934 and 1940 the city gained a new downtown post office, courthouse, city market, and two public housing complexes, one for whites and one for blacks. Berry Field airport opened in 1937. In 1938 the Public Works Administration funded a school building program that delivered eight new schools, additions to three existing structures, and renovations to thirty-two others. Federal dollars paid for the reconstruction of Fort Negley and improvements to the park system; the Warner Parks, the primary beneficiary, got a golf course, picnic shelters, miles of limestone walls, and a steeplechase course. The Works Progress Administration spent $2.5 million to pave and expand the city's street system. The state received the Supreme Court Building and John Sevier Office Building. The Tennessee Valley Authority brought cheap electricity rates to town.

As a consequence of all this largesse, local

The Post Office on Broadway (now the Frist Center for the Visual Arts) under construction.

(Photograph, April 2, 1934: Marr and Holman Collection, The Tennessee Historical Society, Tennessee State Library and Archives)

business and civic leaders, who had previously viewed the public sector with suspicion or even disdain, "warmed to the idea of using government to shape the city," according to historian Robert Spinney.[20] This was a pattern repeated throughout the urban South. "[B]ecause the federal funds came to the cities with few strings attached, civic boosters found that the works pro-

WPA workers removing abandoned streetcar tracks on Church Street as part of the repaving of the street.

(Photograph, 1930s: www.historicnashville.com)

grams modernized their cities at minimal local cost and left the existing political and social order intact."[21]

One of the first government tools Nashville's boosters endorsed for city shaping was a planning commission. The New Deal had mounted a campaign to create local planning commissions, and offered the reward of funding for planning studies if they were performed by commissions staffed with professional planners. Local support for the commission came, not from city bureaucrats or elected officials, but from the Chamber of Commerce, whose members "were concerned about the intrusion of undesirable commercial activities—like gasoline stations—into residential and commercial neighborhoods," according to historians Lester Salamon and Gary Wamsley. "The four businessmen named to the Nashville Planning Commission therefore made zoning their

first priority" when the commission was established and began meeting in 1932.[22] An interim zoning code was adopted by the city council within four months, and a permanent code followed the next year that divided the city into residential, commercial, and industrial zones.

Planning director Gerald Gimre secured federal funds for five planning studies in the 1930s: a land use study, a traffic safety study, a public transportation study, a housing study, and a six-year capital improvements program.[23] These studies helped Nashville secure federal aid for the construction of a number of public works projects. But commission members were more interested in zoning than in proactive planning. Because zoning came relatively late to Nashville, the first code lagged behind development. The zoning code was thus used to protect existing land uses—at least those in the locations where the business elite were heavily invested, the downtown and the affluent suburbs—from potential disruption.

The character of this early code is known in planner jargon as "pyramidal" zoning. The code established a hierarchy of land uses and forbade the intrusion of "lower" uses (commercial and industrial) into areas set aside for "higher" ones (single-family residential). But the early codes did not defend higher uses in areas set aside for lower ones. In the areas of the city zoned for lower uses, therefore, any combination of land uses was possible and property owners were rendered defenseless against neighboring land uses with negative impacts.

The original zoning code restricted the residential classification to the suburbs located well beyond the commercial and industrial core, but

1904–1910

1904 Carnegie Library opens downtown after a donation by industrialist and philanthropist Andrew Carnegie of $100,000 for construction; in 1963 the building is demolished and replaced with the Ben West Library. Carnegie libraries in North and East Nashville are still standing.

• Downtown streets changed from names to numbers.

1905 Boycott of streetcars by African Americans to protest Jim Crow segregation of accommodations; Reverend Preston Taylor, James Napier, and Richard Boyd form a private company to provide transportation for African Americans. Because the city levies a privilege tax on the system, and the African Americans can put into circulation only a small number of vehicles, the protest fails within a year.

• First National Bank Building, at twelve stories Nashville's first skyscraper, constructed on the corner of Fourth Avenue North and Church Street.

• City Sewer Department established.

• Last stagecoach line discontinues service.

1907 Tony Sudekum opens first movie theater next to the Arcade on Fifth Avenue North.

1910 Hermitage Hotel opens at the corner of Sixth Avenue and Union Street.

assigned the commercial and industrial classifications to large chunks of primarily residential areas interspersed with or adjoining commercial or industrial use, principally in the first-ring neighborhoods. "The land classified as commercial by the zoning ordinance," write Salamon and Wamsley, "was 50 percent larger than the acreage then in use for commercial purposes in the city, even though the planners at the time saw no need for so much additional commercial property and little likelihood of its development." As late as 1973, a year before the comprehensive zoning ordinance (COMZO) that eliminated the "pyramid" was enacted, almost 100 acres zoned commercial and 6,600 acres zoned industrial in the inner city were still not used for either purpose. "By adopting a pyramidal scheme and extending the area assigned to less restrictive uses beyond any reasonable expectations, the ordinance denied protection to precisely those homeowners most in need of it—the inner-city residents whose property was threatened by encroaching commercial and industrial development."

Because of the proximity of the first-ring neighborhoods to the central business district and the industrial/transport belt, and the presence of some commercial and industrial uses within them, the zoning code thus opened up these neighborhoods—even though they were primarily residential in nature—to pretty much any type of commercial and industrial development without regard to the pattern of development. The code implicitly assumed that the urban design of these neighborhoods, with their tradition of fine-grained mixed-use—corner stores and commercial centers surrounded by residential fabric—was in itself a prescription for residential doom. But it was the code that was writing the prescription.

North Nashville, Salamon and Wamsley point out, "provides a classic example of the consequences of pyramidal zoning." The district housing much of the city's African American middle class and its two black institutions of higher learning "was early zoned commercial and industrial despite the predominantly residential character of much of it. As a consequence, when the pressures arising from the aging of the housing stock, the slow spread of downtown commercial and industrial activity, and the crushing impact of Interstate 40 hit the area in the 1950s and the 1960s, the zoning code provided the residents little assistance in protecting the character of their once viable residential community." And the fact that the pyramidal scheme was in effect until 1974 gave "homeowners little confidence that the area would be preserved as a residential area, and this gave little encouragement for home improvement investments." Pyramidal zoning thus encouraged the "blight" that government would subsequently attempt to cure with public housing projects and urban renewal.

The earliest zoning codes also prevented sensible planning of commercial development along the historic pikes by indiscriminately assigning commercial zones to the strips of land flanking these major arterials. These zones were mechanically extended outward with subsequent suburbanization. The result has been miles of low-density strip commercial development, traffic congestion, and the deterioration of the residential fabric on adjacent blocks.

The effects of substituting zoning for planning served to limit the role of the professional planners on the commission's staff, even though these planners were well aware of the challenges to the city posed by the car and the expanding rings of suburbs, which would eventually need basic city services. The commission's inattention to proactive land use planning allowed growth

Trailer camp for defense workers at Vultee aircraft plant. (Photograph, May 1941: Peter Sekaer, Library of Congress)

to occur without regard for the social, economic, and physical implications for the community at large.

Planning for Growth

World War II "launched Nashville and the South into an unprecedented era of sustained growth," writes historian Don Doyle.[24] The war in effect extended the New Deal economic stimulus programs by means of defense industries. The Vultee Aircraft plant touched down near the airport in 1941, employing 7,000 workers to build the "Vultee Vengeance" bomber. Existing industries adapted to make the materials for war. Middle Tennessee's mild climate and rolling terrain were optimal for army maneuvers, which between 1943 and 1944 engaged 600,000 troops. Camp Campbell was established near Clarksville. All these soldiers came to town on leaves and weekends.

But it was the postwar period that concerned Nashville's planners, who realized that the end of the conflict would release the pent-up demand for housing and the associated city services such as transportation infrastructure and utilities. These concerns were echoed by liberal civic leaders such as Silliman Evans, Sr., the publisher of the *Tennessean*, who as early as 1943 began advocating for an official and organized

Defense workers clocking out.
(Photograph, 1942: Jack Delano, Library of Congress)

planning process for the city's development. Underlying the push for planning was the ambition to prepare Nashville to take advantage of the expected postwar wave of federal public works expenditures.

In 1945 planning director Charles Hawkins began to meet regularly and informally with officials in the fields of public health, water and sewer service, and public works, as well as representatives of the Chamber of Commerce and the local newspapers, to consider the problems posed by growth. They discussed the need to do something about Nashville's slums, which had been a health threat and a public eyesore since the depression of the 1890s. They also talked a lot about sewers. Suburban development outside the city limits was served only by septic tanks and private disposal companies. These septic systems had begun to contaminate ground water, especially in the area near Richland Creek.

Hawkins and his staff predicted that the low-density development pattern of the newer suburbs would continue in subsequent decades. They recognized that this development pattern would not provide the tax base to pay for the necessary infrastructure, and that this infrastructure would be more expensive per household because the larger lots necessitated longer utility lines and streets to serve each home. They also understood that suburban commercial development would force the construction of new roads, in particular circumferential streets to connect the major spoke roads. And they realized that as more development occurred outside the city limits in Davidson County there would be escalating demand in these areas for city services, such as sanitary sewers, parks and playgrounds, and fire protection, that the county government had no authority to provide.

These discussions, and the planners' response to them, laid the groundwork for urban renewal, the interstates, and Metro government.

Housing for the Public

Public housing, urban renewal, and the interstates were inextricably linked in the comprehensive plans laid for the future. But public housing came first chronologically because that was where the federal government decided to target its initial funding.[25] The National Recovery Act of 1933 provided for a federal housing program whose purpose was to increase employment in the construction industry and supply decent, safe, and sanitary homes at low cost to the "temporarily poor."

Improvement in housing conditions was sorely needed. A third of Nashville's population lived in slums where most housing was "unfit for human habitation," according to a 1937 report by the city's Planning Commission. These slums lacked paved streets and had few parks or playgrounds and miserable schools. Some areas were not served by city water and sewer or streetcar lines. Death and disease rates were considerably higher than in the city as a whole.

With the passage of the National Housing Act of 1937, public housing was directly linked with slum clearance. The federal government gave funds to local housing agencies for the construction and administration of the housing projects. The Act stipulated that for every unit built, a substandard one had to be demolished. This gave housing agencies an incentive to tear down houses that may not necessarily have been substandard, and did not increase the amount of housing available to the poor.

Local realtors and landlords fiercely opposed the first public housing constructed in Nashville by the federal government.[26] When the City Council proceeded with the housing program, significant concessions were made to these antagonists. The original intention for public housing to serve as a yardstick against which to measure private housing quality and fair rentals was redefined. Instead public housing would be "a mechanism for controlling property values," Doyle writes. A belt of public housing "would ring the existing slums of the central city and serve as a barrier to protect the residential sections in the suburbs…This agreement allowed existing slums to fester and perpetuated—even accentuated—the residential segregation of blacks and whites in Nashville."

The original design concept for public housing was an English-style village whose scale would differ little from the surrounding neighborhood. Cheatham Place (for whites) on Eighth Avenue North at the edge of Germantown, and Andrew Jackson Court (for blacks) on Jackson Street near Fisk University were completed in 1938 and turned over to the newly constituted Nashville Housing Authority to administer the following year. The first section of Boscobel Heights (now James A. Cayce Homes) in East Nashville and James C. Napier Homes in South Nashville opened in 1941. These later projects established the pattern of housing superblocks.

In the 1940s planners became aware that much more affordable housing was needed.

1920–1928

1920 Tennessee's vote to ratify the Nineteenth Amendment to the U.S. Constitution gives women across the country the right to vote. The Hermitage Hotel served as headquarters for both suffragist and anti-suffragist groups, whose members converged on Nashville to lobby the Tennessee legislature.

- First Nashville Symphony organized. The symphony plays in Ryman, then Vendome Theatre, moving to War Memorial in 1925.

- Work begins to replace temporary Nashville Parthenon of wood and stucco with a permanent concrete version; the new building is finished in 1931. Restoration of this structure is completed in 2001.

1925 Tennessee War Memorial Building constructed to honor dead of World War I.

- WSM—"We Shield Millions"— radio, owned and licensed by National Life and Accident, goes on the air and the Grand Ole Opry soon follows.

1926–1927 Major floods along the Cumberland during the winter; the river floods parts of downtown again in 1937.

1927 A promotional brochure by the Illinois Central Railroad proclaims that Nashville is one of the two largest commercial fertilizer manufacturing centers in the United States, and one of the two biggest hardwood markets in the world; the city also has factories turning out ten thousand pairs of shoes a day.

1928 First airport opens to the public; McConnell Field, located on the present site of McCabe Golf Course, operates until 1939.

1929 A national city planning survey finds Nashville "notably lacking in city planning, zoning, and subdivision control"; in 1931 the Nashville Planning Commission is created.

1930 Local banking and brokerage firm Caldwell and Company declares bankruptcy on November 14; in response, 120 banks across the South go under. By 1931 armies of transients are camping on the Cumberland's banks and roaming the streets looking for work.

1933 Tornado tears through East Nashville, taking a path remarkably similar to the tornado of 1998.

1934 Tennessee Valley Authority formed by Congress.

1936 City Hall and Market House, as well as the 1855 Davidson County Courthouse designed by William Strickland's son, Francis, demolished to make way for the current Metro Courthouse.

1937 Federal government constructs Cheatham Place (for whites) and Andrew Jackson homes (for African Americans) as first public housing in Nashville. Nashville Housing Authority is created to administer these projects in 1939.

• Nashville sculptor William Edmonson first African American to have a one-man show at the Museum of Modern Art in New York City.

• American Airlines lands first commercial plane at Berry Field, which was named for Col. Harry S. Berry, a World War I pilot and the state WPA administrator. A new terminal is built in 1961, the first year of jet service. In 1987 another new terminal is constructed, and the name is changed to Nashville International Airport—but the initials on the luggage tags are still BNA.

Beautiful Low-Cost Quarters Will Replace Slums

· TYPICAL · COURT · CHEATHAM · PLACE ·
NASHVILLE · TENN.
· NASHVILLE · ALLIED · ARCHITECTS ·

BOSCOBEL HEIGHTS
PROJECT TENN. 5-1
NASHVILLE HOUSING AUTHORITY
MARR & HOLMAN – ARCHITECTS
NASHVILLE, TENN.
1940

Top: Cheatham Place, the public housing "village" for whites constructed by the New Deal. The federal government used high-quality materials to establish a national standard of decency for low-cost housing.

(Reprint of a drawing in the *Tennessean*, 1938: photograph by Gary Layda)

Bottom: Boscobel Heights (later James A. Cayce Homes), constructed in the second round of public housing for Nashville. Note the large housing blocks and the obliteration of the street grid in the site plan, which would be typical for subsequent projects. Additions in the 1950s would make this the largest public housing complex in the city.

(Drawing, 1940: photograph by Gary Layda)

The idea was that private developers would be more willing to invest in blighted areas if land acquisition and assembly was made easier by local housing agencies. But private developers did not see a profit in redeveloping much of the land cleared of slums for residential use. So the concept of slum clearance shifted to the redevelopment of cleared sites for commercial uses, with the displaced residents relocated to new public housing projects elsewhere. In Nashville plans were soon initiated to construct 2,625 new units of affordable housing, which were completed in 1954.

There were good intentions behind public housing, which initially provided much better living conditions than the private sector alternative for those accepted in the program. But with the rise of welfare in the 1960s the concept behind this housing changed to one of warehouses for the permanently poor, which had seriously negative impacts on the projects and on the stability of the traditional neighborhoods around them. Subsequent federal policy exacerbated this effect. In 1981 the federal government established preferences for those eligible for public housing that ensured the concentration of those with the lowest incomes. Between 1981 and 1996, when the preferences were dropped, the average income in the projects declined from 33 percent of

Almost two thousand Nashville families had been accommodated in public housing, but thirteen thousand more families were still living in substandard conditions according to the 1940 U.S. Census. In response to the national shortfall, the 1949 Federal Housing Act established objectives for slum clearance and new housing, provided funds for the relocation of residents displaced by slum clearance, and encouraged the inclusion of the private sector in redevelopment.

Top: Capitol Hill was a neighborhood, however shabby, before urban renewal.

(Photograph, 1952: Metro Archives)

Bottom: Street scene in the Capitol Hill neighborhood. Note the primitive housing and lack of paved streets.

(Photograph, 1952: Metro Development and Housing Agency)

Nashville's median income to 17 percent.

It was only with the federal Hope VI program that the Metro Development and Housing Agency began to deconcentrate the poverty of public housing with the demolition of the Vine Hill and Preston Taylor projects in 2000. In their place the agency has constructed houses that address the street, rather than superblocks that turn away from it, and restored the network of streets. But the remaining housing projects still make it hard to move forward in the first-ring neighborhoods that surround them.

Reshaping Capitol Hill

The late '40s in Nashville featured the first manifestation of the perennial question: "What are we going to do about downtown?" In the automotive age, the central city was suffering from congested streets, the steady migration of retail to suburbia, and the decay of its building stock because rehabilitation seemed a poor investment.[27] A growing number of old structures were being demolished for parking lots. While some civic boosters "advocated a revival of rapid transit as a remedy to the auto-glutted town," Doyle writes, "most retailers feared that if they did not welcome the automobile with more parking space and better [read "wider"] thoroughfares, the rising suburban shopping centers would." The concept of civic renewal thus became linked with the reconstruction of the city for the automobile.

Nashville's planners stood ready for the new wave of federal dollars with a land use study for

1940–1956

1940 Nashville Housing Authority designates more than 90 percent of the housing between Capitol Hill and the railroad trestle to the north as unfit or substandard, paving the way for the Capitol Hill Redevelopment Plan; this urban renewal project, which eliminated six historic African American churches, is the first in the nation to receive Congressional approval in 1949.

• Cumberland River freezes solid.

1941 Buses replace electric streetcars.

1950 Music City USA term coined by Nashville DJ David Cobb of WSM radio.

1951 Z. Alexander Looby and Robert Lillard elected to the City Council, the first African Americans to win seats in that body since 1911.

1952 Scarritt College becomes the first racially integrated private school in Tennessee. Two years later, when the newspapers publish graduation photographs that include two African Americans sporting their mortar boards, the administration receives phone calls from irate Nashvillians yelling that the school can't mix the races. The president's secretary calmly replies, "We've already done it."

1954 Farmers Market moves from 1937 City Market building opposite the Metro Courthouse to Jackson Street north of the Capitol; the old market is now the Ben West Building and houses Metro traffic courts.

1956 Owen Bradley knocks out the floor of an old house and brings the first music enterprise to what would become Music Row; subsequent now-historic recordings issue from Bradley's quonset hut and RCA's Studio B.

1957 Life and Casualty Tower, the tallest building in the Southeast, opens for business.

- Public school desegregation begins on September 9 with the Nashville Plan, a gradualist approach allowing one grade per year to be desegregated beginning with the first grade. In the early morning hours of September 10, a wing of the Hattie Cotton School in East Nashville is destroyed by a dynamite blast in an act of violent resistance to desegregation.

1959 Construction of Briley Parkway begins.

1960 Protests against whites-only lunch counters begin at downtown department stores, five-and-dime stores, and bus terminals; boycotts by black shoppers follow. On April 19 a crowd of more than three thousand march from Fisk University to the steps of the courthouse, following the bombing of black leader Z. Alexander Looby's house; there they hear Mayor Ben West throw his support behind demands for the integration of the city's lunch counters.

- Grandstand at Tennessee State Fairgrounds burns; it hosted the first Tennessee State Fair in 1907.
- One half of all American recordings come from Nashville.

1961 Maxwell House burns on Christmas Day; the hotel was built by John Overton and opened in 1869. The brand of coffee named after the hotel went into production in 1900.

Capitol Hill after urban renewal has begun. (Photograph, ca. 1964: Metro Development and Housing Agency)

the Capitol Hill Redevelopment Project. When the Housing Act was passed by Congress in 1949, Nashville's application was the first submitted and the first approved. The Nashville Housing Authority purchased ninety-six acres north and west of the State Capitol and proceeded to demolish what had been Hell's Half Acre, a black slum featuring unpaved streets and dilapidated structures, many with outdoor privies, as well as six historic African American churches. What replaced the slum was the six lanes of James Robertson Parkway, which carried traffic around the base of the hill and across the Cumberland via the new Victory Memorial Bridge. The hill below the Capitol was terraced for parking for state workers and the rest planted with trees and grass. The state constructed the State Library and Archives and the Cordell

Hull office building. The city laid plans for a municipal auditorium, although actual construction was not completed for more than a decade because of protests from black business and professional men whose offices would be displaced. Private developers purchased more than half of the land and constructed motels, apartment and office buildings; the land north of the railroad tracks was sold for industrial uses.

One result of the Capitol Hill Redevelopment Project was renewed civic pride and commitment to reinvest in the central city among downtown businessmen. Another was renewed criticism from African Americans that urban renewal was "Negro removal." From the standpoint of urban design, the problem was that the fine-grained street grid—even if it was a network of dirt—was destroyed and replaced with a wide road and buildings along it that related poorly to it. The city was being reengineered for cars to pass around the city and to be stored within it. And while it was obvious that much of the housing in the neighborhood was in appalling condition, it was nevertheless a neighborhood. The lack of residential replacements for the demolished houses, except for the small number of apartments that came to be used primarily as temporary quarters for visiting state legislators, meant that it was a neighborhood no more. The underlying presumption for all this renewal was that downtown Nashville was to be primarily a place to do business.

With the Capitol Hill project, Nashville's planners had demonstrated their ability to get federal monies and then use them for massive reconstruction. It was a pattern that was to be repeated through the 1970s, as the ideology of moving residents to make way for commerce and the car played out across the older parts of the city with increasingly radical effects.

The City from the Air

A Hollywood musical is an unlikely occasion for urban planning principles. But the opening frames of the film version of *West Side Story*—released in 1961, the same year that *The Death and Life of Great American Cities* by Jane Jacobs appeared—provide a visual primer that could have been created by Robert Moses, New York *über*-planner and the target of much of Jacobs's wrath.

The film's musical overture plays against an aerial abstraction of the New York City skyline. As the overture ends, abstraction condenses into reality, then shifts to a panoramic overhead sequence—bridge to cloverleaf to park to tops of skyscrapers to massive apartment blocks—before homing in on the roofs of tenements. During the overhead sequence, minuscule cars and trucks move in orderly processions—no traffic jams. People are invisible. The soundtrack, except for a lone whistle, is eerily quiet, the cacophony of the streets stilled by the lofty perspective. Seen from this distance, the city has all the beauty of a humming, well-oiled machine.

It is only when the camera comes to earth in an arid playground that people appear. They are the proverbial inner-city youths, troubled kids with time on their hands—hence all that dancing and fighting and finger snapping. And their neighborhood is an ethnic war zone that the forces of civic order—police and recreation director—haven't a clue how to pacify.

The American planners of the 1950s and '60s took a similarly lofty perspective because they had a similarly jaundiced view of city living. For them, the city had become a disorderly, socially dysfunctional, hard and unlovely place. Lots of people living cheek by jowl and mixing it up on the streets was a scenario straight out of Darwin—Jets vs. Sharks.

Unlike *West Side Story*'s cops, however, planners such as Moses had a pacification strategy.

Manhattan from the air. (Photograph, n.d.: National Archives)

To save the city, they reasoned, it must be disciplined, its complexity simplified. Abstract analysis produced plans featuring a simple series of relatively self-contained uses: housing, transportation, recreation, commerce, education, culture. The urban form this arrangement took goes back to the 1920s, when architect Le Corbusier first proposed his "Radiant City": a series of skyscrapers in a park crossed by limited-access highways and skywalks. In this vertical city, the street is bad for humans, so they must be elevated above it or isolated from it by greenery.

Jane Jacobs calls this civic discipline "pretended order, achieved by ignoring or suppressing the real order"—the intricate social and economic patterns under the seeming disorder of cities— "that is struggling to exist and be served." This kind of planning, which Jacobs likens to bloodletting, fails to see how a city really works, disregarding the organized complexity underlying the messy mixture of uses, the intimate if casual social encounters of sidewalks and stoops. The Robert Moses kind of planning—which dominated Nashville's planning until the 1990s—is made from the air, not the street.

It is an interesting intersection of fiction with reality that many of the scenes in *West Side Story* that were shot on location used abandoned tenements on New York's Upper West Side. These buildings were available for backdrops because they had been condemned by the mayor's Slum

"There is nothing economically or socially inevitable about either the decay of old cities or the fresh-minted decadence of the new unurban urbanization. On the contrary, no other aspect of our economy and society has been more purposefully manipulated for a full quarter of a century to achieve precisely what we are getting."

Jane Jacobs,
The Death and Life of Great American Cities
(1961)

1962–1969

1962 Interstate arrives in Davidson County with the construction of a segment of I-40 near the Cheatham County line; cynics note the apparent coincidence that Governor Frank Clement has a home in Dickson.

1963 *Central Loop General Neighborhood Renewal Plan* by Clark and Rapuano for Nashville Housing Authority—the urban renewal plan for Nashville.

- Construction begins on Percy Priest Dam; completed 1968, finalizing control of the currents of the Cumberland River. Old Hickory Dam began operating in 1957.

- Metro Government established, one of the first combinations of city and county governments in the nation.

- Harding Mall becomes the first shopping center in Tennessee. Soon followed by One Hundred Oaks Mall, named for the One Hundred Oaks Thompson mansion demolished for its construction.

1966 Metro Historical Commission formed to preserve Nashville's heritage.

- The Hermitage (1835) of Andrew Jackson becomes first building in Davidson County on the National Register of Historic Places.

1967 Davidson County voters approve the sale of liquor by the drink.

- Country Music Hall of Fame—inspired by the Cowboy Hall of Fame in Oklahoma City—debuts on Music Row on the former site of the Tony Rose Park playground.

- Construction of Ellington Parkway begins.

1969 Nashville leading city in the world in the number of electrically heated homes, courtesy of TVA's cheap rates.

Aerial view of pre-interstate Nashville.

(Photograph, 1959: Metro Planning Department)

Clearance Committee (chaired by Robert Moses) for the "urban renewal" that would bring forth in their stead Lincoln Center: ghetto to culture ghetto. The Lincoln Center groundbreakers were led by President Dwight Eisenhower, whose administration delivered the interstate highway system.

What is ironic is that the condemned territory, admittedly grimy and in need of rehab, exhibited all the basic characteristics of good urban form: narrow streets with on-street parking, continuous street walls of five-story (human-scaled) buildings, a mixture of land uses with residential over retail, small shops like Doc's candy store, fruit and vegetable stands, and a rec hall for social occasions. This urban fabric seems—to the early twenty-first century—a more likely candidate for a makeover than a bulldozer. But bulldozers are what the cities got.

The itinerary for the bulldozers in Nashville was crafted in response to the 1954 Federal Housing Act, which coined the term "urban renewal" and used it to describe a broader, more comprehensive approach to the problems of slums and urban blight.[28] The first urban renewal project in Nashville under the 1954 act was in East Nashville and began in 1959. The targeted area covered 2,052 acres and contained 8,617 dwelling units and 5,750 buildings. While the housing authority initially proposed to tear down only the worst of the housing and repair the rest, the Federal Highway Act of 1956 made rehabilitation less necessary, or even possible.

By the terms of the 1956 act, the federal government would pay 90 percent of the cost for Nashville's segments of a national, limited-access superhighway system. The city's planners had determined that one of these segments linking several interstates would go on the East Bank. The urban renewal plan for East Nashville called for 126 acres to be used for the interstate right-of-way and an additional 374 acres to be cleared along the river for industrial uses. The most important impact on the remaining acres was new water and sewer lines for the neighborhood.

As with East Nashville, the 1956 highway act also played a dominant role in the Edgehill urban renewal area, which stretched from what is now Music Row south and east to the path selected for I-65. It was the job of local planners to establish the routes through the city for the interstates that the federal government had planned to converge on Nashville. City planners hired as consultants the New York firm

"Beneath this slab / John Brown is stowed. / He watched the ads, / And not the road."

Ogden Nash,
"Lather As You Go,"
Good Intentions
(1943)

The Case of I-40

When land acquisition for I-40 began in 1964, the total impact of the right-of-way on North Nashville became apparent. The chosen corridor passed through a major African American business district and near three black colleges. In 1967 black civic leaders learned that this route represented a modification of earlier plans for a more southerly course through a predominantly white area parallel to Charlotte Avenue. Defenders of the northern path alleged that it was necessary to change the route in order to have the desired number of interchanges for downtown with the federally required three miles between interchanges.

Agitation turned to outrage when the black community discovered that the final blessing for the northern route was given at a 1957 public hearing that was less than completely public. The notices for the hearing bore the wrong date, "were posted only in post offices in white neighborhoods, and were not distributed to the news media," according to legal historians Allan Gates, et al. And "the transcript of the hearing, required by law to be taken, was very incomplete." Charging that no proper hearing had been held, the citizens of North Nashville formed the I-40 Steering Committee and went to court. But the District Court for the Middle District of Tennessee held that "the 1957 corridor hearing, while a poor example of admin-istrative procedure, was not legally in-adequate." And "the crippling effect of the highway on the community was not deemed enough to warrant an injunc-tion." Higher courts upheld this decision.

The effects were indeed crippling. The highway disrupted businesses, split up neighborhoods, dead-ended streets, and radically altered the traffic flow. To this day the noise and air pollution re-main a nuisance, as a recent public meet-ing on these problems demonstrates. But the case of I-40 in North Nashville illus-trated one lesson: public action against a major road project cannot wait until bids are about to be let and be successful. It would be several decades, with the fight over the Franklin Corridor, before Nash-villians learned it.

Christine Kreyling

The history of the I-40 controversy is from "Nashville Model Cities: A Case Study," by Allan Gates, Richard W. Creswell, Paul M. Kurtz, Paul R. Regens-dorf, Samuel W. Bartholomew Jr., and Richard W. Greenstein, in Growing Me-tropolis: Aspects of Development in Nashville, *edited by James F. Blumstein and Benjamin Walter (Nashville, Tenn.: Vanderbilt University Press, 1975, pp. 196–99).*

Vision for the interstate loop. From the air the highway is a ribbon of white, like a necklace adorning the central city. (Drawing, 1963: Metro Planning Department)

of Clarke and Rapuano—the same consultants used for the Capitol Hill Redevelopment Proj-ect—to recommend paths for the roads after studying population density, land use and street patterns, topography, locations of undeveloped land, existing neighborhoods, and the all-impor-tant land values. Edgehill was typical of the kind of neighborhood selected to eat the puree of ur-ban renewal and interstate—lower income, large minority population, and partially blighted.

The urban renewal project in Nashville with the highest visibility, however, was the one for the city center. The Central Loop General Neighborhood Renewal Plan of 1963 was de-vised by the firm of Clarke and Rapuano, the perennial consultants to the Nashville Housing Authority, for the area inside the interstate inner loop west of the Cumberland River. It is a classic of the Robert Moses school of civic reformation.

In the vision for the Central Loop, new build-ings are a gleaming white, while existing build-ings that the plan retains are represented in dun colors. And the form these new structures take is the stand-alone surrounded by lavish landscaping and open plazas—the suburban ideal of buildings in a park—decidedly different from the older, shared-wall structures that fill up the blocks and reach to the sidewalks to form continuous street walls. The streets are wide—many of them six lanes—and carry primarily one-way traffic; there

Central Loop: General Neighborhood Renewal Plan. Views from north and south. (Aerial rendering, 1963: Clarke and Rapuano for Nashville Housing Authority; perspective sketch, 1963: Clarke and Rapuano for Nashville Housing Authority)

are few vehicles and fewer parking lots.

First Avenue North has been eliminated entirely as have all the historic buildings between this street and Second Avenue, which have been replaced by a large park and a series of high-rise towers. Second Avenue itself has grown to eight lanes, the center half of which tunnel under the Metro Courthouse. Of the city's significant historic buildings, only the State Capitol and the Downtown Presbyterian Church are visible in the rendering, although the site map shows the Customs House and Post Office still standing—goodbye Ryman Auditorium. A new baseball stadium lies in Sulphur Dell north of the Capitol.

Much of the Central Loop Plan was never implemented. But its impact on the heart of downtown between Union and Deaderick Streets, the Metro Courthouse and Eighth Avenue, was dramatic. War Memorial Park was replaced by Legislative Plaza, which was elevated above the street to accommodate parking and offices underneath. The city demolished the existing structures along Deaderick Street, widened the street to four lanes, installed broad sidewalks lined with trees, and sold the vacant sites to the state and to private developers for new office construction and civic space such as the Tennessee Performing Arts Center. The form these new buildings took is that suggested in the Central Loop Plan: stand-alone towers rest on high, blank podiums that provide little visual interest at street level, fail to define a continuous street wall, and lack the mixture of uses that would help to socialize the street.

The public square and the historic buildings around it were bulldozed, replaced with a surface parking lot in front of the courthouse, the

1970–1979

1970 All twelve grades of the public school system are officially integrated, but the vast majority of students still attend schools predominantly of their own race. Busing to achieve integration begins in 1971; in that same year seven new private schools are organized.

1972 Opryland USA theme park opens.

1973 First building in Metro Center office park placed atop a former landfill; in 2002 Watkins College of Art and Design occupies abandoned cineplex; the Watkins Institute had held its first classes on Church Street in 1889.

1974 Parking lot constructed in front of the Metro Courthouse, replacing the public square; the last of the historic nineteenth-century buildings surrounding the square are razed.

• Legislative Plaza replaces War Memorial gardens; renovations to repair leaks to state offices and parking garage below commence in 2004.

1977 *Nashville: Conserving a Heritage* published by the Metro Historical Commission, drawing attention to Nashville's historic neighborhoods; creates ethic to preserve districts and neighborhoods as well as individual buildings.

1978 Nashville Sounds debut in Greer Stadium; professional baseball returns to Nashville.

• Edgefield first Nashville neighborhood to receive protection of historic zoning overlay.

• Amtrak ends passenger rail service to Nashville.

1979 Vanderbilt University and Peabody College merge.

1981–1993

1981 Tennessee Performing Arts Center opens downtown in the James K. Polk Building, which also houses the Tennessee State Museum and state offices.

1983 Riverfront Park dedicated on July 10, replacing large TVA tower and the Nashville wharf at the foot of Broadway.

1985 I-440 construction begins; the limited-access highway linking I-40 west of the city with I-65 and I-24 to the south is completed after neighborhood activists force changes to its design.

1988 First Southern Festival of Books in downtown Nashville.

1991 Construction of 840 Loop begins with the southeast segment; fierce battles over the road's design and right-of-way in southwest Williamson County are only resolved when Gerald Nicely becomes TDOT Commissioner in 2001; Nicely also suspends plans for the equally controversial northern segment of 840.

• Father Ryan High School moves from Elliston Place to Franklin Road, one of a number of private schools to seek greener pastures in the newer suburbs.

• Center City Plan is the first Subarea Plan for downtown; updated in 1997.

1992 Sudekum Building—an Art Deco landmark on Church Street— detonated for surface parking; Cumberland Apartments are later constructed on the site.

1993 Tennessee Bicentennial Capitol Mall and State Capitol Area Master Plan accepted by the Building Commission. The centerpiece is the proposed seventeen-acre urban park. Followed in 1997 by the Bicentennial Mall Urban Master Plan.

Demolition of the American National Bank Building, Fourth Avenue North and Union Street.
(Photograph, 1973: Metro Historical Commission)

giant First American Center (now AmSouth), the Gay Street Connector, and the wide, curving road that connects the Woodland Street Bridge to Union Street.

Nashville was using urban renewal to make a government investment in the business district to entice the private sector to do likewise, at a time when companies such as National Life were contemplating a departure to the suburbs. At the same time the city and county worked out a plan to limit the taxes a 1907 state law gave the county sole power to assess on insurance companies headquartered in Davidson County. The assessed cost of new construction was to be written off as a credit against the county tax so that a dollar spent on building was a dollar saved in taxes. In the short run these strategies worked. Along Union Street Nashville's bankers and insurance barons followed the government's lead and constructed mammoth new office buildings. National Life built a 31-story tower of travertine marble (now the state-owned Tennessee Tower) set back from the street in an expansive plaza.

These gestures toward downtown revitalization were well-intentioned. But the simplification of the core from a complex and finely-woven mixture of land uses into a central business district, and the anti-urban form the envelopes for the businesses took ignored the perspective of the man on the street. The broad sidewalks and open plazas became increasingly depopulated. Urban renewal kept the companies downtown—for a while—but it gave the people employed by these businesses less reason to walk around in the city.

Going Metro

By 1960 there were more people living in Davidson County outside the city limits than in Nashville itself.[29] The car—and most families had one—enabled people to live anywhere on the expanding system of roads and highways. Suburban developers mass produced thousands of inexpensive tract houses on cheap land in the about-to-be-not-country. Low-interest mortgages for this new housing were frequently underwritten by federal programs.

People who migrated to the suburbs were exchanging decaying urban neighborhoods for a brand new house, a green lawn, and new schools and stores. "Many white suburbanites also left the city out of an unspoken fear of blacks," Doyle points out, "an effort to maintain social distance by creating more physical distance between the races at a time when the legal barriers of racial segregation were beginning to crumble."

The problem for local government was to plan for future development and provide services to a metropolis that was an economic unit but divided politically. The migration of residents, as well as commerce and industry, eroded the city's tax base. The county had neither the legal authority nor the funds to provide adequate services. Many suburban communities relied on individual subscriptions to pay for police and fire protection and garbage collection. County residents took advantage of urban amenities such as parks and libraries without paying the property taxes that supported them. As satellite cities such as Berry Hill, Oak Hill, and Forest Hills incorporated, many feared that the political balkanization and fierce competition among vested interests would lead to metropolitan disintegration.

One solution was the annexation of county land by the city, but promoting this was suicide for any politician. Residents of the county

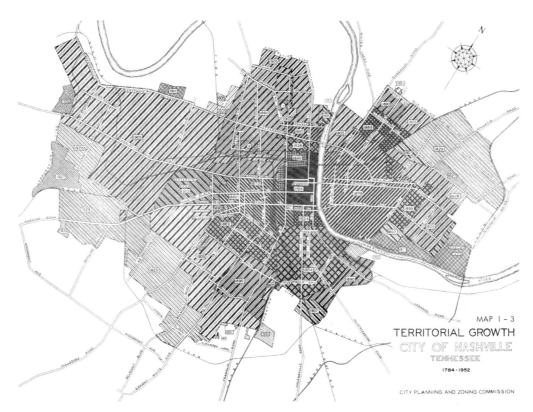

Nashville growth patterns, 1784–1952.

(Map, February 1965: *History and Physical Setting: Nashville and Davidson County, Tennessee,* Planning Commission of the Metropolitan Government of Nashville and Davidson County)

MAP 1 - 3

TERRITORIAL GROWTH
CITY OF NASHVILLE
TENNESSEE
1784-1952

CITY PLANNING AND ZONING COMMISSION

paid much lower property taxes, and the resulting poor level of services was less of an issue for them than retaining the personal funds to pay off the mortgage and acquire the car, TV, and other consumer goods that had become *de rigueur* in suburbia.

Another strategy was the consolidation of city and county government, which was advocated by a 1952 report, *A Future for Nashville,* published by a joint commission of city and county representatives created to study the provision of services. The report noted, however, the state constitutional obstacles to consolidation, and recommended as a stopgap measure major annexations of sixty-nine square miles and ninety thousand people into a metropolitan government.

In 1953 a limited state constitutional convention enabled the merger of city and county governments, if a majority in both areas voted for

the change. In 1958 the first public referendum on consolidation passed in the city but failed in the county. Mayor Ben West then turned to annexation to improve the city's tax base. The City Council authorized extensions to the city limits that took in fifty-two square miles and eighty-two thousand residents of the county, many of whom were outraged when their property taxes increased and services didn't. Having experienced annexation, the disgruntled began to call for another referendum on consolidation.

After a brutal political battle that pitted Mayor Ben West against County Judge and soon-to-be-Mayor Beverly Briley, consolidation was approved by the voters in 1962. The charter for the metropolitan form of government differed little from the one proposed in 1958. Both called for two tax districts distinguished by levels of service. Residents of the General Services District (GSD) would pay a base property tax

"Metro Nashville was the most important thing we did since John Donelson got off the boat at this part of the Cumberland River."

Mayor Bill Purcell,
interview
(July 28, 2004)

1994 BellSouth building rears its "Batman" profile over the Nashville skyline, joining the L&C tower as an icon for the city.

- Zoning in the central core changed to permit residential construction.

- Ryman Auditorium reopens after renovation; threatened by demolition after the Grand Ole Opry migrated to the Opryland complex in the Pennington Bend suburbs in 1974, the historic building was saved by a national preservation campaign. In 2001 the Ryman is named a National Historic Landmark.

1995 Groundbreaking for Shelby Bottoms Greenway.

1996 Bicentennial Mall opens to the public on May 31. The Mall, with the new Farmers Market, which debuted on the Mall's western flank in 1995, propels redevelopment in Germantown and Hope Gardens neighborhoods.

- The Nashville Arena opens with a Christmas concert by Amy Grant; in 1998 the professional hockey team the Predators leap onto the ice of what is now the Gaylord Entertainment Center.

1997 Opryland Theme Park closes and is replaced by Opry Mills Mall in 2000.

- *The Plan for SoBro* is published by the *Nashville Scene*, the result of a design charrette that focused on the area south of Broadway to the interstate.

1998 Tornado hits downtown and East Nashville. The massive destruction of homes and trees spurs the 1999 ReLeaf Nashville campaign and R/UDAT plan for East Nashville.

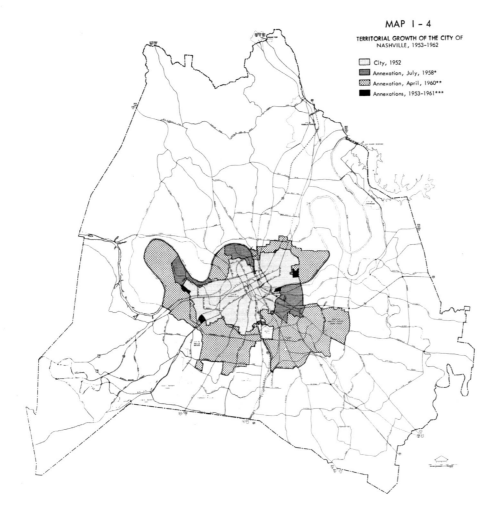

MAP I – 4

TERRITORIAL GROWTH OF THE CITY OF NASHVILLE, 1953–1962

- ☐ City, 1952
- ▦ Annexation, July, 1958*
- ▧ Annexation, April, 1960**
- ■ Annexations, 1953–1961***

Nashville growth patterns, 1953–1962. (Map, February 1965: *History and Physical Setting: Nashville and Davidson County, Tennessee*, Planning Commission of the Metropolitan Government of Nashville and Davidson County)

rate for the essential services of schools, roads, and police. Residents of the Urban Services District (USD) would pay a higher rate for additional services such as sewer lines, fire protection, and garbage collection. The USD would expand as sewer lines were laid. The distinction between the two charters was the size of the Metro Council. The 1958 proposal featured a Council with twenty-one members. The charter of 1962 had a forty-one-member Council, with five representatives of the county at large, to assuage suburban residents who feared underrepresentation in the new government.

On April 1, 1963, Metropolitan Nashville–Davidson County government became a reality. A city of 73 square miles and 171,000 people became a new political entity of 508 square miles and more than 400,000 people. The city's tax base was stabilized, duplication of government bureaucracies and services was eliminated, the school systems merged, city/county rivalry ceased, and a new civic consciousness emerged in the suburbs. In addition, Nashville now had a coherent government structure for long-range planning that would serve as a magnet for federal public works grants.

But there were downsides for residents of the old city. Because the provision of services was a key component of the campaign platform for consolidation, the coming of Metro refocused the commitment of government resources to infrastructure in the outlying areas.[30] The immediate need was for sewer lines in the suburban hinterland, not only in those locations served by septic systems, but also in brand new subdivisions springing up at the periphery. Some of these areas were of such low development densities that the installation of sewer lines was economically impractical. The increased tax base that came from the expansion of the Urban Services District never paid for the high cost of building new sewers. And the hook-up fees charged to residents and developers when the sewer lines arrived did not remotely cover the actual cost of the lines' construction. One result was large hikes in water/sewer bills for residents of the older suburbs that already had sewer lines. Another was deferred maintenance for much of the existing infrastructure in the central city.

The flaw of the new Metro government was that it ignored the implications of land use patterns and thus failed to make more compact development a prerequisite for urban services. In reports and studies of the 1950s and '60s and '70s, Nashville's planners warned that the low-density development patterns of the suburbs would make the provision of infrastructure and services to these areas prohibitively expensive, dilute the level of services in the traditional neighborhoods, and make it all but impossible to establish an efficient and economically feasible mass transit system for Metro Nashville. Metro government solved many problems, but it missed the opportunity to begin to address the dilemma of sprawl.

The Second Reconstruction

Nashville "was the first major city in the South to experience widespread desegregation of public facilities," writes historian Don Doyle.[31] The city's geographical position on the northern edge of the South, its history of Union occupation during the Civil War, and its self-image as a leader of the progressive New South all played a part in Nashville's failure to mount a massive and violent resistance to civil rights of the sort staged in Birmingham and Little Rock. More important was the unique combination of strong local black leadership—lawyers, clergy, and educators—and young activists from other parts of the country who came to Nashville to attend the city's institutes of African American higher education and brought with them an unwillingness to accommodate to the established racial customs of the city.

Those customs were decidedly racist. African Americans had to sit in a separate waiting room at Union Station and use separate bathroom facilities at the city hall and county courthouse. Of the city's thirty-two parks encompassing 3,650 acres, blacks were permitted in fewer than fifty-five acres in six parks. Blacks could buy goods at downtown department stores but were not served at their lunch counters, nor at most white-owned restaurants and bars. The War Memorial Auditorium featured segregated show times for performances by African American musical groups. Jim Crow seating was the rule at the Ryman Auditorium, the Sulphur Dell baseball stadium, and movie theaters, except for the Bijou, which had been a black-oriented venue since 1916. This historic theater, along with the rest of the black commercial and entertainment district on Fourth Avenue North, was demol-

Urban renewal obliterating the African American commercial and entertainment district on Fourth Avenue North; the Bijou Theater is still standing in the background.

(Photograph, 1957: Metro Archives)

ished in 1957 as part of the Capitol Hill Redevelopment project, and replaced by the Municipal Auditorium.[32]

The job market was also highly segregated. There were almost no African American sales staff in the retail and wholesale trades. The banks and insurance companies employed no blacks except in porter and janitorial positions, and the state of jobs in government was similar. Fewer than 4 percent of the twelve thousand jobs in new industries such as the Ford Glass plant and Gates Rubber were held by blacks.

Residential segregation became increasingly pronounced between 1940 and 1960 as neighborhood racial patterns were shaped by public housing and urban renewal, city zoning policies, the practices of home mortgage lenders and realtors, and the exodus of whites to the suburbs.

"In 1940, 120,084 whites lived within the city's boundaries; by 1960 that number had declined to 98,085," Doyle writes. "At the same time the number of whites in [Davidson] county beyond the city limits grew from 80,386 to 224,826," where they made up 98 percent of the county's population outside the city.

Enabled by the 1954 U.S. Supreme Court decision in *Brown vs. Board of Education of Topeka, Kansas*, separate and unequal public schools were the first target of the campaign for civil rights. A class action lawsuit on behalf of Nashville's black school children led to the court-ordered school desegregation plan of 1957. The so-called Nashville Plan, which was adopted by other Southern cities, allowed one grade per year to be desegregated beginning with the first grade. This gradualist approach included the

"The problem of the Twentieth Century is the problem of the color-line."

W. E. B. Du Bois,
The Souls of Black Folk
(1903)

1999–2003

1999 Coliseum football stadium welcomes the Tennessee Titans (formerly Houston Oilers); construction necessitates relocation of industrial uses on the East Bank. In their first year in their new home the Titans emerge as AFC champs.

2000 Mayor Bill Purcell announces the foundation of the Nashville Civic Design Center.

2001 *USA Today* names Nashville the nation's most sprawling metropolitan region with population of one million or more.

• Frist Center for the Visual Arts, Country Music Hall of Fame and Museum, and the downtown Nashville Public Library open to the public.

• Union Station train shed dismantled after decades of neglect; the site is used for surface parking. With the shed gone, Union Station loses its designation as a National Historic Landmark in 2003.

• Nashville Rescue Mission relocates to the old Sears building on Lafayette Street. The Mission's former quarters, a 1914 Spanish-style building that housed the exclusive Centennial Club for ladies until 1960, was demolished in 2000 for surface parking after a suspicious fire.

2003 Construction begins on Schermerhorn Symphony Center.

Civil rights march, April 1961.
(Photograph, 1961: Nashville Public Library, The Nashville Room)

The campaign to desegregate white-only lunch counters at department stores, five-and-dime stores, and bus terminals, which began on February 13, 1960, was a disciplined exercise in the tactics of non-violence practiced primarily by black students attending Fisk University, the American Baptist Theological Seminary, and Tennessee A & I (now Tennessee State University). When the sit-ins failed to yield the desired result, boycotts of downtown stores by supportive shoppers followed. The turning point came on April 19, when three thousand protesters marched from Fisk University to the Metro Courthouse following the predawn bombing of civil rights leader Z. Alexander Looby's house. Mayor Ben West met the marchers on the courthouse steps, and, when pressed to take a personal and moral stand, finally threw his support behind desegregation of the lunch counters.

Subsequent protests focusing on segregated movie theaters and hotel accommodations, as well as fair employment practices—which targeted the H. G. Hill grocery stores—gradually yielded positive results. "Segregation had all but disappeared in most Nashville public accommodations by 1964," Doyle writes.

The federal government took note of Nashville's comparatively peaceful acceptance of civil rights by showering the city with Great Society program funds. By the early 1970s, Metro Nashville was simultaneously involved in over 170 federal grants and ranked well above larger cities in the South in the amount of federal dollars it received. But as the map of 2000 U.S. Census figures illustrates, desegregation of public places did not bring about integration in the residential living patterns of the city.

racial gerrymandering of school zones, which left only 115 of the 1,400 black first-graders eligible to enter formerly all-white schools in 1957, as well as a policy that permitted students to transfer, upon written request from their parents, when they were zoned for a school that was predominantly of the other race. This plan was token desegregation, but it at least started Nashville down the path of compliance, not defiance.

The number of black children in formerly all-white schools grew from nine in 1957 to 728 by 1963. In 1966 the Metro School Board voted to abandon the grade-per-year approach and integrate all twelve grades of the public school system. But by 1970, the combination of residential segregation and the patterns of neighborhood school zones ensured that the vast majority of students still attended schools with predominantly their own race. In response, federal judge L. Clure Morton ordered the creation of a new plan whose aim was to create a unified public education system in which each Metro school was integrated roughly in proportion to the percentage of blacks and whites in the population of Metro Nashville as a whole. This meant busing, and the gradual erosion of the concept of neighborhood schools.

Yellow school buses began shuttling children across Metro Nashville in 1971; in that same year seven new private schools were organized. Many white parents moved to distant suburbs beyond the district busing plan, or left the county entirely. By 1979 the white enrollment in the schools ordered by the court to desegregate had declined by 53 percent. The disjunction between the goals of balanced integration, and the American tradition of the neighborhood school that lies within walking distance of a child's home and serves as a center of a community's life and culture, has still not been resolved.

36

THE PLAN OF NASHVILLE

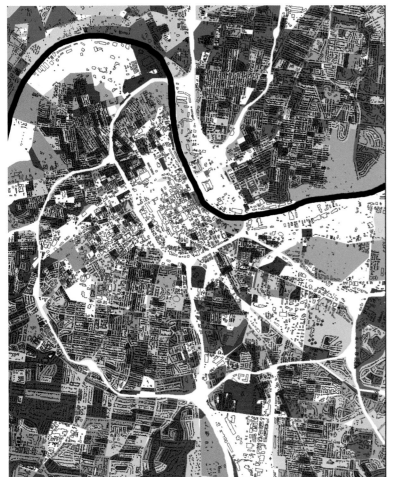

Map Key

☐	0–33%
■	33–50%
■	50–66%
■	66–75%
■	75–85%
■	85–95%
■	95–99%
■	99–100%

Percent of residents that belong to the majority race in the census block group.

Map of 2000 U.S. Census figures illustrates the residential diversity of Nashville's neighborhoods. The map was devised by selecting each area's most prominent race, and then measuring the exclusivity of that race, to determine neighborhoods that are more homogeneous (shades of red) and those that are more heterogeneous (shades of blue), regardless of which race is dominant. The map thus shows areas where those of different races are currently more likely to be neighbors.

(Map, 2000: U.S. Census, with interpretive text by Brian Christens)

Saving History in Three Dimensions

It was urban renewal, ironically enough, that empowered the historic preservation movement in Nashville, and in the nation as a whole.[33] Before what Jane Jacobs calls "the sacking of cities" in the 1950s and '60s and '70s, the preservation of architecture focused on the houses and public buildings where "great white men" lived and worked. As early as 1813, Independence Hall in Philadelphia was saved from demolition, and the Mount Vernon Ladies' Association was formed in 1814 to guard the home of George Washington. The first local manifestation of this phenomenon was the Ladies' Hermitage Association, which in 1889 acquired the house that Andrew Jackson built from the state to preserve it as a public shrine. These structures were deemed worth keeping, not necessarily because of their architectural virtues, but because of the historical importance of the people who owned and used them.

With the exception of buildings that satisfy our interest in the lifestyles of the rich, famous, and dead, Americans have a tendency to think that a new structure, or even a whole new city, is obviously superior to what it superseded. This attitude is rooted in the nature of our national origins. "History was part of the baggage we threw overboard when we launched ourselves into the New World," explains California writer Wallace Stegner in "The Sense of Place."

The demolition derby of urban renewal threw history overboard with a vengeance. Old landmarks were routinely imploded to make way for new skyscrapers, parking lots, and roads. When the congregation of First Presbyterian Church moved to the suburbs in the 1950s, their historic downtown home in the Egyptian Revival–style church by William Strickland, where many of Nashville's most prominent citizens had worshipped, was scheduled to be razed for surface parking until a core group of members stepped in to stop the bulldozers. The six historic African American churches in the neighborhood of the State Capitol were not so lucky; all were eliminated by the Capitol Hill Redevelopment Project.

Preservationists became a political force at the national level in 1966, with the public outcry over the destruction of the grand vaulted halls of New York City's Penn Station. The protests were motivated, not by the loss of a building that had housed eminent people, but by the loss of magnificent architecture. In that year, Congress passed the National Historic Preservation Act, which established preservation roles for federal, state, and local levels of government, and created the National Register of Historic Places. In that same year, Metro government established the Metro Historical Commission (MHC). The

"The most important thing about preservation is not the creation of the illusion of an old place, but the visibility of the arc of time, of generations of architecture working together to create a sense of place. We preserve not to take us back to the past but to make for a better present."

Paul Goldberger,
Preservation
(January/February 2004)

2004 Construction begins on new public square park—with parking garage below—in front of the Metro Courthouse; renovation of the courthouse commenced in 2003 after the mayor and Metro Council took up temporary quarters in the former Ben West Library.

- Gateway Bridge restores vehicular connection between East Nashville and SoBro, lost when the Shelby Street Bridge closed in 1998; Shelby reopened as a pedestrian bridge in 2003.

- Thermal Plant, which had burned Nashville's garbage to heat and cool many downtown buildings, demolished—to the cheers of environmentalists.

2005 The Plan of Nashville is published by the Nashville Civic Design Center.

Sources for timeline images include: Library of Congress, Metro Archives, Nashville Public Library, Tennessee State Library and Archives, and www.historicnashville.com.

The old West End Methodist Church, whose steeple once punctuated the pivot from Broadway to West End Avenue, was demolished ca. 1940 for what became part of West End's "Auto Row," an early example of the impact of the car on fine architecture.

(Photograph, n.d.: Nashville Public Library, The Nashville Room

Demolition of the east side of the public square.

(Photograph, 1974: Nashville Public Library, The Nashville Room, Warterfield Collection)

The Ryman Auditorium, which opened as the Union Gospel Tabernacle in 1892. Identified as "obsolete" in the 1963 *Central Loop Plan* for downtown urban renewal, and targeted for demolition in the 1970s, the "mother church of country music" survived to reopen for performances in 1994 and today stands as one of the crowning glories of Nashville's preservation movement.

(Photograph, 2003: Vanderbilt University, Neil Brake)

commission's early efforts were primarily devoted to getting such obvious landmarks as The Hermitage, Belle Meade Plantation, Travellers Rest, and Union Station listed on the National Register, and developing a historical marker program.

By the 1970s, some Nashvillians had begun to perceive that the new office buildings, interstates, shopping malls, and subdivisions, coupled with the invasion of chain stores and fast-food franchises, were turning their home place into what urban critic James Kunstler calls "the geography of nowhere"—a city less and less distinguishable from other Sunbelt cities of similar size. The purging of Nashville's civic heart, with the demolition of the historic buildings around the public square and the supplanting of the square itself by wide roads and surface parking, was a classic illustration of the exchange of local character for generic function.

When National Life and Accident announced its intentions to move the Grand Ole Opry to the new Opryland complex in 1973 and demolish the Ryman Auditorium—and to use the historic bricks to construct the "Little Chapel of Opryland"—preservation in Nashville became a public issue. A sometimes uncivil war broke out between those determined to save one of Nashville's most sacred spaces and the prominent families who owed their fortunes to the insurance company. The turning point came when Ada Louise Huxtable, the architecture critic of the *New York Times*, challenged National Life's position as "a mixture of architectural ignorance and acute business venality." This national shame campaign kept the building standing, padlocked shut except for the occasional tour group, until the revival of downtown as an entertainment destination. The rebirth of Second Avenue as a tourist hot spot in the 1990s induced Opryland, Inc., to see new revenue opportunities in a structure it once scorned as hopelessly passé. Renovation to the building began in 1993, and the following year music finally returned to Nashville's most hallowed hall.

With the case of the Ryman, local government learned that some civic monuments were so significant to our sense of who we are as a community that Nashvillians would not let them be lost. When the fates of the Customs House and Union Station were in question, their salvation was accomplished, not by public protest, but by a close collaboration between preservationists and city officials. The concept of protecting the character of a whole district rather than a stand-alone structure, however, took longer to sell for downtown.

123 South Eleventh Street in the East End neighborhood, remuddled and restored; a good example of the neighborhood success stories that form the backbone of historic preservation in Nashville.

(Photographs, 1986 and 1996: Metro Historical Commission)

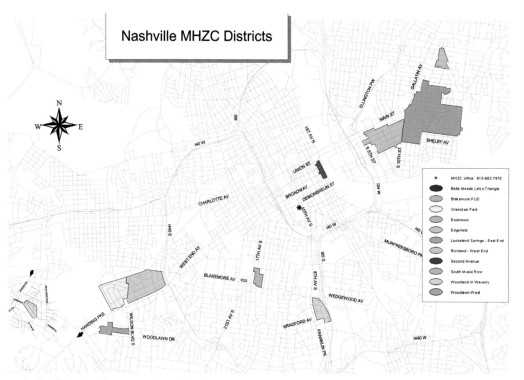

Nashville MHZC Districts

* MHZC office: 615-862-7970
Belle Meade Links Triangle
Blakemore PUD
Cherokee Park
Eastwood
Edgefield
Lockeland Springs - East End
Richland - West End
Second Avenue
South Music Row
Woodland in Waverly
Woodlawn West

Nashville's historic and conservation zoning districts. (Map, 2004: Metro Historic Zoning Commission, Fred Zahn)

The warehouse precinct of Second Avenue North was, in 1972, the first historic district in Nashville to be listed on the National Register. In 1985 a fire destroyed an entire block on the eastern side containing the oldest buildings on the street. As a replacement, an Alabama developer proposed a glitzy, twenty-one-story tower that was initially supported by elected officials. But the Metro Historical Commission and the nonprofit Historic Nashville, Inc., realizing that such a structure would seriously erode the architectural coherence of the street, filed a lawsuit challenging the variances for the tower that had been granted by the Board of Zoning Appeals, and won. Efforts to control demolition, exterior rehabilitation and new construction by applying

a historic zoning overlay to the district, however, failed in 1986; Second Avenue received this protection only in 1997.

District preservation came sooner to the neighborhoods, perhaps because it was only a small cadre of long-term residents and true believers who saw any value in the older suburbs, and the low property values did not promise windfall profits to developers. In 1977 the Metro Historical Commission published a seminal study, *Nashville: Conserving a Heritage*, that identified twenty-four historic neighborhoods and made recommendations for their preservation and revitalization. Many of the neighborhoods singled out in the study were the same ones that urban renewal had targeted for slum clearance as "blighted." That same year the city passed legislation enabling historic zoning and created the Metro Historic Zoning Commission to administer it. The following year Edgefield became the

first neighborhood to receive this protection from demolition and architecturally inappropriate exterior rehabilitation. In 1985 the East End and Lockeland Springs neighborhoods pioneered the concept of conservation zoning, a slightly less stringent set of rules for preservation.

In the struggle to save and repair Nashville's old neighborhoods, "preservation was a side issue, really," says Metro Historical Commission executive director Ann Roberts. "The problems were absentee landlords, lack of codes enforcement, deteriorating properties, and redlining by financial lending institutions." Preservation overlays were the only means available to neighborhood activists for recognizing the virtues of traditional urban design and enforcing its basic principles. That the zoning has been effective is demonstrated by the rising property values in the districts with the overlays, and the continued growth of the program, which today includes eleven historic and conservation zoning districts covering approximately 3,300 properties.

Other government agencies have become more responsive to the goal of preserving and restoring the traditional urban fabric. The Metro Development and Housing Agency carefully monitors historic structures in its redevelopment districts and has established design guidelines for several of them—the East Bank and Five Points districts in East Nashville and for parts of the Phillips-Jackson district in North Nashville—that mandate compatible infill. The Planning Department now takes historic properties into account in its community planning process, and has put in place an urban zoning overlay to encourage urban rather than suburban development patterns within the pre-Metro city limits.

The recent history of preservation in Nashville is a narrative of victories alternating with defeats. In the former category are the restoration of Cravath Hall on the Fisk University campus, the Nashville Parthenon, and the Shelby Bridge, as well as the broadening of the definition of what's worth conserving to include public works infrastructure, such as the City Reservoir and gauge house, and the Omohundro waterworks. Outstanding among the latter are the destruction of the Art Deco Sudekum building on Church Street, the Jacksonian apartment building on West End Avenue, the Nashville & Decatur railroad depot on Fourth Avenue just south of the City Cemetery, and the National Landmark Union Station train shed in the Gulch.

The significance of the preservation movement goes beyond the fact that it has changed the way Nashvillians and their government think about old buildings. By focusing on continuities of architectural fabric in whole districts, preservationists brought attention to the larger issues of traditional urban design and the need to build the future on the solid foundations of the past. Perhaps even more important, the grassroots nature of the movement's evolution demonstrated that listening to the community is a crucial component of city planning.

Looking for the Soul of the City

The closer the historian comes to the present, the more difficult it is to find the telling detail in the welter of circumstances. For it is only in the fourth dimension of time that significance—the relationships between causes and effects, positives and negatives—can be even remotely apprehended. But some things about the recent shaping of the city can be told, even now.

The past decade in Nashville has witnessed a dramatic animation in the life of downtown. The reopening of the Ryman Auditorium and the Shelby Bridge, the rehabilitation of Second Avenue and Lower Broad, the transformation of the Broadway Post Office into the Frist Center for the Visual Arts, the construction of the Arena (now Gaylord Entertainment Center), the Coliseum, the Country Music Hall of Fame and Museum, and the downtown library—all these initiatives have brought people back to the streets and sidewalks of the city beyond the eight-to-five of office hours. The change in zoning rules to permit residential construction in the central core has led to a new apartment tower and the rehab of the upper floors of old buildings for urban living, with more on the way. Construction began on the Schermerhorn Symphony Center in 2003 and the Thermal Plant was demolished in 2004, the same year that the city commenced the building of a new park to replace the parking lot that had replaced the public square in front of the Metro Courthouse.

Outside the city center in the first-ring neighborhoods, the Farmers Market and Bicentennial Mall have begun to generate new residential development north of the Capitol. East Nashville got the Shelby Bottoms Greenway and turned the devastation of the 1998 tornado into a great leap forward. The Metro Development and Housing Agency is proceeding with plans for a new neighborhood on Rolling Mill Hill to the south, a mixed-use village is taking shape in the Gulch, and the upper reaches of Demonbreun Street have been transformed from a tourist trap into a hangout for cafe society.

These specific developments were more than matched by changes in the city's planning policies, but the latter did not come without a battle. The occasion of combat was the Franklin Corridor.

In 1995 Metro's planning and public works departments announced plans to tear down the 1909 Shelby Bridge and replace it with a new bridge as part of a six-lane high-speed corridor south of Broadway linking two interstates. Also part of the plan was the demolition of the Demonbreun viaduct, to be superseded by a road swooping south of Cummins Station before reconnecting with Demonbreun Street and I-40 to the west. A few incredulous Nashvillians questioned the wisdom of demolishing the city's only remaining historic bridge and building a Berlin Wall through an area that had the potential to become a crucial buttress in the support structure of downtown. They also challenged the premise that what downtown needed for rejuvenation was more asphalt for more cars.

During the long but ultimately successful effort to turn corridor into urban avenue, south of Broadway became SoBro. The Nashville Urban Design Forum was established to bring public debate to the development of the city. And the *Nashville Scene* staged the "SoBro Charrette" to create a positive vision for the area as an alternative to Metro's corridor fixation, and published the results as *The Plan for SoBro*. The Forum eventually led to the founding of the nonprofit Nashville Civic Design Center as a watchdog

The Shelby Bridge, which reopened as a pedestrian and bicycle connector between downtown and the East Bank in 2003, is one of Nashville's most recent preservation and urban design successes.
(Photograph, 2004: Frederic Schwartz Architects, Dave Anderson)

for the built environment, which was announced by forum-member-turned-Mayor Bill Purcell in December 2000. In 2002 the Design Center began work on the Plan of Nashville, a fifty-year vision for the city.

The corridor struggle was evidence of an ever-widening realization by Nashville's design professionals and interested citizens of the crucial role of transportation infrastructure in determining urban form. It was not enough to preserve old buildings and design fine new ones. Architecture could only play its part in the three-dimensional life of the city if it was considered as part of a larger context that included how a city works as well as how it looks.

The understanding of the interconnectedness of transportation and land use had its counterpart at the regional level with the 840 wars. Plans by the Tennessee Department of Transportation (TDOT) to encircle Nashville with a ring road through the surrounding counties at a distance of thirty-five to fifty miles from the city center initially engendered no opposition; construction on the southeast quadrant began in 1991. But when the route for the right-of-way through south-

west Williamson County was announced, TDOT found itself with a fight on its hands. Critics playing catch-up charged that the limited-access highway would beget sprawl that would gobble up forests and farm land, destroy high-quality watershed and the creatures who dwell there, and suck the life out of Nashville proper.

Peace was only restored with a new governor, former Nashville mayor Phil Bredesen, and a new TDOT commissioner, Gerald Nicely, former executive director of the Metro Development and Housing Agency, in 2001. Nicely agreed to the design of the southwest segment of State Route 840 in a more environmentally-friendly manner and suspended planning and construction of the northern half of the road entirely. The Commissioner also mandated more citizen involvement in future TDOT projects, and instituted a long-range planning process whose goal is a more balanced transportation system. By-products of the 840 controversy include an increased awareness of the mutual dependencies between the farmer and the downtown booster, the nature lover and the city dweller, as well as the creation of the nonprofit Cumberland Region Tomorrow as a re-

gional counterpart to the Nashville Civic Design Center.

Complementary to these specific events were changes in planning personnel and policies. The Roads-R-Us chiefs at the state and local levels were replaced by officials with a better grasp of urban design and the need for a balance among transportation options. Citizen involvement has become an important rite of planning. Nashville's media now covers urban planning and development as major local news rather than ghettoizing the subject in the business pages. More Nashvillians have come to grasp, as the Plan of Nashville testifies, that the way that we form our city in turn forms the quality of the life we lead in it.

The exact form the Nashville of the future will take is still undecided. "Cities are like individuals," explains urban scholar Joel Kotkin. "They evolve in unique ways. Every city has a soul. You have to try to understand what that soul is first, and then you get a better sense of what the problems are. You start by looking at a city's history and thinking about ways to help nurture its intrinsic strengths."[34]

For more than fifty years in Nashville the tide ebbed from urb to suburb, as people moved to the periphery and government investment followed them. Now it seems, with the citizen-based vision that is the Plan of Nashville, that the tide may be about to turn. The Plan charts the reverse flow of resettlement into the first-ring neighborhoods and back to the city center, to come home to the public square from whence we embarked to first shape the land more than two hundred years ago.

Nashville at 2000

Using data from the U.S. Census Bureau's 2000 Census, it is possible to examine various areas in Nashville, with respect to population, housing, and transportation characteristics.

The purpose of these maps is not to criticize Nashville or individual districts or neighborhoods, but to provide detailed information and to establish a baseline against which prog-ress can be measured. As Nashville evolves into the future, these characteristics of the city will change.

Brian Christens
Ph.D. student in Community Research
and Action, Department of Human and
Organizational Development,
Peabody College, Vanderbilt University

This map illustrates the average travel time in minutes to work for those who work outside the home; these times should be doubled to calculate the amount of time that these workers are spending commuting in their cars each day. Also, since these are the averages, many people in these areas take much less or much more time to get to their jobs. It is clear that as proximity to downtown increases, travel time decreases, no matter where the commuter works. The lack of desirable, affordable housing close to job centers is leading many people to commute for more than an hour, or sometimes two hours per day.

(Map, 2000: U.S. Census)

Map Key

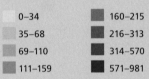

0–34	160–215
35–68	216–313
69–110	314–570
111–159	571–981

Residents per square kilometer

Map Key

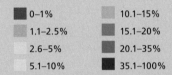

0–1%	10.1–15%
1.1–2.5%	15.1–20%
2.6–5%	20.1–35%
5.1–10%	35.1–100%

Percent of residents using public transport to travel to work

This map illustrates the relative density or compactness of Nashville's neighborhoods, allowing us to determine which geographic areas already house a higher number of residents, and which have the greatest potential for infill.

(Map, 2000: U.S. Census)

Public transit usage is generally low in Nashville. This map illustrates the areas of the city where people currently travel to work via the public transportation system. If Nashville is to move toward the vision set forth in the Plan, a much greater use of public transit will be necessary.

(Map, 2000: U.S. Census)

A vision for Church Street.
(Ink on paper, 2004: NCDC, Mark Schimmenti)

AVENUES

AVENUES TO A GREAT CITY: THE TEN PRINCIPLES

As MANY AVENUES lead into a city, so planners and designers have pursued many paths of collaboration with the community to arrive at the Plan of Nashville.

A Vision Plan

The Plan outlines an ideal vision for Nashville that respects the city's cultural history, natural landscape, and built legacy. While the Plan cannot foresee all future challenges and opportunities, its "Ten Principles" provide guidance with flexibility for future decision making. Achieving the civic ideal is not merely possible but realistic—with coordinated efforts, with a sense of common purpose, and with the common vision embodied in the Plan.

The intellectual foundation of the Plan of Nashville is the concept of a "community-based vision plan." The Plan was developed through numerous public meetings staged from late 2002 through the course of 2003 at community centers and other public gathering places within the study area, and involved more than eight hundred citizens who raised and discussed issues that affect their sense of community and quality of life.

The product of this collaboration between planners and the community is a vision plan, not a master plan. The latter is a plan for a clearly defined site developed in response to a fairly specific program. For example, the master plan for Rolling Mill Hill—an area south of the central core—involved a market study to predict the amounts of residential, retail, and commercial square footage that the market could absorb in approximately ten years. The plan then plotted these different land uses onto the thirty-four-acre site, with design criteria to guide the forms that build-out can take.

A vision plan openly engages the optimal; it is more daring in that it strives for the ideal of the matter rather than the fact of the matter. Such a plan presents possibilities and opportunities, usually for a larger and less specifically defined territory than that encompassed by a master plan, and projects further into the future.

As a vision plan, the Plan of Nashville is intended to guide public policy with regard to the city's physical form, to serve as a litmus test to help determine the acceptability of future development proposals. By enabling each part of the city to be understood in relation to the whole, the Plan can empower public policy makers to avoid the piecemeal planning that Nashville has endured in the past.

> "The best city is, of necessity, a utopia. The actual city we live in is the best imitation we can make of that city."
>
> Carroll William Westfall,
> *Architectural Principles in the Age of Historicism*
> (1991)

A Nashville for Everyone

In 1966, I became the founding pastor of Edgehill United Methodist Church. As far as I can learn, it was the first significantly integrated (Black and White) congregation in the city.

From 1966, when we were fifteen members, until my retirement in 1996, when we were right at three hundred members, the congregation was always between 35 and 40 percent minority. Shared Black pastoral leadership included such distinguished clergy as Darrell Rollins, Vincent McCutcheon, and Moses Dillard.

My thirty years as Edgehill's pastor were fulfilling and joyful. We were also blessed, because of our proximity to universities, with a wonderful participation of foreign students from many countries.

But counter motions were occurring during those years as well. From the end of World War II and the expansion of suburbs, many aspects of public policy, at all levels of government, were shaped by racial and class biases—policies around zoning and codes, urban renewal, FHA and VA loans, eminent domain, etc. The result was a high degree of "Balkanization"—a term designating the drawing of boundaries based on race or class or ethnicity. Neighborhoods were increasingly segregated—not by simple choice, but by public policy. Many aspects of life were affected negatively—tax base, urban schools, housing choice, geographical separation.

Many of the worst attitudes about race and class have improved (though they have not disappeared). According to a study by the University of Wisconsin–Milwaukee, Nashville has an above average share of "integrated blocks," primarily within the pre-Metro city limits. But we have a long way to go in becoming a city which sees diversity at a neighborhood level as a blessing, instead of a curse.

Like most other cities, there is an acute shortage in Nashville of low-income rental units. The 2000 Census reminded us: in Davidson County, among households whose income is below $20,000 a year, and who pay more than 30 percent of income for rent, the number is 25,472! Some cities have resorted to unusual methods to achieve a greater degree of diversity and additional affordable housing for low-income families, methods such as housing trust funds, transfer fees, other "dedicated financing sources." Inclusionary zoning has also been enacted here and there. Surely, where there's a will, there's a way.

Nashville has an abundance of resources to promote acceptance and diversity: a strong multiple-source economy, universities, faith communities, excellent private and public leaders, creative non-profits, and on and on. Recently, with so many immigrants settling here, we have seen our diversity multiply. We can see through a gaping window of opportunity, and we can maximize our potential.

I read recently about an older Native American who was asked about how his life was going. He replied that his internal state was like two dogs fighting—one good, the other bad. "What determines which one wins?" he was asked. "Oh, the one wins that I feed the most," he replied.

My hope and prayer is that my city will so "feed the good dog" in us that we will continue, more and more, to rejoice in diversity, welcome it into our neighborhoods, and be sure that none are left behind.

Reverend Bill Barnes
Edgehill United Methodist Church
(retired)

Because the vision springs from the community, the Plan is a testament to the collective ambition to make the best Nashville possible, a "great city" that delivers a high quality of life to its citizens and visitors alike.

The Process

The validity of the Plan of Nashville, and its eventual success, hinge on the acceptance of community-based planning assisted by professional design expertise. This process produces principles and goals developed by, and reflective of, the will of the people at large. These principles serve as the guidelines for future development proposals—for example, a new downtown elementary school or convention center.

The process had four stages:

1. Research by design professionals, planners, and historians on Nashville's history, culture, and prior planning led to a better understanding of why the city looks and works the way it does today.
2. Citizens identified current concerns and priorities in the neighborhoods, in the city, and in the region.
3. The community's aspirations and ambitions for the city directed the development of the principles and goals of the Plan.
4. A team of design professionals—particularly the staff of the Nashville Civic Design Center—assisted by writers and editors, formulated the Plan of Nashville as the embodiment and amplification of the three prior stages.

The community meetings during the visioning process helped set the geographical scope of the Plan: the downtown and its "first ring" neighborhoods, i.e., the original suburbs surrounding the downtown. The study area contains the inner loop of the interstate highway system as well as the east and west banks of the Cumberland River.

THE TEN PRINCIPLES

During the visioning process, consensus emerged regarding ten principles to guide public policy, development practice, urban planning, and design:

1. Respect Nashville's natural and built environment. *Goals are:*
- The preservation and enhancement of the landscape's natural features;
- Environmentally sensitive building practices;
- Preservation and continued use of our historic buildings.

2. Treat the Cumberland River as central to Nashville's identity—an asset to be treasured and enjoyed. *Goals are:*
- Protection of riverbanks, waterways, and wetlands;
- Environmentally sensitive uses of the river and riparian areas, balancing habitat, recreation, transportation, and water supply issues;
- Amenities and public access along the riverfront;
- A variety and multiplicity of connections across the river;
- Strong connections between neighborhoods and the river.

3. Reestablish the streets as the principal public space of community and connectivity. *Goals are:*
- Physical connections among the neighborhoods and downtown by means of a rational network of streets and avenues;

- Design standards for streets that ensure a high level of quality—physical and aesthetic—for the pedestrian.

4. Develop a convenient and efficient transportation infrastructure. *Goals are:*
- The road and street system reconfigured to distinguish between the mobility needs of high-speed through traffic and the access needs of local traffic;
- A system that balances the needs of pedestrians, bicycles, mass transit, and automobiles, including car storage;
- An interconnected network of mass transit opportunities that fully integrate a 24-hour life style.

5. Provide for a comprehensive, interconnected greenway and park system. *Goals are:*
- Greenways and parks linking public spaces, streets, neighborhoods, and the Cumberland River;
- Parks for all neighborhoods equipped for a variety of recreational, generational, and cultural activities.

6. Develop an economically viable downtown district as the heart of the region. *Goals are:*
- More, and more diversified, residential opportunities in downtown;
- Public investment leveraged with private development;
- A variety of uses that support workers, residents, and visitors, e.g., schools, retail, after-hours, and weekend activities;
- A downtown that is "Nashville" and not an average or generic place.

7. Raise the quality of the public realm with civic structures and spaces. *Goals are:*
- Civic buildings and spaces that reinforce a sense of civic pride;
- Locations that are significant sites in complementary relationships;
- Connections to the city network by means of vistas, streets, and greenways;
- Civic buildings and spaces that set high standards for the design of the city at large.

8. Integrate public art into the design of the city, its buildings, public works, and parks.

9. Strengthen the unique identity of neighborhoods. *Goals are:*
- Strong neighborhood centers and boundaries;
- A mixture of land uses and residential diversity within each neighborhood;
- Cohesive organization for each neighborhood, with a hierarchy of streets as well as a range of parks;
- Appropriate private development directed by public policies that reinforce each neighborhood's natural features, cultural history, and built heritage and that support commercial needs;
- Continued community involvement through strong neighborhood organizations.

10. Infuse visual order into the city by strengthening sightlines to and from civic landmarks and natural features. *Goals are:*
- View corridors to and from significant landmarks, especially the State Capitol;
- View corridors and vistas of all types, from small and intimate to sweeping and grand.

For Life, Liberty, and the Pursuit of Happiness, We Must Have Cities

We are citizens at the same time of a nation, a state, and a locality, but our local citizenship is the most tangible. That is where we live in the most direct contact with others who touch our lives and whose lives we touch. Citizens shape their city, and it in turn shapes them.

Suburbs, strip malls, and business parks serve people's needs, but they hardly offer a larger happiness. These are developments, not neighborhoods. They do not promote citizenship. And neither do dead-at-night downtowns. All of these offer a lesser happiness than the full-bodied happiness found in active participation in a full-blooded community.

Only an urban core alive with a variety of people and their 24/7 activities offers that happiness. Here are old and new buildings and civic spaces built over time and adapted to changing times. Identified by its visual vitality, good design, and attention paid to civic art and beauty, the center will promote the interaction between people that sustains citizenship throughout the city.

Such a place can only be made and sustained by people who live their lives as citizens. In our complex modern world, cities require commercial prosperity, transportation efficiency, and much else besides. But that is not enough. A Nashville that has a vibrant and diverse appearance and a population focused on an appealing, visible, and accessible visible core, will allow her citizens to pursue their happiness as they live and work together and fulfill their civic duties. In return, Nashville offers all her citizens a richer happiness both for themselves and for their neighbors.

Carroll William Westfall
School of Architecture
University of Notre Dame

The Plan

THE PLAN OF NASHVILLE

NASHVILLE IS NOT ONE but several cities. In the mind of America, it is Music City USA. On the map of the nation, it is marked by the star for a state capital. Within a tighter perspective, Nashville is the downtown of the Middle Tennessee region. Looking more closely still, we see a city of neighborhoods.

As the capital of Tennessee, Nashville houses the institutions that serve the state's citizens and collectively symbolize the state to all Tennesseans. Capitol Hill is the state's acropolis, the Bicentennial Mall the park that embodies the land, the history, and the culture of the state.

As the downtown of the region, Nashville is the center of commerce and culture, health care and higher education for Middle Tennessee. This city is tied to the region by the Cumberland River and its tributaries, by a web of roads and railroads, and by patterns of commerce that stretch back to the eighteenth century. Its performing and visual arts, sports events and other entertainment, universities and hospitals draw patrons from all of Davidson and the surrounding counties—and beyond.

Nashville, the city of neighborhoods, is home to an economically and ethnically diverse population. The center of this city, in the words of Mayor Bill Purcell, is "the neighborhood we all share," the place where every Nashvillian is a stakeholder. Surrounding it are the first-ring

neighborhoods, the streetcar suburbs that buttress the inner city. It is in this central core and enframing ring that the Plan of Nashville is rooted.

The Plan that follows is presented in three sections. The first deals with designing connections to enhance Nashville's identity as a regional center. The second concentrates on the downtown area and the creation and enhancement of civic space. The focus of the third is on reconstructing a sense of place in the neighborhoods that encircle downtown. Taken together these sections map a vision for the three-dimensional future of the city.

"Whatever our place, it has been visited by the stranger, it will never be new again. It is only the vision that can be new; but that is enough."

Eudora Welty,
"Place in Fiction"
(1956)

The Arcade, the room within the rooms that are Nashville's public spaces.
(Photograph, 2004: Vanderbilt University, Daniel Dubois)

Opposite: The Plan of Nashville.
(Drawing, 2003: NCDC)

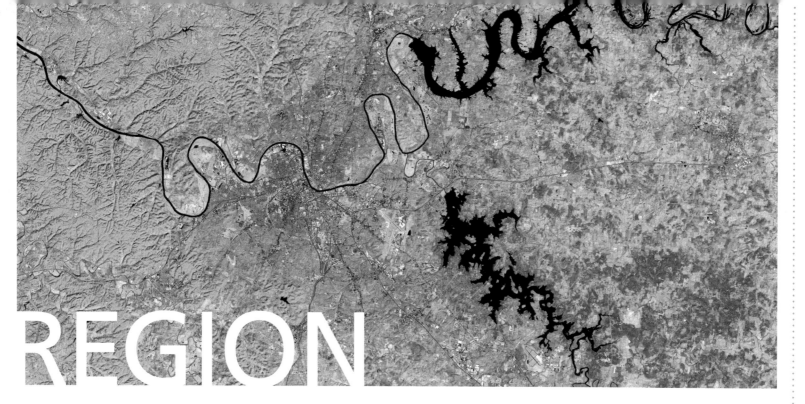

REGION

The Middle Tennessee Region: densities in a continuum. High-density areas are red; low-density areas green; cluster of red in the center is Nashville. Bodies of water are purple, with Old Hickory Lake in the upper right corner and Percy Priest Lake below. Note development along the radial pikes entering downtown Nashville.

(Satellite photograph, October 1999: Department of Geosciences, Middle Tennessee State University)

NASHVILLE AND ITS REGION: MAKING CONNECTIONS

THE HISTORIC LOGIC OF URBAN form is centripetal: purveyors of the most valuable offerings of commerce and culture located their goods and services in a dense concentration within the city's core so that they were most accessible to the greatest number of consumers. The traditional neighborhood repeated this logic in miniature, placing stores and schools, libraries and churches at the center of the residential fabric.

Country headed to town on the spoke roads —in Nashville called pikes—that fed the city center. Residents of outlying small towns could also reach the larger city by railroad. The city's downtown and neighborhoods were closely linked by a tight network of roads and streets and transit lines.

In the second half of the twentieth century, however, a centrifugal force fractured Nashville.

The necessities of daily life spread all over the map in a diffuse pattern of destination locations. Today it takes many trips to get the children to school, to go to church, to buy groceries and clothes, and to earn the money to pay for it all. The gaps between destinations are episodes of denial, of ignoring the clutter of signs, the honking of horns, and all the asphalt. And the roads that once knitted together public and private life have become barriers between them.

For the citizens who participated in the Plan of Nashville process, more and better connections within the region—between a commuter's home and job space, between neighborhood and neighborhood, between work and play, shops and schools—was a pervasive theme. After decades of exercising the personal liberty of the car culture—living atomized lives, trapped within

the confines of a steel frame with headlights and a rear view mirror—Nashvillians are seeking the physical connections that bind a people into a community.

Making an Entrance

Entering a city is experiencing a David Hockney photo collage: a shifting series of snapshots. At a certain point in the sequence, images coalesce into portrait, and you know you are "there."

Entering New Orleans, for example, you land at the airport, get on the interstate, and pass through a suburban landscape more blighted than most. But then you take the Carrollton Avenue exit, turn right, and, before you know it, you've hit the "tree line" that stretches to downtown. The live oaks—undeformed by utility companies—arch over the street. Low-rise

"Only connect."

E. M. Forster,
Howard's End (1910)

The traditional pikes (highlighted in orange) were once Nashville's primary connection to the Middle Tennessee region. Note how most of the pikes terminate at Broadway, Nashville's most important street.

(Photograph, 1934: Metro Planning Department; diagram, 2004: NCDC)

"General View of Nashville—circa 1855." View from river bluff south of the city—what is now called Rolling Mill Hill. Note dominance of the State Capitol and the twin towers of the First (now Downtown) Presbyterian Church.

(Lithograph, 1855: J. F. Wagner; reprint, 1973: Elders Bookstore)

buildings grow to the sidewalk, columns and gingerbread appear. Traffic slows. The Big Easy has arrived.

Historically, Nashville "arrived" when the State Capitol came into view. When Union troops reached the then-separate town of Edgefield on February 23, 1862, they could see architect William Strickland's recently completed temple of Tennessee democracy—the vertical punctuation of the city—across the Cumberland River to the west. The army stood on the threshold of the capital it would occupy two days later.

In 1975 the satiric film *Nashville* presented a much different sense of arrival than the Federal troops encountered. Director Robert Altman staged a massive traffic accident and the resulting gridlock on I-40 between the airport and downtown as a visual metaphor for "Welcome to Nashville." On the interstate turned parking lot, stalled drivers alternate between episodes of road rage and down-home neighborliness, defining the character of the city as small town run amok.

The modern condition of Nashville—and most other American cities—is Altman minus the humor. The Nashville skyline is a more emphatic vertical marker than the Capitol ever furnished. But actually reaching the city once you've glimpsed the towers of downtown is a journey on streetscapes of generic ugliness. The vast majority of city seekers arrive by car, via a highway and street system designed to get the highest number of vehicles in and out of town as fast as possible. This emphasis on traffic engineering has strongly negative implications for the visual and physical quality of these public spaces.

Taking the High Road

One sequence of arrival involves jockeying and weaving on the limited-access highways—the interstates—followed by an abrupt landing on a series of wide-wide streets lined with gas stations and other marginal uses, before reaching the grid of downtown.

The journey from the north on I-24/I-65 is a plunge through a concrete canyon of Jersey barriers and noise walls—some scored to resemble stone in crude mimicry of the limestone beneath the hills—flanked by the relentless march of billboards. The vista of the city ahead is broken by the rapid repeat of cobra-headed sodium vapor lights, and by bright green signs telling you how to avoid Nashville on your way to Chattanooga or Knoxville, Huntsville or Memphis.

In recent years the interstates that loop around the center of Nashville—shared by local and through traffic—have reached their capacity and become dysfunctional many hours of the day. The limited-access highway currently offers neither a visually compelling nor particularly efficient entrance into the city.

Taking the Low Road

An alternative sequence of arrival is the stop-and-go rhythm of the older regional roads. The pikes once provided a gradual introduction to the city, moving from country to town through the first-ring neighborhoods in a pattern of evolving density. But the widening of these arteries, and the erosion of their architectural character by out-front surface parking with re-

Nashville's automotive history stacked up on I-40.
(Photograph, n.d.: Vanderbilt University)

curring curb cuts, now provides an introduction to the placeless society.

On the historic Gallatin Pike, for example, there are but few vestiges of the road described in the 1939 WPA guide to Tennessee as lined with farms and manor houses, suburban villas and cottages, and small commercial villages.[1] Today the venerable National and Spring Hill cemeteries offer a green and dignified—if all too brief—respite from the asphalt slum of car dealers and big box retail. And Evergreen Place—an 1850s country house that was more recently the Jim Reeves museum—still stands, albeit battered by the sound pollution of Briley Parkway. Closer to town in Inglewood are scattered remnants of an older and more genteel suburbia—Tudor bungalows and the spires of churches, a small Deco shopping strip and the occasional

old-fashioned commercial building pulled up to the sidewalk.

But the overwhelming impression is of a cacophony of signs, webs of utility lines, and the repeated sequence of pawn shops, discount tobacco sheds, fast food franchises, chain stores, and parking lots.

Where Gallatin Road bends into Main Street, near East Nashville's Five Points, stands an historic marker of what civic entrance used to signify. Facing north on its triangular patch of earth, away from downtown, East Library was—at the time of its completion in 1919—the first notice to travelers that they had arrived in the city. The architecture told them so.

In contrast to the irregular profiles and shifting seasons of the rural landscape, the library celebrates the obviously manmade. The

Entrance sequence to Nashville from north via I-24.
(Photographs, 2004: NCDC)

Entrance sequence into downtown Nashville from north along Gallatin Pike and Main Street.

(Photographs, 2004: NCDC, Gary Gaston and Raven Hardison)

building's simple rectangle of limestone blocks, set on a raised base to give it civic standing, with a classical pediment front and center over the entrance, speaks a language of calm and order, rationality and hierarchy, stability and permanence.

Now East Library is just an urban blip on the radar screen of sprawl. Between the library

building and the State Capitol in the distance, the remaining stretch of Main Street reverts to the wilderness of the drive-by culture.

Nashvillians are proud of the image of their city beamed to the world from the Goodyear blimp during a Titans game. Pride would turn to shame, however, if the broadcasters filmed the overland route into the Nashville of today.

Healing the Pikes

To create a fitting sense of arrival into the city, the Plan of Nashville concentrates on remaking the traditional pikes. The goal is not to return the historic roads to their more bucolic, pre–World War II character—an impossible task given the growth that has occurred in the intervening years. Care should be taken to preserve

Existing buildings and building types currently found along Gallatin Pike that are worth preservation.

(Watercolor, 2004: Susan Barbera)

and restore historic roadside elements, including the small commercial buildings—former groceries and pharmacies—that line the sidewalk. New development should be of an urban character, with a gradual increase in density and intensity of development the closer to town the roads approach.

Ingredients in road remake include:

Building placement—Pull to sidewalk and define the corners.

Building heights—Establish a range of permitted heights that form an architectural fabric sufficient to the degree of urbanization appropriate in the context.

Using the northeast entrance into the city as an example, the section from Trinity Lane to East Library would have a height range from two to six stories since the building placement would be more piecemeal. The section from East Library to the Cumberland River, however, would have a height range of three to five stories since a more continuous street wall is desirable. Height ranges are given in stories not feet to promote some visual variation in profiles since height between floors may differ.

Location of off-street parking—Place parking lots to side and rear of buildings and limit curb cuts.

Buildings at street level—Orient usage and transparency of facade (lots of clear glass) to sidewalk traffic.

Right-of-way usage—Restore the block pattern to concentrate turning to predictable intervals.

Establish rights-of-way that include all of the following: travel lanes for motor vehicles, travel lanes for bicycles, on-street parking, planting strips with trees, and wide sidewalks.

Signage—Eliminate billboards and pull signage to the pedestrian level.

Lighting—Decrease the height and increase the frequency of lighting standards for pedestrian friendliness.

The Plan of Nashville is not the first public recognition that major arterials into the city need to be urbanized. In 2000, the Metro Planning Department amended the zoning code to enable—although it does not force—the placement of new buildings to reflect an urban condition, i.e., to be pulled to the sidewalk, defining street walls and corners. Prior to this time, Nashville zoning mandated suburban-style setbacks for new construction. This new Urban Zoning Overlay (UZO) applies to the area of Metro Nashville lying within the city limits as they existed in 1956, and thus where urban design is appropriate.

The Metro Development and Housing Agency (MDHA) has also tried to nudge these roads in the right direction. On two major

Existing conditions on Gallatin Pike in Inglewood.

(Photographs, 2004: NCDC)

Same sections envisioned as a more pedestrian-friendly and inviting entrance into the city. Note the absence of tangled power lines that mar the view.

(Watercolors, 2004: Susan Barbera)

arterials—sections of Nolensville Road and Main Street that retained at least fragments of urban character—the agency has undertaken streetscaping projects. MDHA has funded the placement of special pavers in selected crosswalks, and the planting of street trees in sidewalk extensions—concrete "bulbs"—that shelter space for on-street parking. In the case of Main Street, the agency also commissioned design guidelines for new building construction that encourage the urbanization of the street.

Streetscaping is merely an amenity, however, and does not in and of itself create true urban form. Until the architectural fabric lining the roads is redeveloped to form the appropriate walls for these public spaces, the entrances to Nashville will remain the corridors of Anywhere USA.

Gradually increasing intensities of color indicate areas of higher density. The traditional pikes and main streets have a higher scale than the fabric that surrounds them, culminating in the tallest structures of downtown.

(Map, 2004: NCDC, Raven Hardison)

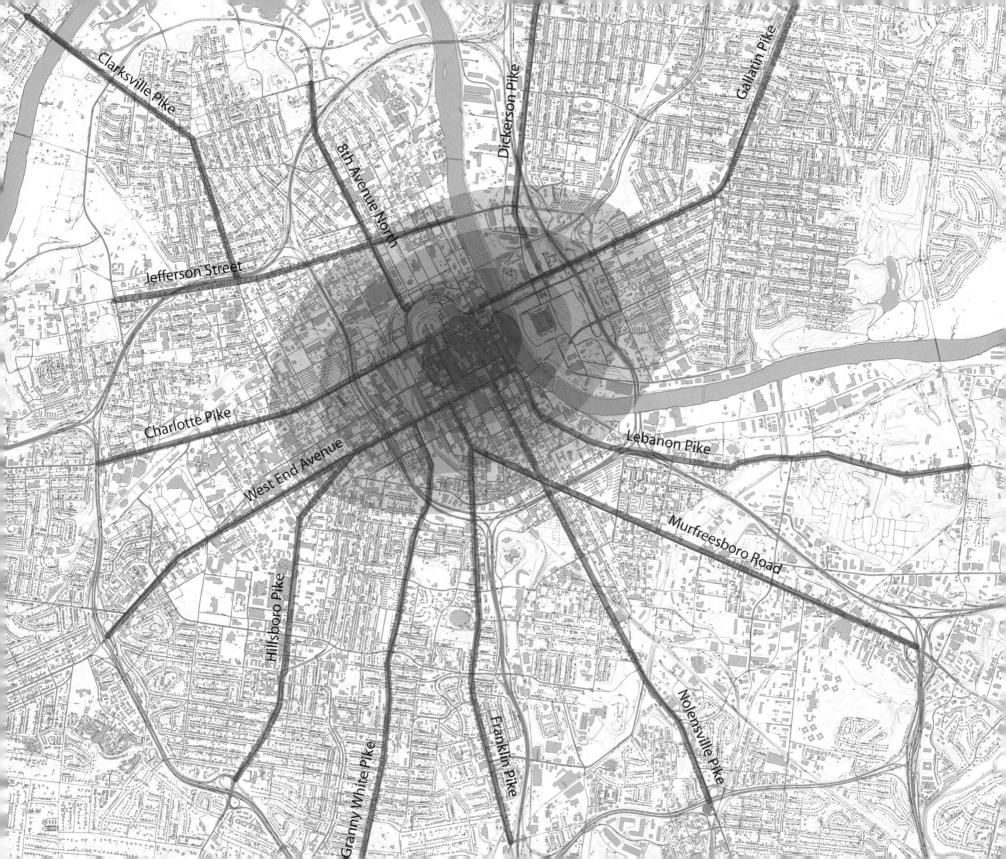

Clarksville Pike

8th Avenue North

Dickerson Pike

Gallatin Pike

Jefferson Street

Charlotte Pike

West End Avenue

Lebanon Pike

Murfreesboro Road

Hillsboro Pike

Granny White Pike

Franklin Pike

Nolensville Pike

"Nashvillians have spent the last one hundred years turning away from the river. Let's focus the next one hundred years on turning towards the river."

Kim Hawkins, community workshop participant

EMBRACING THE CUMBERLAND RIVER

NASHVILLIANS once thought of the Cumberland River as a road that moves. When the river ceased to be the main commercial artery to and from the city, however, we turned away from it, toward rails of iron, the spokes of highways, the runways of the airport—newer and speedier links with the rest of the world.

There are signs that Nashville has begun to look to the Cumberland River once again. The central chain in the green necklace that is Metro's greenways master plan is the fifty-seven miles of the river that churn through Davidson County. To improve the quality of the runoff water that flows into the river, Metro Water Services has spent $685 million—with another $125 million planned—to reduce sewer overflows from manholes and pump stations.

Further, the Metro Development and Housing Agency has a master plan for a brand new neighborhood on the river bluffs south of downtown called Rolling Mill Hill. And in 2004 Mayor Bill Purcell commissioned a study of current and projected uses of the riverfront in the city center to coordinate future planning for the banks of the Cumberland.

Citizens are turning back toward the river, as well. A group of citizens concerned about the health of the entire Cumberland watershed founded the not-for-profit Cumberland River Compact in 1997 as an education and advocacy group. CRC is currently working on a pilot project to build sustainable housing within the watershed, including an urban site near the Cumberland River.

Among the citizens who participated in the Plan of Nashville, redefining the relationship of the city to the Cumberland—with an emphasis on public access—emerged as the dominant theme in the planning process.

Nashvillians have recalled the Cumberland River's real and symbolic importance, this time not primarily as an avenue of trade and travel, but as a natural resource to be treasured and enjoyed. We drink the river's waters and float our boats in its currents. A wide variety of wildlife depend on the river for habitation and sustenance. From a larger perspective, the river and its watershed are Nashville's most enduring connection to the Middle Tennessee region.

Nashville has, of course, despoiled the Cumberland. We've dammed the river into tranquility, cut down the vegetation that held its banks, and polluted it with the runoff of our lives. But the river has not been abused beyond reclaiming. The Plan of Nashville maps a path of reclamation.

The Plan envisions a careful balance among the river's various uses as drinking water source and habitat, for transportation and recreation. An imbalance of uses could have negative impact on other uses. For example, the development of numerous marinas could damage water quality through dredging and the effluents from boats.

In the Plan, the uses of the land along the river change to reflect the current needs of the city. Industries not dependent on the river relocate to more appropriate sites, for example, near interstate nodes. The sheds of industry are replaced with mixed-use neighborhoods and an interlaced park system stretching from Tennessee State University to Shelby Bottoms. The public has much greater access—through parks and other points of interest—to the riverbanks.

Historically, the river has been viewed as an edge, a dividing line or barrier. The 1963 *Central Loop General Neighborhood Renewal Plan* by Clarke and Rapuano illustrates this attitude painfully, failing to even visually consider the river's east bank. (See "The City from the Air," page 31.) The Plan encompasses both banks, and provides greater physical and visual connections between them.

Physical Connections: A City of Bridges

In the Plan of Nashville, new bridges—three for automobiles and two for pedestrians—work with existing bridges to link the Cumberland River's east and west banks. The locations for these new connections were determined by planner/citizen collaboration during the planning process. Existing automobile bridges are made pedestrian and bicycle friendly through better avenues of access, widening of sidewalks, lighting at a pedestrian scale, and buffers between travel lanes and sidewalks. Increasing the total number of bridges to sixteen within the Plan's study area establishes the physical unity of the riverbanks, connects neighborhoods on either side of the river, and links the greenway system across the waterway.

Industrial uses dominate both banks of the Cumberland River. (Photograph, 2003: Metro Planning Department)

Below left: Industrial district above Jefferson Street Bridge. Warehouse buildings lining the riverfront taint views to the Cumberland and preclude pedestrian access and recreational enjoyment.

Below center: The Rolling Mill Hill neighborhood—planned for the former site of Metro General Hospital—will be located on the river bluff directly opposite the Philip Metal scrap yards, providing the residents with a less than ideal river view.

Below right: East Nashville residential neighborhoods—James A. Cayce Homes and Boscobel Heights—shown on the upper part of this photograph are cut off from the riverfront by warehouses along the water's edge.

(Photographs, 2003: Metro Planning Department)

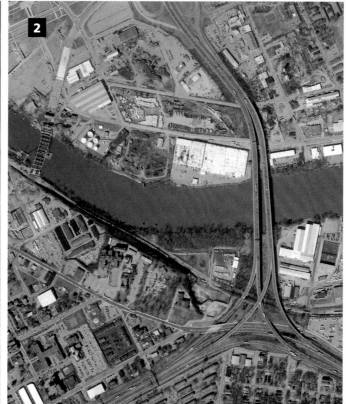

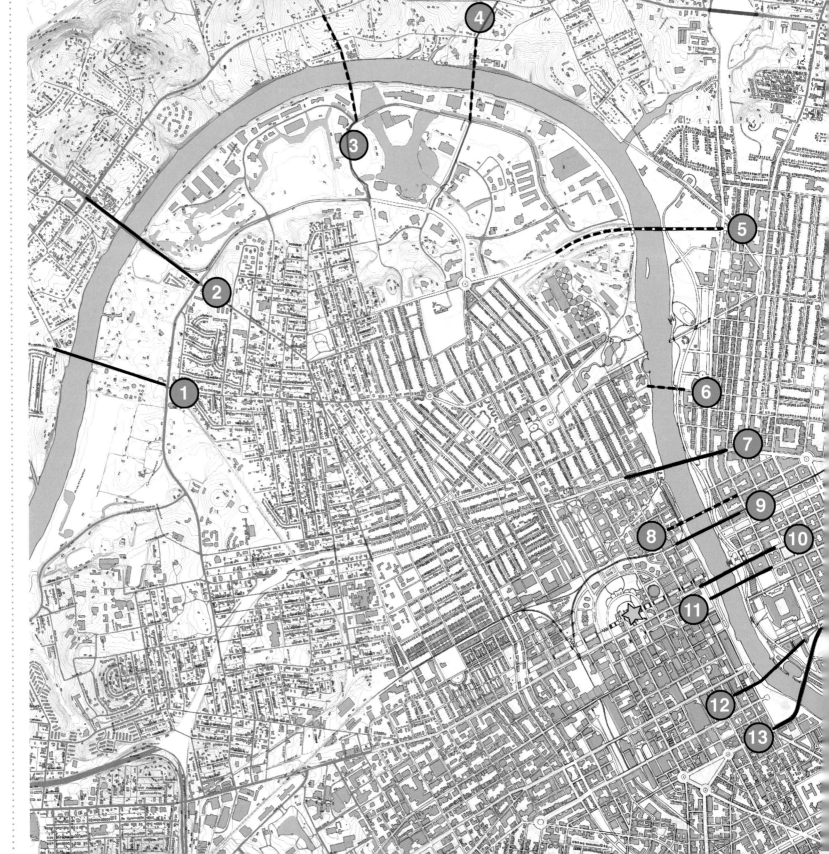

Existing and proposed bridges across the Cumberland River. New bridges would bring more Nashville neighborhoods to the water's edge and literally tie them together across the river.

(Map, 2004: NCDC, Andrea Gaffney and Raven Hardison)

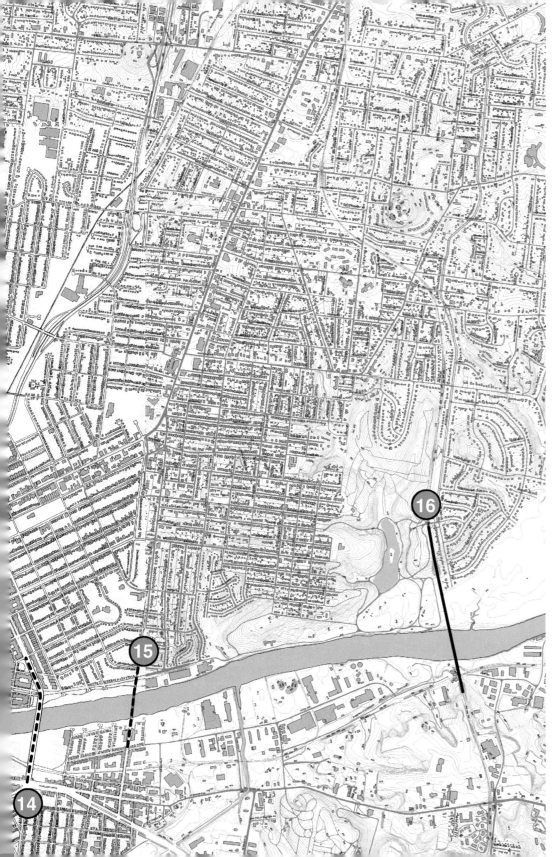

Map Key

Solid lines: existing bridges
Dashed lines: new bridges, also listed in bold

1. Nashville & Ashland City Railroad Bridge

2. Clarksville Highway Bridge

3. **Old Buena Vista Pike Bridge**
   Connects to Trinity Lane, Buena Vista Pike, Whites Creek Pike, and Old Hickory Boulevard.

4. **Trinity Lane Bridge**
   Connects to Trinity Lane and Whites Creek Pike.

5. **Interstate (I-265) Bridge, reconfigured**
   Existing interstate bridge avoids the city rather than links pieces of the city. Furthermore, the form of the bridge makes viewing the Cumberland while crossing it difficult. The bridge should be reconfigured along boulevard lines to calm traffic and provide better access for pedestrians and bicyclists. (See "Getting Around," page 77.)

6. **Neuhoff Pedestrian Bridge**
   Connects Neuhoff complex (Nashville Cultural Arts Project; International Center for Living Watersheds) to new Cumberland Northeast Park, thus providing a link from Germantown to new open space and recreation on the east bank. Citizens suggested that this bridge should be a public art project.

7. Jefferson Street Bridge
   Made pedestrian and bicycle friendly.

8. **Bicentennial Bridge**
   Connects northeast Nashville neighborhoods to the state government district and the Bicentennial Mall. The bridge also links the new East Transit Hub and East Boulevard with downtown.

9. CSX Railroad Bridge

10. Victory Memorial Bridge

11. Woodland Street Bridge

12. Shelby Pedestrian Bridge

13. Gateway Bridge
    Made pedestrian and bicycle friendly.

14. **East Boulevard Bridge**
    (Treatment same as 5, above.) Carries new urban boulevard across the river.

15. **South Eleventh Street Pedestrian Bridge**
    Links new neighborhoods in East Nashville and along the south bank. This bridge also connects the greenways on both banks, making access to the Stones River Greenway much easier.

16. CSX Railroad Bridge

"The river banks should shake hands with each other."

Tom Hardin,
community workshop
participant

Brush Creek Corridor, Kansas City, Missouri. Bridges create a high level of connectivity across Brush Creek Corridor in Kansas City. Beautifully integrated waterfront greenways and parks link the surrounding areas to the creek's edge and create a rich asset for the citizens of the city.

(Photograph, 2002: Alex S. MacLean/ Landslides)

Visual Connections: Seeing the River

Being able to see the Cumberland River and to see across it contributes significantly to a collective consciousness of the city's "wholeness." Because the sense of the river should be omnipresent, view corridors to the Cumberland should be unobstructed. Each neighborhood near the river should have a visual point of reference to the river. In the Plan these are defined by a tower, pylon, or other structure that punctuates but does not block sightlines to the Cumberland.

John A. Roebling Suspension Bridge, Cincinnati, Ohio. Visually interesting bridges add aesthetic value to riverfronts and provide cities with unique visual identities.

(Photograph, 2004: Metro Planning Department, Keith Covington)

The East Bank Greenway (1999) and Shelby Street Bridge (renovated for pedestrians, 2003) provide beautiful views across the Cumberland River to downtown, enhance Nashvillians' connection to the river, and help to create a sense of place.

(Photograph, 2004: NCDC, Raven Hardison)

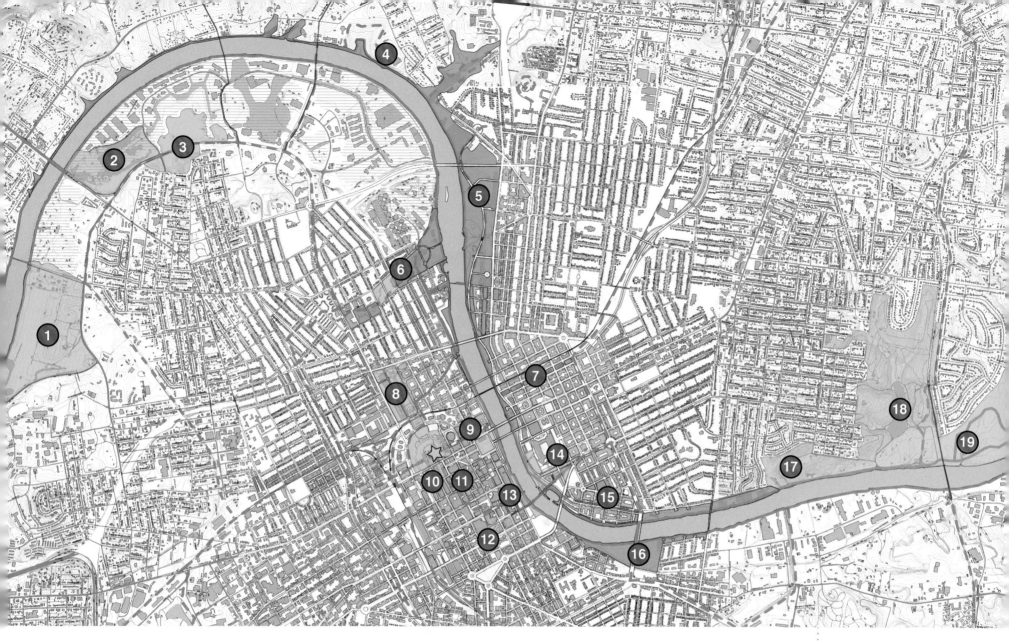

Map Key

Proposed sites listed in bold.

Dark green: proposed parks,
   also listed in bold
Light green: existing parks
Solid green lines: existing greenways
   and greenways currently under
   construction
Dashed green lines: proposed greenways
Hatching: proposed Buena Vista
   Bottoms (see pages 143-46)

1. TSU Agricultural Campus
2. Ted Rhodes Golf Course
3. Athletic Fields
4. Lock 1 Park
5. **Cumberland Northeast Park**
6. **Governor House and Green**
   (includes Morgan Park)
7. **Ellington Linear Park**

8. Bicentennial Mall and Capitol Hill
9. Public Square and Courthouse
10. Legislative Plaza and War Memorial
    Building
11. Church Street Park
12. Hall of Fame Park
13. Riverfront Park
14. East Bank Greenway

15. **East Bank Neighborhood Park**
16. **Southside Riverfront Park**
17. Shelby Golf Course
18. Shelby Park
19. Shelby Bottoms

Existing and proposed park
system along the Cumberland
River; note how greenways and
parks form one continuous,
integrated network.

(Map, 2004: NCDC, Andrea Gaffney and
Raven Hardison)

Map Key

Yellow: existing neighborhood development

Orange: proposed neighborhood development, also listed in bold

1. **Northeast**
2. **Ellington**
3. **East Bank**
4. Cayce
5. Boscobel Heights
6. Rolling Mill Hill
7. SoBro (South of Broadway)
8. Downtown
9. **Sulphur Dell** (proposed in *Bicentennial Mall Urban Master Plan;* see page 98)
10. **East Germantown**

New "river neighborhoods" along the Cumberland. Areas like Boscobel Heights and SoBro, no longer isolated from the river by industry, will also become treasured for their proximity to the Cumberland.

(Map, 2004: NCDC, Andrea Gaffney and Raven Hardison)

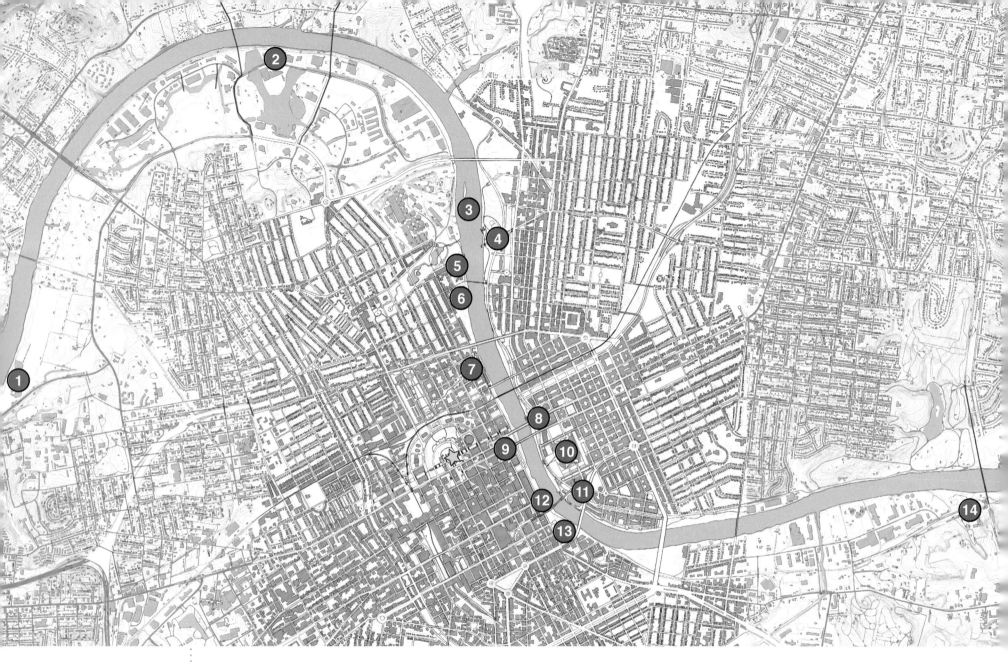

Existing and proposed points of interest along the Cumberland River.

(Map, 2004: NCDC, Andrea Gaffney and Raven Hardison)

Map Key

Proposed points of interest listed in bold.

1. **Tennessee State University Boat Dock**

2. Metro Center Lake and Greenway

3. River Island

4. **Cumberland Northeast Park Band Shell**

5. **River Overlook**

6. Neuhoff Complex

7. **Sulphur Dell Boat Dock**

8. **East Capitol Axis Terminus Marker**

9. Public Square

10. Coliseum: Titans Stadium

11. **Downtown Marina**

12. Broadway Terminus

13. Site of former Thermal Transfer Plant; any redevelopment plan should preserve public access to water's edge.

14. Omohundro Water Plant

Greening the Cumberland

For the citizens who contributed to the Plan of Nashville, parks are a necessity rather than an amenity. They repeatedly emphasized that they want more access to public greenspace, and that this greenspace should take the form of an interconnected system.

The Plan of Nashville envisions this system of parks and greenways as lining the Cumberland River and having strong links—in the form of pedestrian and bicycle paths, as well as lanes for vehicles—to the adjacent neighborhoods. An extensive park system along the river will celebrate and beautify living within the city while providing places to exercise and find aesthetic relief from urban life.

River Neighborhoods

In many cities, property within sight and walking distance of a waterway is prime living space. In places as distinct as New York and Chicago, Cincinnati and Memphis, rooms with a view of the river are prized possessions.

Nashville, however, hasn't exactly been drinking in the view of the Cumberland, even though the river is a scenic one. This is because the land along the river, to a large extent, still exists in its industrial state, marred by scrap yards, parking lots for trucks, and chunks of concrete or rocks tossed as rip rap to hold the banks.

With the relocation of riverfront industry and the development of greenways along the banks, living near the Cumberland becomes eminently desirable. The Plan, therefore, grows new mixed-use neighborhoods to the public greenspace at the river's edge.

Points of Interest

To accentuate the Cumberland River's importance to Nashville, the Plan defines points

Coal Harbor Shoreside Promenade in Vancouver, BC: a vibrant waterfront that integrates a working harbor with bike lanes, walking paths, parks, and mixed-use development.

(Photograph, 2003: NCDC, Gary Gaston)

The East Bank Greenway is one of Nashville's most recent steps in reclaiming the riverfront for public use. This section of the greenway, located on land formerly devoted to industry and now the site of the Coliseum, incorporates preexisting train tracks into the design to serve as a visual reminder of the area's past.

(Photograph, 2003: Hawkins Partners)

Residential development and parks along the Charles River in Boston (top), and the Allegheny River in Pittsburgh (bottom). Note that while dwellings have fine river views, the rivers' edges are secured for public use.

(Top photograph, 2003: NCDC, Andrea Gaffney; bottom photograph, 2003: City of Pittsburgh)

of interest to draw people to the water's edge. These focal points are scattered along the river, linked with each other by greenways, and take many forms.

Points of interest include marinas and smaller boat docks, the Coliseum and the Neuhoff complex, historical markers and public art. Streets that end at the river have their termini converted into pocket parks or overlooks. Each terminus has a distinct identity yet conforms to an overall civic standard.

If the bridges are the physical links that stitch the river and its neighborhoods together, the points of interest focus attention on the Cumberland in and of itself. They are places for recreation—for renting a canoe or kayak—as well as moments in space for contemplation—watching the sun set or a heron fish. These focal points enable us to realize that the Cumberland River is a thing of beauty in motion.

Conclusion

One of America's most famous civic agendas, the *Plan of Chicago* (1909), oriented the urban fabric toward its waterfront, "giving over this land to public recreational use and integrating the lakeshore drive and parks with the city street pattern and park system," according to historian Kristen Schaffer.[2] The Chicago plan's co-author, Daniel Burnham, saw the city—both its physical fabric and its public services—as a formative agent in the lives of its citizens. And he envisioned Lake Michigan and the Chicago River as tools that could positively accommodate the city to the people who lived in it.

The Plan of Nashville presents the Cumberland River as having a similar potential to shape and improve the lives of Nashvillians.

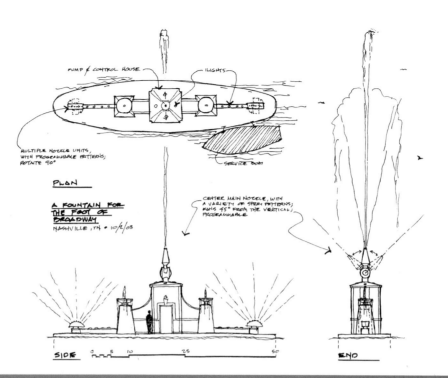

PUMP & CONTROL HOUSE

LIGHTS

MULTIPLE NOZZLE UNITS, WITH PROGRAMMABLE PATTERNS; ROTATE 90°

SERVICE BOAT

PLAN

A FOUNTAIN FOR THE FOOT OF BROADWAY
NASHVILLE, TN • 10/2/03

CENTER MAIN NOZZLE, WITH A VARIETY OF SPRAY PATTERNS; RUNS 45° FROM THE VERTICAL; PROGRAMMABLE

SIDE   0 5 10   25   50

END

Left top: Sculptural bridges like this one in the Metro Center Greenway add visual interest to the linear park system.

(Photograph, 2003: NCDC, Gary Gaston)

Left bottom: Overlook or gateway along riverfront greenway.

(Drawing, 2003: Tuck Hinton Architects, Blaine Kimbrough)

Right: "Water cannon" in the Cumberland River. Such urban interventions become powerful focal points for adjoining neighborhoods and treasures of the city at large.

(Drawing, 2003: Frank Orr)

The Shelby Street Bridge is the only connection across the Cumberland restricted to pedestrians and bicycles. Lighting emphasizes the simple, yet striking beauty of the bridge's structure. The Plan features two additional pedestrian bridges similar in scale and level of design.

(Photograph, 2003: Frederic Schwartz Architects, Douglas Romines)

Composite diagram of river-oriented development. The Plan envisions the Cumberland lined with parks and housing as well as public gathering places and interest points. Greenways weave along the river and through adjacent neighborhoods, connecting the city to its most valuable natural resource. Note how each layer of development combines to form a system of connectivity.

(Map, 2004: NCDC, Andrea Gaffney and Raven Hardison)

Map Key

Solid black lines: existing bridges

Dashed black lines: new bridges

Solid green lines: existing greenways and greenways
    currently under construction

Dashed green lines: proposed greenways

Dark green: proposed parks

Light green: existing parks

Hatching: proposed Buena Vista Bottoms

Yellow blocks: existing neighborhood development

Orange blocks: proposed neighborhood development

Red dots: points of interest along the river

I-65/ I-440 interchange.
(Photograph, 2003: Metro Planning Department)

"Our national flower is the concrete cloverleaf."

Lewis Mumford
Quote
(October 8, 1961)

GETTING AROUND

TRANSPORTATION infrastructure is a means to an end, not an end in itself. The purpose of the infrastructure is to enable people and goods to move from place to place as efficiently and economically as possible.

For much of Nashville's history, the framework of movement was diversified because it served different vehicles and was relatively task specific. The long-distance corridors were first the river for boats, then rails for trains, then runways for airplanes. Streets were for local traffic—biped and quadruped, then trolleys and cars, and later buses. Sidewalks distinguished paths for human foot traffic. The turnpikes, or farm-to-market roads, bridged the gap between short- and long-distance travel.

After World War II, however, Nashville—like much of the nation—declined from a mul-timodal transportation system into a transportation monoculture. City planners designed an infrastructure dedicated overwhelmingly to a single mode—the internal combustion engine—to serve patterns of newly segregated land uses.

The traditional pikes by which farmers had delivered their products to city markets became major arterials, increasingly shared by long-distance travelers and commuters dwelling in new subdivisions adjacent to these roads. Zoning rules encouraged commerce to migrate out of neighborhood centers to the arterials. Suburban villas were replaced by motel courts and gas stations and strips of shops; farms, by shopping malls. These developments served as magnets for more traffic. The traffic lights and curb cuts required for all this retail slowed traffic. The arterial, serving long-distance

and local needs, served neither very well.

The traffic engineer's solution was the limited-access highway: what we now know as the freeway, expressway, or interstate. The theory behind these roadways is a simple one. Limiting access to a highway to a widely-spaced series of ramps and cloverleafs restricts the occasions when vehicles on the highway must decrease their speed to allow vehicles accelerating from the slower speeds of the urban condition to enter the flow of the highway. There are no stops for signals at intersections, because there are no intersections. Drivers feel comfortable at maximum speeds because of wide lanes and the separation from oncoming traffic by a median or Jersey barrier. Cars do not slow for turning because there are no right angles.

The limited-access highway was envisioned

for long-distance travel—hence the term *interstate*. This highway system was to be the concrete equivalent of the rivers and railroads of the past. As avenues for through traffic, the highways would bypass cities; connections between motorway and city would be by boulevards and surface streets.

But the cities fought to bring the interstates into town; the first one arrived in Davidson County in 1962. City officials across the nation reasoned that the highways would deliver tourists as well as the trucks that were supplanting trains as the carriers of goods, and make commuting easier for the suburbanite crawling on the arterials. To accommodate local as well as through traffic, the number and frequency of access points to the highway had to be increased. The limited-access highway was asked to serve contradictory needs—just like the arterials—and its design purpose was compromised.

Despite much recent demonization, the interstate is not inherently evil. And no one wants to go back to the days of driving all the way from Nashville to Florida on a two-lane state highway. But as a design for long-distance travel adapted to provide local circulation, the limited-access highway does not perform well. Neither does the arterial lined with strip malls, curb cuts, and cul-de-sacs.

Both road patterns concentrate rather than disperse traffic. Cul-de-sac subdivisions feeding arterials offer no alternative routes. And once you're on the interstate, you pretty much have to stay on it until you reach your destination. Concentration is the bane of the automotive age, as is apparent in the congestion and growing length of Nashville's rush hours. And the congestion—and air pollution—will get even worse. The Federal Highway Administration predicts a doubling of freight truck through traffic on the interstates in the next fifteen to twenty years.

The relentless fixation of transportation planning on a single mode—the automobile—and the demands on the highway infrastructure to serve both local and through traffic has, at the beginning of the twenty-first century, produced a system that, as a means of traveling within or into cities, is no longer economical nor efficient.

Nashville needs a variety of transportation modes for local circulation: mass transit, bicycles, and the good old-fashioned human foot, as well as cars. And the most economical and efficient infrastructure for a multimodal system serving local transportation needs is the traditional urban street system.

An interlocked network—usually a grid of blocks—supplies vehicles and pedestrians with access points to a particular thoroughfare at each intersection. The driver thus has multiple options for getting from place to place. If an accident clogs traffic on one road, for example, a driver can turn right or left and use an alternative route. The speed of such a system is limited by stop signs and signals, by trolleys or buses pausing to take on or discharge passengers, by cars slowing to turn at corners and drivers looking for an on-street parking space. The limits to speed make for pedestrian-friendliness.

"After all, what is a pedestrian? He is a man who has two cars—one being driven by his wife, the other by one of his children."

Robert Bradbury,
New York Times
(September 5, 1962)

A typical day on a Nashville interstate.

(Photograph, 2003: Vanderbilt University, Daniel Dubois)

Strategies for arterial reformation: Gallatin Pike between Ordway Place and Greenwood Avenue.

(Drawings over photograph, 2004: NCDC, Raven Hardison)

Left: Existing street with curb cuts indicated by red lines. Most of the sidewalk is eroded by curb cuts, which is dangerous for pedestrians. Traffic is slowed by countless turning opportunities.

Center: By eliminating curb cuts along Gallatin and providing parking access from the side streets, the number of turning opportunities is reduced from forty-one to twelve; sidewalks can be repaired, making the street safer for pedestrians and increasing traffic flow.

Right: Gallatin Pike redeveloped with buildings (illustrated in gray) constructed up to right-of-way, which provides definition and scale to the pedestrian areas already enhanced by the elimination of curb cuts.

Reforming the Arterials: Streets That Move Cars and Create Great Places

The arterial gets its name by way of analogy to the artery in human anatomy, which carries blood from the heart through the body. Historically, arterials have functioned as the main channels in a branching system of roads and streets, carrying traffic to and from the heart of the city.

Over the past fifty years, Nashville's arterials have passed through three stages: from multimodal mixed-use corridors, to high-speed single-mode commercial arteries, to roads characterized by excess vehicle capacity and decayed and under-utilized low-density commercial buildings. Today Nashville is suffering from a clogging of its arteries. We have tried to make these roads carry heavy traffic, yet zoned them almost entirely commercial. These goals work in opposition to each other.

Fast flow of traffic happens when cars stop in-frequently. Commercial areas, however, require frequent cuts in the curbs of these roads for cars to access parking lots. Cars slowing and stopping to turn all along a block reduce mobility to a crawl. Lots of curb cuts also endanger pedestrians by interrupting the sidewalk and forcing walkers and cars into conflict—guess who wins? The congestion created by cars slowing to turn at each retail outlet undermines efficient mass transit. Commuters in cars, frustrated by the stop and start rhythm of the arterials, take to the interstates, contributing to these highways' increasing dysfunctionality. Commercial properties suffer from the loss of traffic. Our arterials have thus become a non-sustainable—functionally and economically—segment of the infrastructure of transportation.

Places and markets change. The belief that the commercial-only arterial is best must be rethought in favor of concentrated commercial nodes linked by higher density mixed-use corridors. There is much more property along our arterials zoned for commercial use than can be economically sustained. And the amount of existing arterial commercial development—in the form of the big box and the strip mall—cannot be supported under today's economic realities.

According to Kennedy Lawson Smith, the director of the National Trust's Main Street Program, the amount of retail space per capita has outgrown the nation's needs. In 1960, the United States had four square feet of retail per person; in 1990, eighteen square feet; by 1998 the figure had grown to thirty-eight square feet. Yet Smith says that our existing buying power can only support sixteen square feet of retail per capita. At the same time, there is not enough residentially-zoned property in proximity to mass transit to provide the ridership to make transit viable.*

An important challenge of the Plan of Nashville is to recapture Nashville's historic pikes-turned-arterials as the means to link and enhance all elements of the city. To reestablish our traditional pikes as great corridors we must do nothing more—or less—than apply the lessons of urban avenues and boulevards:

- Use a participatory process to develop a public consensus as to the redevelopment potential of individual corridors.

- Identify important commercial nodes. At these nodes, create places where people feel comfortable by slowing traffic and providing interesting uses and convenient access.

- Intensify the development that flanks our corridors with increased residential and office activity connected with appropriate pedestrian linkages and mass transit service.

- Develop a plan that, in addition to recommending land uses, provides clear visual examples of how to enhance the physical environment through properly placed and scaled buildings, properly located parking, efficient access, and easy wayfinding.

- Develop strategies for the arterial street system that provide for motor vehicles, pedestrians, bicyclists, and mass transit with equal attention. Buildings placed next to the sidewalk, with direct pedestrian access from the primary street, encourage walking. Parking located to the rear shields the undesirable appearance of parking lots while leaving the street available for more interesting building frontage. The network functions best with few vehicular access points or curb cuts—except from alleys or lanes to parking in the rear—and short blocks (six hundred feet maximum, preferably four hundred feet) with properly signaled intersections.

- Finally, make it easy for builders and developers to do the right thing. All too often, developers support the vision of the community discussed above and would develop in ways that are pedestrian-friendly and supportive of transit use. But time is money. Unless the development review system is redesigned to speed up the process of obtaining permits for projects such as the community envisions, developers are forced to revert to previous building patterns because they cannot wait for more flexibility.

Great streets—such as King Street in Charleston, Mulberry Street in Boston, Washington Avenue in Miami, St. Charles Avenue in New Orleans, and even Second Avenue in downtown Nashville—are great places. Nashville currently has few great streets, and none of them are our major arterials. But all have the potential to become pleasant to drive on and, more importantly, reward pedestrian traffic, if we take the steps outlined above.

Nashville's urban form was at one time seamlessly integrated with its pikes and avenues. They provided the means of commerce, communication, and community structure. The city's major streets were the conduit for walkers, streetcars, and automobiles and reflected the diverse urban experience. Our objective is to recapture that balance.

Rick Bernhardt, FAICP, CNU
Executive Director
Metro Planning Department

*Kennedy Lawson Smith, interview by Rick Bernhardt, May 11, 2004.

But Nashville's urban street system has been fractured by limited-access highways. These highways, in addition to their inability to meet the current variety of transportation needs, are also hostile to the form that a city must take to be successful.

The Model Transportation System

For a city to succeed as the downtown of the region, transportation infrastructure must provide a dignified and appropriate sequence of arrival, diverse and accessible links to the region, and access to attractions with regional appeal, such as sports venues and cultural centers.

For Nashville to enhance its identity as a city of neighborhoods, transportation infrastructure must define several elements including neighborhood form, i.e., clear and distinct edges and centers, and links among the neighborhoods and between each neighborhood and downtown. A network of streets, as well as bicycle and pedestrian paths, must be organized into a clear hierarchy: boulevards/avenues, collector streets, local streets, alleys, and sidewalks. A block structure must be strongly related to the street network and sized at pedestrian scale. In addition, the placement of buildings on the blocks that define street walls must be of human scale.

The fundamental obstacle to Nashville as the downtown of the region and the city of neighborhoods is the arterial and highway infrastructure.

"The automobile has not merely taken over the street, it has dissolved the living tissue of the city. Its appetite for space is absolutely insatiable; moving and parked it devours urban land, leaving the buildings as mere islands of habitable space in a sea of dangerous and ugly traffic."

James Marston Fitch,
New York Times
(May 1, 1960)

Uncommon Sense

In 1776, Thomas Paine wrote a pamphlet that questioned the divine right of kings and defined the rights of man, to advocate for the American Revolution. He called it *Common Sense*. At the time Paine's sense was decidedly uncommon, and he was decried as a radical.

The transformation of the highway system in the Plan of Nashville may seem, at first glance, to call for a new American revolution. Actually, what the Plan proposes is an evolution.

The truly radical gesture—in the sense of practices and policies of extreme change—was the introduction of the limited-access highway into the urban fabric in the first place. Today a proposal to carve concrete canyons through our traditional neighborhoods—often African American and always low income—would be rejected as politically impossible. Metro officials would undoubtedly reject a plan encouraging massive numbers of residents and businesses to flee to surrounding counties while at the same time permanently removing thousands

of acres from Metro tax rolls. Watchdogs of the public health would protest the negative impacts on air and water quality. Most importantly, Nashvillians would refuse to ransom the long-term welfare of their city for short-term gains in motoring speed.

We know more now. What we need to remember, from our history as a community, is that transportation is an evolving art. It is time to begin to recognize that the limited-access highway in the city is a period piece, and move on.

Christine Kreyling

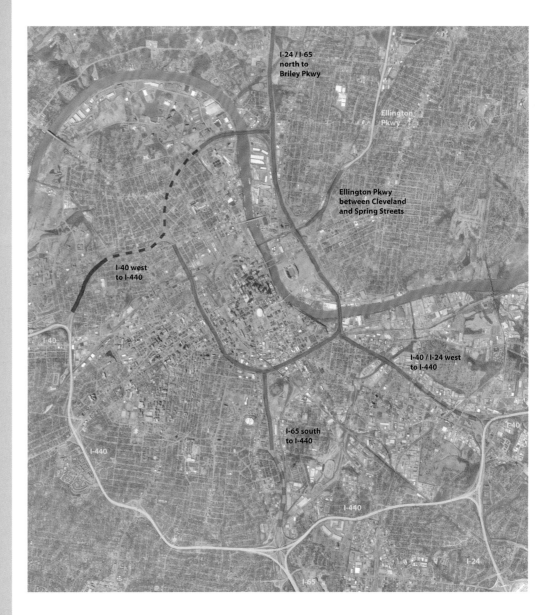

The citizens of Nashville recognize the obstacle to a better city presented by the limited-access highways. Only 6 percent of those who participated in the Plan of Nashville process favored retaining the inner loop highway segments as they currently exist.

(Diagram over photograph, 2004: NCDC, Gary Gaston)

Map Key

Solid red: conversion to urban boulevard
Dashed red: transition from interstate interchange to urban boulevard
Dashed black: removal of interstate, street grid restoration

Solid black: transition from interstate interchange to street grid
Yellow: interstate configuration stays the same

Weaning Ourselves from the Highway: The Four-Step Program

The following reforms of the highways point the way toward a new Nashville: an economically strengthened downtown surrounded by closely linked neighborhoods. The Plan of Nashville, however, does not depend completely on reaching the final steps in the program. Each step is a marked improvement over what came before.

The steps can be followed sequentially, or intervening ones skipped with the proper triggers, such as the reduction of traffic demands or the capacity of bypasses to accommodate through traffic. It is important to remember in designing new thoroughfares, however, that how we design them will determine their viability. If a limited-access highway is transformed into a boulevard that mimics the design of our current arterials, the result will be nothing more than linear sprawl.

Of the four steps presented in the reformation process, the final one is an either/or proposition. A section of limited-access highway right-of-way can become an urban boulevard, or the right-of-way is abandoned altogether and the street system returns to its pre-interstate condition.

The four-step program is a plan for local circulation. Long-distance traffic will not use the urban street and road system (see "The Long-Distance Driver," pages 86–87, for the treatment of through traffic).

I. Cosmetic Improvements

Landscaping, chain link removal, public art, sound walls, and reduction of light glare would improve the quality of life on the roads and on adjacent properties, without modifying the function or capacity of the highway system. This approach, however, is only a "band-aid."

The cosmetic treatment will make arriving in

Existing conditions, East Bank near Coliseum. The interstate cuts off East Nashville from the river while consuming vast amounts of developable real estate.

(Photograph, 2003: Metro Planning Department, Chris Wooten)

Nashville more visually appealing. But connectivity among the neighborhoods and downtown is not improved, nor are there new opportunities for mass transit or other modes of mobility such as pedestrian and bicycle traffic. Neighborhoods experience a superficial gain through aesthetic treatments and the reduction of noise.

II. More Links

The main benefit of more links is the increased connectivity among neighborhoods and to the downtown, as well as new route possibilities for public transit, pedestrians, and bicyclists. Additional land for redevelopment also becomes available at the intersections of the links.

Seattle's Freeway Park, a wide greenspace near the city's convention center that crosses a highway to connect downtown with neighborhoods, is one example of such a linkage. Another is a plan by the city of Minneapolis for a two-block-wide "bridge" across a highway that will contain primarily residential development.

III. Rationalized Interchanges

A right-angle interface between the highways and the public streets is pedestrian and bicycle friendly—because right angles slow traffic down—and provides opportunities for bus stops, dedicated transit lanes, and multimodal transportation hubs. Reclaimed land—hundreds of acres—is returned to the downtown and neighborhood fabric, and to Metro tax rolls.

IV. Option 1. Highway to Boulevard

The segment of interstate on the East Bank of the Cumberland River has the following characteristics that make it a good candidate for highway-to-boulevard conversion. The highway conforms to the geometry of the street system around it. The land on either side of the highway could be easily organized into neighborhoods that would use the boulevard as a "high street." The type of medium-scale development and land uses associated with an urban boulevard would be in keeping with the density desirable for this area.

Cosmetic Changes: The East Bank riverfront develops while interstate configuration stays the same. Increased landscaping and better lighting make the city more attractive.

(Drawing, 2004: Earl Swensson Associates, Ken Henley and Corey Little)

EAST NASHVILLE ENVISIONED

More Links: As the East Bank continues to develop, new linkages are added. The Coliseum's expansive parking lots are pulled into the urban fabric of the East Bank, while parking needs are accomplished within mixed-use garages.

(Drawing, 2004: Earl Swensson Associates, Ken Henley and Corey Little)

EAST NASHVILLE ENVISIONED

EAST NASHVILLE
ENVISIONED

Rationalized Interchanges: As the East Bank neighborhood becomes more dense, the cloverleaf intersections are reformed to a less land-hungry design, allowing increased development. Note the transformation of the Ellington Parkway terminus in upper right corner.

(Drawing, 2004: Earl Swensson Associates, Ken Henley and Corey Little)

EAST NASHVILLE
ENVISIONED

Highway to Boulevard: The East Bank Neighborhood is now fully connected to the rest of East Nashville. The former interstate right-of-way is occupied by new development and the grand East Boulevard. Note the two new bridges now crossing the Cumberland.

(Drawing, 2004: Earl Swensson Associates, Ken Henley and Corey Little)

If the highway is converted to a boulevard lined with trees and mid-rise buildings, the aesthetics of arrival into the city is greatly enhanced. Because the boulevard is—unlike the interstate—integrated into the existing street system, what had been a barrier between East Nashville and the East Bank and downtown now becomes an avenue and a destination pulling the sections of the city together. A right-of-way that served only motor vehicles now also provides for mass transit, non-motorized vehicles, and pedestrians, possibly with dedicated lanes for transit and bikes. Significant housing and retail can be programmed into the old interstate right-of-way which is now freed for redevelopment, thus enhancing the adjacent neighborhoods.

IV. Option 2. Street System Restoration

The River District is a series of neighborhoods once organized around Jefferson Street. I-40 plowed through these neighborhoods without

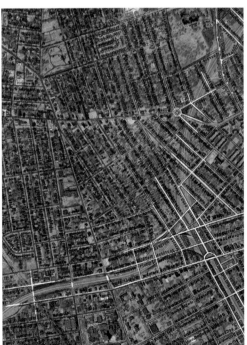

Left top: Diagram illustrating North Nashville with I-40 right-of-way restored to the pre-interstate public street system. This step serves cases that require major repairs of the public street system in areas where an urban boulevard is not appropriate.

(Drawing over photograph, 2003: NCDC, Raven Hardison)

Left bottom: Development fills in reconnected grid and heals fractured neighborhoods in North Nashville.

(Drawing over photograph, 2003: NCDC, Raven Hardison)

Right top: Existing conditions in North Nashville and Fisk–Meharry area, to right. Note how I-40 closely parallels Jefferson Street, effectively cutting off the street from North Nashville to the left.

(Photograph, 2004: Metro Planning Department)

Right bottom: Street system restoration: The River District neighborhoods are reunited by the removal of the interstate and reconfiguration of the historic street grid, allowing Jefferson Street to return to its former prominence.

(Drawing, 2004: NCDC, Mark Schimmenti)

Urban boulevards, Kansas City, Missouri.

(Photographs, 2002: Alex S. MacLean/Landslides)

Left: Note how interstate at upper left metamorphoses into tree-lined boulevard, the Paseo, with walking paths, gardens, and public gathering spaces.

Right: Median of Ward Parkway at Meyer Circle has been programmed with lawns, large fountains, and gardens.

But Where Will the Traffic Go?

Any proposal for road modifications that threatens to reduce capacity or speed—such as converting some Nashville interstates to boulevards—immediately raises the challenge, often belligerently posed, "But where will the traffic go?" The presumptive answers are always disastrous: gridlock, eight-mile back-ups, economic ruin, and losing out to rivals Memphis and Chattanooga. To many, reducing road capacity, and thereby inviting more congestion, is like falling short in sewer or electrical capacity. Sewer deficiencies create a public health menace; voltage drop causes the physical failure of electrical appliances.

With traffic, however, we simply move to a different point on the "supply and demand" curve when the supply changes. As travel becomes more expensive (in terms of travel time, the only "cost" immediately felt by the driver), we simply consume less of it. And the accommodations that drivers make, when free-flowing road capacity is less available, are not at all like the apocalyptic gridlock that transportation planners are fond of predicting. Drivers are smarter than this.

One of the immediate adjustments that drivers make to congestion is simply to reschedule their travel away from the peak work trip times, by far

the most congested periods, and often the only congested periods. Information industry employees, now a majority of Nashville's workers, are more than ever able to vary their office hours. Voice mail, e-mail, pagers, cell phones, personal digital assistants, and laptops favor flexible working hours, even when the worker must daily visit a home office. A vehicle trip shifted from the peak period is better than adding the same amount of new capacity, since the existing road is being more efficiently used, at no additional cost.

When capacity or service is reduced, drivers are also quick to reroute themselves. Rather than simply dumping themselves onto the nearest available alternative, as the "doomsday" view of traffic congestion warns, drivers actually reroute themselves in an elaborate cascade of route changes. While drivers shifting from their primary route may simply divert to the nearest available alternative route, the rerouting does not stop at this simple stage. Drivers already on the alternate route do not simply ignore the new traffic and meekly sit in increased congestion. Rather, some of these drivers at the margin of choice between routes move instead to yet another alternate, and so on, through an elaborate chain of reroutings. The "trip assignment" in travel forecast models can reflect millions of daily decisions that drivers make in the Nashville area, and thereby project the traffic. In other words, a conventional transportation planning tool gives us a livable answer, unexpectedly.

Paradoxically, the same traffic models that seem to be always telling us that we need more road capacity to keep traffic flowing, also tell us, on the other hand, that if we remove capacity, the system will continue to function quite nicely, with drivers making, in the aggregate, sophisticated decisions to keep the system operating.

By far, the most interesting response to congestion is change in the pattern of origins and destinations. The choice of home location is one of the most volatile in this respect. When major new road capacity was added—to the interstates around Nashville, for example—many homeowners living in older parts of Nashville and reinvesting in their neighborhoods chose to move their households to a new suburban tract home inevitably spawned by the road addition. Conversely, if congestion had not been removed, the same households would have remained in place, continuing to reinvest in an existing neighborhood.

Who then is victimized by road congestion that causes residents to stay in place? It is difficult to find any victim. Certainly not the city of Nashville, where the homeowner lives now. The city has a deep interest in its homeowners staying in place and reinvesting. Nor is the school district the victim, since it is not interested in adding capacity in one place while abandoning corresponding amounts of capacity elsewhere. Perhaps the suburban tract-home developer might be a stakeholder who loses when road

capacity lags. But, on the other hand, doesn't this homebuilder, with a shift in product and location, have every opportunity to develop and redevelop in the existing settled areas, where values are increasing due to location?

Trip destinations also react to congestion. Free-flowing, high-speed traffic is a promise to the retail industry that large catchment areas of population can be delivered to a single location, within the acceptable travel time needed for big-box retailing (typically fifteen to twenty minutes). The result: even larger big boxes, with a corresponding ever-increasing amount of travel required for the same amount of purchase. Endlessly expanding the scale of big-box retailing is contrary to every planning objective in the Nashville region. Yet, at the same time, a policy of maintaining free-flowing traffic at all times presents an irresistible incentive to further concentrate retailing in very large boxes.

What happens to retailing when the promise of free-flowing traffic is withdrawn, through an action as visible as reducing capacity or speed? Does the retail industry abandon the area? Of course not. The industry is smarter than that.

Grocery stores will choose to run neighborhood-sized stores of forty thousand to fifty thousand square feet at more locations, rather than fewer big-box stores of three or four times the size. Franchise retailers will reduce their threshold requirements, yielding more locations with smaller market areas and less travel time. Some retailers, accustomed to operating only in single-owner, closed-environment malls, will make the leap into multi-owner open environments such as main streets, downtowns, and neighborhood centers.

Information technology favors a pattern of more, smaller commercial destinations rather than fewer large ones. Automated warehousing, self-replenishing inventory systems, self-service checkout, and electronic theft prevention systems let retailers operate at more numerous smaller locations efficiently.

Again, it is difficult to find any "victim" of these reactions by retailers to increased traffic congestion. The customers, with more and closer shopping destinations, are certainly not victimized. Nor is the development industry, which is building more units and more floor area. Nor are local communi-

ties, many of which are seeing long-neglected main streets or neighborhood centers reoccupied by retail businesses. Nor are the retailers themselves, who are mastering, even if reluctantly, more sustainable ways to retail.

Traffic engineering, it is now clear, is full of unintended consequences, in both directions. The intended consequence of high capacity, to reduce costs and to reduce delay, soon gives way to the unintended consequences of drivers going farther, not faster, soon followed by the moving around of households, businesses, and all of the daily destinations. None of the ultimate results—more travel, more congestion, abandonment of older communities, sprawl across the countryside—were intended.

The unintended consequences of traffic congestion, we are now learning, can run in a positive direction. The presumed dire consequences of reducing capacity—more travel time and cost—prompt a chain of events that, in reality, is anything but dire. Homeowners reinvest in communities. Businesses find new ways to better serve their customers. Unintended consequences of the negative sort are well understood, although they always seem to fly in the face of conventional wisdom. It should not be surprising that the reverse is true; that deliberately tolerating congestion may have unintentional consequences in a positive direction.

Walter Kulash, P.E., Traffic Engineer

Tear It Down!

Milwaukee has done something that might seem astounding, perhaps even un-American: tear down a superhighway. Forty years ago, highway designers planned to surround the central business district with an expressway that was to include a section along the shore of Lake Michigan. This section, which would have separated downtown from its waterfront, generated enough opposition to stop its construction. But more than half of the loop was built, including a three-quarter-mile stretch that separated the north side from the rest of downtown.

The elevated road obstructed what would otherwise have been beautiful views on both sides of the Milwaukee River, and property values near the structure were depressed. In contrast, downtown Milwaukee experienced a housing boom that had developers searching for sites. In 1999, the county, state, and city agreed to remove most of the Park East Freeway and develop the land. The estimated property value increase is $250 million.

It may seem strange, tearing down expressways after fifty years of the greatest road-building binge in world history. But traffic engineers are learning that urban street grids can distribute urban traffic more efficiently than do superhighways. Orlando-based traffic engineer Walter Kulash argues that, "Widening roads to solve traffic congestion is like loosening your belt to cure obesity," and advocates for more smaller streets and roads rather than huge limited-access interstate highways. Traffic engineer Rick Chellman's research in Portsmouth, New Hampshire, demonstrates that the urban street grid generates less than half the car trips of suburban development.

In eliminating a segment of superhighway, Milwaukee is not alone. When the 1989 earthquake damaged the Em-

barcadero Freeway in San Francisco, it was considered an "act of God." San Francisco's political culture embraced the divine message and the city petitioned the state to remove the freeway instead of rebuilding it. The state agreed, nearby property values shot up by more than 300 percent, and views of San Francisco Bay from the North Coast are no longer obstructed.

In the 1970s, Portland removed an elevated expressway separating its downtown from the banks of the Willamette River and replaced it with an avenue and a park. Property values are up dramatically, and the park is one of the most popular gathering spots in Oregon. Similarly, in the 1980s New York City removed the Westside Highway and has since enjoyed huge development in the old freeway corridor.

We're changing our attitudes about highways and transportation. San Francisco, Portland, New York, and now Milwaukee all are deconstructing freeways and replacing them with avenues and boulevards. All four cities are undoing damage done to them, which points out one characteristic of Americans: we make huge mistakes, but we also correct them. Now Cleveland, Akron, and our friends across the border in Toronto are about to remove freeway segments. Urban expressway deconstruction could be one of the biggest public works projects of the twenty-first century.

John O. Norquist
President of the Congress for the New
Urbanism, former mayor
of Milwaukee, and the author of
The Wealth of Cities (1998)

Excerpted from an article that originally appeared in Blueprint Magazine *(September 1, 2000) and can be found at www.ndol.org.*

regard to the geometry of the street system or the natural boundaries of the neighborhoods. The interstate, because it blocks access to Jefferson Street from the neighborhoods, also limits the ability of Jefferson to successfully function as the area's main street. The boulevard option is not appropriate in this case because there is no need for another major street to compete with Jefferson. The commercial health of Jefferson Street would be better served by a restoration of the surrounding street system.

Most of the land within the interstate right-of-way returns to the neighborhood for private development as well as civic use. Pedestrian and bicycle mobility is enhanced through the re-establishment of pedestrian-scale streets. The neighborhood is also easier to serve with mass transit, although this step does not necessarily provide dedicated right-of-way for mass transit.

Both options, highway-to-boulevard and street system restoration, are overdue gestures to the cause of environmental justice. Low-income and minority neighborhoods, which had been fractured and isolated for the sake of the high-speed trips of the suburban commuter and the long-distance traveler, are rewoven into the city fabric.

The Long-Distance Driver

The Plan of Nashville's vision of the ultimate transformation of the interstate loop is rooted in the distinction between the needs of local circulation and long-distance travel. Conflating the two types of traffic, as we have done in the past, serves neither type very well. Planning for through traffic, therefore, requires the planners to designate existing routes as devoted to this purpose—or develop blueprints for new ones, recognizing all the political consequences—and direct future land use and highway design to this end.

According to the Nashville Area Metropolitan Planning Organization (MPO) and the Tennessee Department of Transportation (TDOT), only approximately 35 percent of the traffic on the interstate inner loop is long-distance through traffic. When the inner loop is transformed into boulevards or returned to the traditional street system, as the Plan presents, these streets will not be designed for high-speed vehicles passing through town.

The Plan anticipates that long-distance drivers will reroute themselves to the high-speed bypasses: Briley Parkway and I-440. For this assumption to succeed, long-range planners must determine that the future of these highways is primarily to serve high-speed through traffic and then develop strategies to manage the traffic count or number of vehicles, and the mobility of these roads, to enable this traffic to efficiently bypass the city.

The Traffic Count
Local Usage

The citizens who participated in the Plan of Nashville process look forward to a time when there is a drastic reduction in local usage of the limited-access highways. This reduction depends on changes in how we plan and build our city. Planning and development must enable the greater use of public transportation for mobility and access across the city, as well as the use of bicycle and pedestrian modes for trips of shorter distance, to achieve fewer car trips per household.

When the arterials are reformed and the inner loop is transformed, the resulting network of streets and boulevards should absorb the local traffic—including trips by mass transit and bicycle—that represents 65 percent of today's interstate usage. More of the remaining limited-access highway's capacity is thus available for through traffic.

Spaghetti Junction

The D.C. suburbs have the "Mixing Bowl." In Rochester, the most infamous is the "Can of Worms." Drivers in other cities employ other derisive nicknames: "Orange Crush," "Hillside Strangler," and "Malfunction Junction." These ominous labels evoke the psychological impact caused by the tangled confluences of major highways—interchanges on steroids.

These points on the nation's interstate web feed vehicles into a dizzying filtration system that spins motorists about on a roller coaster of ramps and through a dicey succession of lane changes, before spitting them out in some new direction. The saving grace for the weak of stomach is the increasing slowness of the bumper-to-bumper traffic that winds through these concrete tilt-a-whirls.

When viewed from the air, the super-interchange is often sculptural in form, an artistic interweaving of pavement that belies its negative attributes. Chief among them is that "interchange art" consumes massive amounts of a limited commodity: urban land.

Nashville boasts several of these bloated interchanges. None is larger—or more confusing—than the convergence of Ellington Parkway, I-24, Main Street, Spring Street, and Dickerson Pike in East Nashville. "Spaghetti Junction"—actually it's more like lasagna—devours ninety-five acres of urban property. Nashville's entire central business district could fit within the confines of its sweeping ramps. If those ninety-five acres were built out as a medium-density mixed-use neighborhood—as envisioned in the Plan of Nashville—the site that now drains tax dollars for road maintenance would instead generate huge cash flows.

In the Plan's scenario for this East Nashville site, there would still, of course, be a need for roads, parks, and other public spaces. But approximately seventy acres would remain for private development. The worth of this land today is approximately $15 million, based on the current value of adjacent commercial and industrial properties. That figure could rise to $100 million—or more—as the property becomes increasingly valuable to urban developers.

Suppose, as the Plan does, that this land were redeveloped as three- and four-story buildings mixing substantial amounts of residential with some office and retail uses—a total of around nine million square feet of space. A rough estimate of the aggregate value of construction would be $1.3 billion in today's figures.

Annual tax revenues to Metro on the "Spaghetti" site alone would, at current rates, exceed $20 million when built out. And that figure does not take into consideration the financial benefits of all that development money rippling through the economy, or the sales tax revenue generated by new urban residents spending their dollars in the city. The obese interchange is a field of gold waiting to be mined.

David Koellein
Development Program Manager
Metro Development and Housing Agency

> "Stick a fork in that road spaghetti and wind it up!"
>
> Carol Norton,
> community workshop
> participant

Left: East Nashville, 1934, superimposed over 2003. Note how the neighborhood of East Nashville reached almost to the river.

Center: The construction of major highway interchanges erased what were once fine-grained neighborhoods.
(Photographs, 1934 and 2003: Metro Planning Department)

Right: "Spaghetti Junction" superimposed on Nashville's central business district. The amount of land occupied by the East Nashville super-interchange is roughly equal to the area of Nashville's CBD.
(Diagram over photograph, 2004: NCDC, Raven Hardison)

"Bypasses are
devices that
allow some
people to dash
from point A
to point B very
fast while other
people dash
from point B
to point A very
fast."

Douglas Adams,
*The Hitchhiker's Guide to
the Galaxy*
(1979)

Bypass Capacity

The feasibility of the interstate transformation depends on the ability of Briley Parkway and I-440 to handle the diverted through traffic. This capability in turn depends on a collective agreement among planners that a primary purpose of these highways is to provide high-speed routes to bypass the city. Some gains in mobility may be realized by reconfiguring intersections and limiting local access. The Plan strongly recommends that there be no increase in the actual size of the rights-of-way. American transportation history has already demonstrated that adding new capacity to roadways just induces more traffic to use them.

The changes the Plan of Nashville presents for the arterials and interstates cannot occur in isolation. The timing of the changes is dependent upon many factors that will require close coordination between land use and transportation planning.

The relocation of freight hubs out of the urban areas would remove the need for highways designed to accommodate semis. Increases in density, particularly for residential population in the study area of the Plan, could subtract cars from the interstates and add them to the urban streets or mass transit systems. An increase of twenty-five thousand people who both live and work in downtown, for example, would remove a comparable number of single-occupancy vehicles (SOV) from the highways during rush hour. The changes are also contingent on a shift in our transportation investment from adding road capacity to increasing mass transit opportunities. More residential development within quick walking distance of the arterials and collector streets would enable mass transit to function more economically and efficiently.

Ultimately, getting the interstates out of urban Nashville is a long-term vision that will

Long Distance

Interstate trucking represents up to 30 percent of Nashville's through traffic, according to TDOT data. Travelers in cars make up the rest. Economic forces and the availability of alternate forms of travel and freight movement will determine the through traffic counts of the future.

TDOT has plans for passenger rail linking the major cities of Tennessee. But preliminary estimates indicate that train speeds will not reach that posted for vehicles on the interstates.

TDOT needs a more ambitious plan for passenger rail, with speeds at least comparable to that of cars and trucks—and the state must have the political will to fund it—if we are to pull drivers off the interstates and onto the trains.

Investment at the state and federal level in the rail freight infrastructure would increase the speed and capacity of the rails. Such investment could mitigate the projected doubling of freight truck traffic on the interstates in the next fifteen to twenty years.

require many large and small steps—all coordinated and moving in the same direction. By making that vision a goal on our civic horizon, and then evaluating current and future land use and transportation plans in terms of their respective abilities to reach that goal, we can make a system that works equally well for long-distance and local traffic.

Mass Transit for Local Circulation

It doesn't take a rocket scientist to figure out that, in the competition to move more people using fewer vehicles and less road capacity, mass transit has it over the automobile every time. Yet the Plan of Nashville citizen survey of April 2003 found that 88 percent of the approximately five hundred who participated had never used Nashville's public transportation system. Only 7 percent responded that they used transit one to three times per month, 3 percent used the system one to three times per week, and only 2 percent took the bus every day. Why are the figures so dismal?

For starters, the service the Metro Transit Authority (MTA) offers is not particularly

The relative amount of space in a right-of-way occupied by forty people using various modes of transportation. (Photographs, 1999: *Tampa Tribune*)

Top left: Cars, bumper to bumper.
Top right: People spaced as if they are in cars.

Bottom left: People spaced as if they are in a mass transit vehicle.
Bottom right: Bikers and pedestrians.

ment levels: federal, state, and local. Higher appropriations would enable MTA to offer more frequent service as well as direct service to more dispersed origins and destinations.

Because of this underfunding, Nashville buses are not cheap to ride. The cost per trip in 2004 is $1.45, which is the highest fare among Tennessee's larger cities. An unlimited weekly pass is $14.70, an unlimited monthly pass $48.00, not big discounts if you use the bus to commute to work five days a week—and for little else. If you are one of the approximately fifteen thousand state office workers in downtown, for example, and are provided with free parking, there is little economic incentive for you to take the bus.

The ultimate villain in Nashville's under-utilization of mass transit, however, is the city's sprawling, low-density development patterns. According to *USA Today*'s 2001 sprawl index, Nashville is America's most sprawling city. Most routes lack the ridership pool to make them economically viable. Providing all of Metro—including subdivisions on one-acre lots—with comparable levels of service would pretty much guarantee that the level of service would be mediocre.

frequent. Service is also organized in a radial route plan, which works for commuting to and from downtown. But riders seeking other points on the map—East Nashvillians going to the Vanderbilt medical complex or South Nashvillians to Green Hills, for example—must go through downtown and engage in time-consuming transfers. Inconvenient service is not a good strategy for getting people out of their cars and onto mass transit.

The system is also underfunded at all govern-

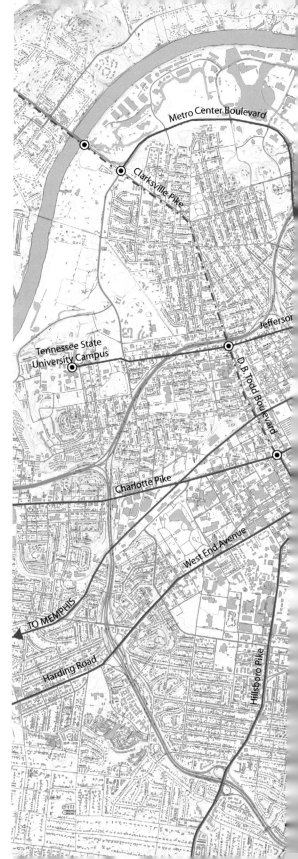

The Plan of Nashville's vision for the future public transit system.

(Diagram over map, 2004; NCDC, Raven Hardison)

Nashville's Future Transit System

Blue Network represents the primary routes for rapid transit service, which requires a dedicated lane on those streets so that the transit vehicle's travel times are not affected by automobile congestion. Blue-dash markings represent the subsequent phase of rapid transit development.

In the initial implementation, rubber-tired transit vehicles would run in the dedicated lane. As ridership grows, Nashville could then add the track, overhead electric wires, and other infrastructure needed to convert to a full BRT or light rail system.

Although MTA buses serve many more routes than are shown here, the blue routes are designated for much more frequent service—every fifteen minutes, perhaps even every ten minutes within the Inner Loop. Routes targeted for early implementation include the corridors that currently boast highest MTA ridership and development intensities: Gallatin Pike/Main Street, Murfreesboro and Nolensville Pikes, Charlotte Pike, Metro Center Boulevard, and West End Avenue/Broadway.

Plans to revitalize Jefferson Street, along with the need to better link TSU's main campus with its downtown satellite campus, indicate that service along Jefferson Street should also be considered in the first phase of rapid transit. Continued redevelopment in Green Hills also suggests the benefit of establishing a rapid transit line on Hillsboro Road, which could link to downtown via the service on West End/Broadway.

Transfer points would be clustered in the downtown area to ensure that commuters, tourists, and downtown residents could easily access all modes of transit within a few minutes' walk. Broadway becomes a key axis where numerous routes intersect. It could eventually be traversed by buses on five-minute headways, with "step on, step off" service at each block between the Gulch and Riverfront rail station.

As of this publication date, MTA is advancing plans to build a new downtown transfer center where passengers will board and depart all regular (non-rapid) bus routes. When city officials select the final site, it will be important to provide easy access between this "local" transfer center and the regional stations planned along Broadway.

Red Network shows regional routes for a commuter rail system, providing service for trips of forty miles or less.

Major hubs include (1) downtown/Gulch, where the majority of rail lines convene; (2) downtown/Riverfront, within easy walking distance of the Coliseum, Second Avenue, and other visitor attractions; and (3) East Nashville near the Spring Street/South Fifth Street intersection.

Future expansion of this network includes intercity passenger rail service connecting Nashville to other large cities such as Atlanta, Birmingham, Knoxville, Memphis, and Louisville (see "Regional Transit" on pages 90-91).

Green Route extends from riverfront station along the river northward, connecting downtown to the Bicentennial Mall, Neuhoff Complex, and Governor Green (see Neighborhood section, "River District," pages 141-55). The line would not be part of the proposed regional commuter system, but developed separately as a tourist-oriented enterprise.

Map Key

⊙ Intermodal Transit Hub

○ Bus Transfer Station

⊙ Transfer Points

—— Regional Rail

—— Local Transit Lines

- - - Future Extensions

—— Green Route

TO BOWLING GREEN / LOUISVILLE

TO HENDERSONVILLE / GALLATIN

TO LEBANON / KNOXVILLE

Nashville International
Airport

The Plan of Nashville envisions
extending RTA's long-range
plan for commuter rail to
intercity service. Note the rail
connection to the airport.
(Diagram over map, 2004: NCDC)

TO MEMPHIS

TO FRANKLIN / BIRMINGHAM

TO MURFREESBORO /
CHATTANOOGA / ATLANTA

Because Nashville sprawls, Nashvillians also drive—a lot. The most recent statistics from the Federal Highway Administration state that the average daily vehicle miles traveled per capita within the Nashville metropolitan region is 34.3 miles. Not coincidentally, Nashville also owns the dubious honor of having received in 2003 an F from the American Lung Association for its air quality. Tennesseans have long claimed to have the best roads in the country. Those roads have taken us to some of the worst air pollution and suburban sprawl.

Getting people out of their cars and onto mass transit could help to mitigate Nashville's deteriorating air quality, as well as ease the congestion on our roadways. To make transit work better for more people, however, we must have more people in greater densities living and working near transit routes—which will require drastic changes in the way we use land for development—and we must provide them with faster, cheaper, and more convenient service.

Some cities, Charlotte, Denver, Pittsburgh, and Atlanta, have begun to expand their transit options beyond the conventional bus which competes with cars for road space. Bus-Rapid-Transit (BRT) and/or light rail, commuter rail, HOV lanes, and dedicated bus lanes are just a few of the new methods that are being used to alter the reliance upon the automobile.

Reliability, convenience, passenger comfort, and the ability to access major destinations are all key in ensuring that a transit system is used by the public. The Plan of Nashville presents a vision of how transit could work in our city.

Regional Transit

Middle Tennessee once had commuter rail. For the first five decades of the last century, the railroads delivered rural residents to Nashville. As Gillian Fishbach and Suzanne Jackson write in

"The Origin and Advancement of Nashville's Transportation System," "The city's retail merchants offered reduced fares on the local trains in an attempt to encourage shopping trips to downtown Nashville. The shoppers boarded the trains in small, rural towns, or at flag stops along the routes."[3] The service was discontinued in 1956, as the automobile became the mode of choice for middle-distance travel.

The Regional Transit Authority (RTA) has a blueprint for returning commuter rail to Middle Tennessee. RTA has plans to develop five routes to link satellite cities to Nashville.

These routes could expand to become intercity lines as well.

Commuter rail will provide an additional layer of regional mobility. The lines have the potential to relieve traffic congestion, as well as supply passengers, both commuters and visitors, with a distinctive way to arrive in the city.

Take the Greenway

For thousands of years, the Natchez Trace and similar footpaths served as the primary transportation network of Middle Tennessee. The region's history began with the foot traffic of the Native Americans, who established an extensive system of trails in order to trade wares and facilitate communication among the various tribes. Metro Nashville's greenways master plan revives this ancient tradition.

As green corridors linking the public parks scattered throughout the county, the greenways are commonly perceived as primarily recreational, providing opportunities for walking, running, bicycling, and other forms of exercise while enjoying nature close to home. But the greenways system is also intended to serve as part of our transportation infrastructure, providing non-automotive routes between home and work, and other destinations. The master plan

Shelby Bottoms Greenway. In the greenways master plan, a biker like this one will be able to ride all the way from the Bottoms to the Tennessee State University campus.

(Photograph, 2003: Hawkins Partners)

envisions the potential for 210 miles of greenways in Davidson County, linking the far-flung suburbs—and the counties surrounding Davidson—with the traditional neighborhoods and the urban core.

Integrating the trails with mass transit, by locating bus stops near greenways and adding bike racks to buses, will enhance the connectivity of the transportation system and provide alternatives to travel by car. Bike and pedestrian modes of travel produce no air or noise pollution, decrease automotive traffic congestion, alleviate parking demand, improve our health, and save energy and tax dollars. These modes are most effectively used in areas of dense and mixed land use, a form of development advocated by the Plan of Nashville. As a transportation alternative to the automobile, greenways are, therefore, a crucial component of the Plan.

"We want a Nashville scaled for humans, not cars."

Sue Mulcahy,
community workshop
participant

THE MODEL TRANSPORTATION PLAN is a vision, made by planners and citizens in collaboration, of a city freed from the noose of its highways. In the plan, Nashville is a city entered along tree-lined boulevards, a place where you can leave home without a car, and where those without cars are more equal members of society.

The social costs of a drive-everywhere culture are high. Chief among them are the loss of independence for children and the elderly—and for the high-mileage moms and dads who are forced to serve as chauffeurs. When Mom or Dad is not available, explains MPO coordinator Jeanne Stevens, "we have the real costs of social service van programs which are inefficient and expensive to operate when compared with a regular transit system. It would be a much smarter use of the tax dollar to build cities in a sensible fashion."

We are also becoming aware of the health costs embedded in our current transportation infrastructure. The roads we build have a huge effect on how much we travel. People who live in areas that contain a tight grid of streets and a mixture of land uses walk more, use transit more, and take half as many automobile trips compared to those who live in typical outer-edge suburbs. Maximizing choice and mobility starts with the pedestrian because every trip begins and ends with walking. By connecting communities, and enhancing the pedestrian environment, we attack the declining levels of personal exercise and growing obesity, as well as our deteriorating air quality.

For several years the American Lung Association has ranked Nashville among the top twenty-five cities with the dirtiest air. "More Highways, More Pollution," a 2004 study by the U.S. Public Interest Research Group, states that Nashville ranks second in the nation in highway capacity and third in the number of miles driven per capita.[4] Not coincidentally, the report found that Nashville leads the nation in pollution from cars and trucks per capita. Poor air quality contributes to asthma attacks, lung cancer, and heart disease.

For too long Nashville has sacrificed its downtown and traditional neighborhoods to the cause of high speeds for commuters in the far-flung suburbs and long-distance travelers and truckers.

The block of Fifth Avenue North between Church and Union Streets features fine urban design; buildings form continuous street walls with good transparency to the sidewalk.

(Photograph, 2003: NCDC, Gary Gaston)

DOWNTOWN

NASHVILLE AND ITS DOWNTOWN: CREATING CIVIC SPACE

To UNDERSTAND WHY a downtown is important, we might as well begin with Jane Jacobs. In *The Death and Life of Great American Cities,* the grandmother of urban commentators writes:

> Probably everyone is aware of certain general dependencies by a city on its heart. When a city heart stagnates or disintegrates, a city as the social neighborhood of the whole begins to suffer: People who ought to get together, by means of central activities that are failing, fail to get together. Ideas and money that ought to meet, and do so often by happenstance in a place of central vitality, fail to meet. The networks of city public life develop gaps they cannot afford. Without a strong and *inclusive* central heart, a city tends to become a collection of interests isolated from one another. It falters at producing something greater, socially,

culturally and economically, than the sum of its separated parts.[1]

Nashville's downtown stagnated in the 1970s and '80s, when the Opry left, sleaze shops and winos took over Broadway, and vacant storefronts littered the streetscape. Today, while there are definite signs of revival, much of this revival is dependent on the programming of special events. The downtown of daily life still lacks animation. The ubiquitous dead zones of surface parking, the absence of retail, and the fact that many new projects in downtown have been subsidized by Metro monies leave open the question of whether Nashville's central city is marching forward or staging the dance of one step forward, one step back.

The march of progress depends on satisfying the needs and expectations of two downtown

constituencies: the regional citizens, who use the city center for its resources and services, and Nashvillians for whom the center holds pride of place as the foremost among the city's neighborhoods. For both groups, downtown should, through its architecture and urban structure, evoke a distinctive sense of place with twin and overlapping identities: a grand capital city that also functions as a self-sustaining neighborhood.

Solids and Voids

The relationship of buildings and spaces—the public rights-of-way of streets and sidewalks, as well as plazas and parks—constitutes the character of a city. This relationship defines, or fails to define, the downtown's sense of place.

To the extent that the traditional urban fabric survives in downtown Nashville, the

> "A place is nothing, not even space, / Unless at its heart a figure stands."
>
> Amy Lowell,
> "Thorn Piece,"
> *A Shard of Silence*
> (1957)

"I think the landscape is everything outside the building footprint. It is the moment you walk out of the house and enter the world."

Martha Schwartz,
New York Times Magazine
(May 16, 2004)

relationship between buildings and spaces strikes a good urban balance between solid and void. What erodes Nashville's urban character, however, is an inattention to the visual opportunities inherent in the urban fabric—the sightline to a major monument, for example—as well as the non-traditional propensity toward surface parking and buildings that do not meet the sidewalk and supply human-scaled walls to the street. The result is too many voids, and too few solids. And the solids that exist are often far *too* solid: blank walls at street level that are hostile to the public right-of-way and offer no visual interest to the pedestrian.

For Nashville to physically affirm its status as capital city and downtown of the region, the central city should feature fine architecture, public art, plazas, and parks. The mere presence of these elements, however, does not constitute a civic realm. The public realm is the space outside the building, including the network—the boulevards and avenues and streets—that unites these elements. This network is the prime location of the "happenstance" encounters that Jane Jacobs stresses as crucial to the city as a "social neighborhood."

Downtown Nashville has some admirable civic architecture: the State Capitol, War Memorial, Metro Courthouse, Public Library. But these structures are often visually and physically isolated from one another—as if scattered throughout downtown rather than placed as parts of a cohesive urban design. Public plazas and parks are underused because they don't successfully function as daily gathering places for Nashvillians.

The Plan of Nashville presents a strategy of connectivity that redefines the relationship between downtown buildings and spaces. There are two scales to this strategy. The grand scale emphasizes Nashville's identity as capital city, and stretches from the city center into the areas surrounding downtown. The secondary scale is the meat and potatoes of the urban fabric, operating locally within downtown as neighborhood. Both scales use elements of urban design that historically evolved from the concept of the axis.

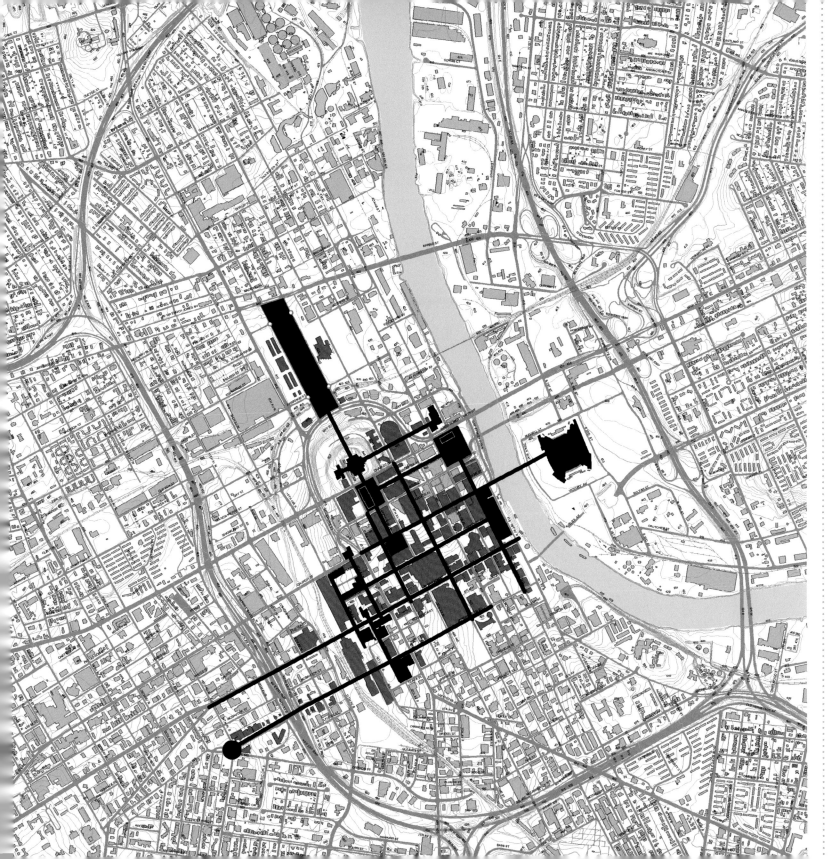

Existing axes and termination points in downtown Nashville. Axes extend from and between important buildings and public spaces.

(Diagram over map, 2004: NCDC, Raven Hardison)

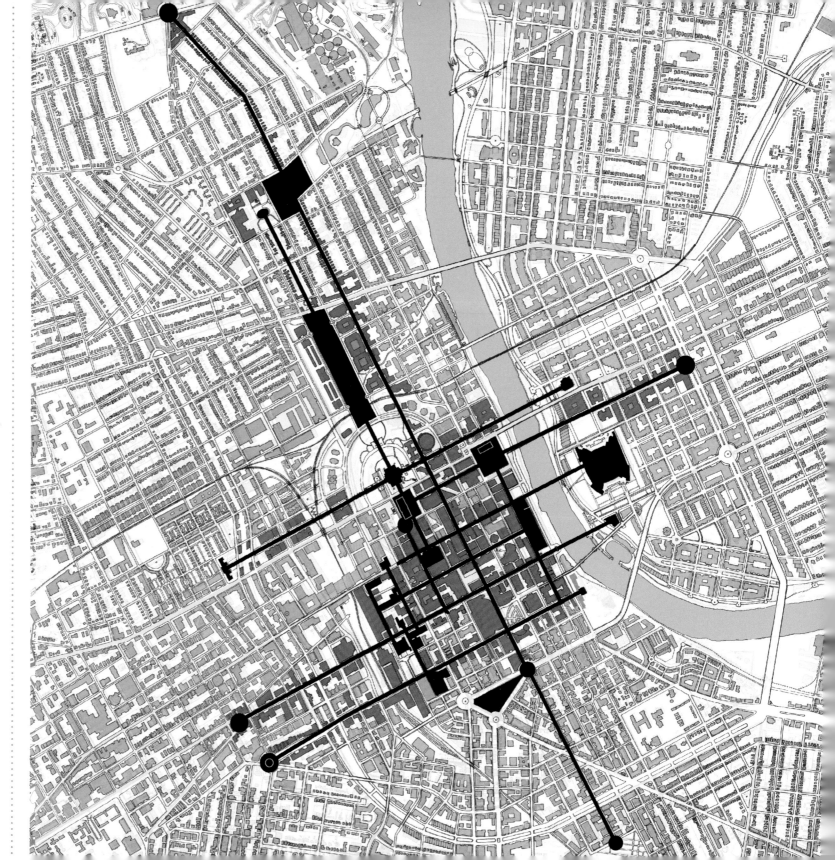

Proposed extensions of axial system strengthening the relationships of buildings and spaces.
(Diagram over map, 2004: NCDC, Raven Hardison)

The Axis in Urban Design

Of the many definitions of the word "axis" given in the *Oxford English Dictionary,* the most literal is "a main line of direction, motion, growth, or extension." In spatial compositions—such as sculpture or architecture—the line is implicit, serving as the organizing principle to which elements in the composition are referred. In the composition of the city, axial design emphasizes long, formal vistas with strongly defined edges; the vista is frequently terminated by a prominent building or monument. The axis itself is invisible, but the perception it creates—of a well-organized city—is definite.

As a tool of city building, the axis is a primary element in the European Baroque tradition, a tradition which urban historian Spiro Kostof describes in *The City Shaped* as the "Grand Manner."[2] The most enduring themes of this tradition were first articulated in the master plan of Pope Sixtus V for sixteenth century Rome: the notion of the vista, the use of the obelisk as a striking spatial marker, and the overarching principle of geometric order for its own sake. France appropriated the Baroque aesthetic, most notably in the replanning of Paris by Baron Eugène Georges Haussmann between 1853 and 1868.

Underlying the Baroque language of urbanism at the time of its inception, according to Kostof, were new ways of considering the relation between streets and buildings. The street is no longer thought of merely as "the space left over between buildings, but as a spatial element with its own integrity." The buildings defining the street channel are viewed as continuous planes rather than independent entities. And straight streets are used to connect churches and other public buildings—creating "constellations of monumentality."

"The European Baroque," Kostof says, "is a phenomenon of capital cities." So it is no coincidence that the District of Columbia is America's most successful experiment in Baroque-inspired planning.

The plan for the nation's capital was drawn by Major Pierre Charles L'Enfant, a French architect and military engineer who had served as an aide to George Washington during the Revolution. L'Enfant combined his knowledge of French planning—his father worked on the famous gardens of Vaux-le-Vicomte—with the ideals of the emerging nation. A brand new capital of a brand new nation undoubt-edly seemed ripe for the Baroque aesthetic because that aesthetic could, as Kostof says, "stage easily perceived, strong urban images that were at once modern—wide, straight streets, open prospects, and the generous distribution of green—and resonant with historical authority." Baroque planning "had become synonymous with the city as a work of art."

As he surveyed the site in 1791, L'Enfant fixed on the two highest ridges for two centers of government: the house of the executive and the house of Congress. From this symbolic division L'Enfant radiated a dynamic web of diagonal avenues overlaid by a rational grid of streets. Within this framework, L'Enfant envisioned a series of classically-styled buildings to convey the same message as the plan: a government aggressively radiating into the future, yet grounded with stable roots in the past.

L'Enfant's plan was revived and enlarged by the McMillan Commission—named after Senator James McMillan, who formed it—in 1902. The resulting plan was overseen by a group of prominent architects and landscape architects who were movers and shakers in the American City Beautiful movement, including Daniel Burnham, subsequently co-author of the *Plan of Chicago*. The plan is largely responsible for the Washington, D.C. we know today.

KEY ELEMENTS

The key elements of the plan for the nation's capital included the following:

- Physical dominance of the buildings housing the legislative and executive branches of government.

- Siting of monuments on major axes to memorialize leaders and events that helped to form the nation.

- Provision of grand public spaces—most particularly the Mall, which occupies the city's grandest axis—in which citizens can congregate for protest and celebration.

- Definition of the edges of the axes through the placement of prominent buildings. The Mall, for example, is flanked by the National Gallery, the Museum of Natural History, the Museum of American History, and the National Air and Space Museum.

Aerial view of Washington, D.C. Axial connectors give the capital a strong visual identity.

(Photograph, 1999: Project for Public Spaces, Inc.)

Diagrammatic rendering of Washington, D.C. Note the axes radiating from the U.S. Capitol Building.

(Drawing over photograph, 2004: NCDC, Gary Gaston)

In commissioning L'Enfant's original plan, George Washington and Thomas Jefferson understood the importance of symbolism and recognized the need to create an instant history to legitimize the New World to the Old. The evolution of this plan, extending its strongly formalistic nature, reaffirms the capital as the physical manifestation of the nation.

In strengthening Nashville's identity as the physical manifestation of the State of Tennessee, the Plan of Nashville is strongly influenced by the example of Washington, D.C. In Washington, however—as in Rome and Paris—the axes are in geometric contrast to the street grid. The Plan of Nashville employs axes within the existing geometry of the streets.

Gary Gaston
Associate Design Director
Nashville Civic Design Center

THE CAPITAL CITY

IN THE PRE-SKYSCRAPER age, the Tennessee State Capitol was the highly visible symbol of Nashville as the home of state government. Today, however, the primacy of the Capitol is no longer self-evident. During the Plan of Nashville's series of community visioning workshops, citizens lamented that Nashville no longer "feels" like a capital—because it doesn't look like one.

To invigorate Nashville's visual identity as Tennessee's capital, planners logically turned to the urban design tradition whose main invention is the capital city: the Baroque, as filtered through the American City Beautiful movement. The Plan of Nashville strengthens the relationship of city to Capitol much as the Mc-Millan Plan revived L'Enfant's plan for the federal capital—by redefining the axes emanat-

ing from the Capitol and extending them deeper into the urban fabric.

The Plan orients the city around the Capitol by formalizing its four axes—north, south, east, and west—using structures to enframe and punctuate them. These axes are like fingers reaching into the surrounding neighborhoods and districts, physically engaging specific parts of the city. Each axis terminates with a public building or monument, which relays the focus back to the Capitol so that the entire region seems to converge upon it. The Capitol building thus becomes the city's unifying element, a frame of reference for citizens and visitors alike.

North Capitol Axis
The Bicentennial Mall defines the north axis, providing an inspiring example of the transfor-

mative power inherent in axial design. Governor Ned McWherter and the Bicentennial Commission decided on the nineteen-acre rectangle as a fitting way to celebrate the state's 1996 birthday by preserving this sightline to the Capitol. As a massive public works project undertaken, not for a strictly functional purpose but for the education and delight of the citizens, the Mall brings urban grandeur to an area formerly occupied by the sheds of light industry and wholesale agricultural produce.

The Plan of Nashville encourages the implementation of the 1997 *Bicentennial Mall Urban Master Plan,* which addresses the area lying east of the Mall. This master plan establishes a thematic building program for the Mall's area of influence devoted to educational and cultural institutions, including the State Library and

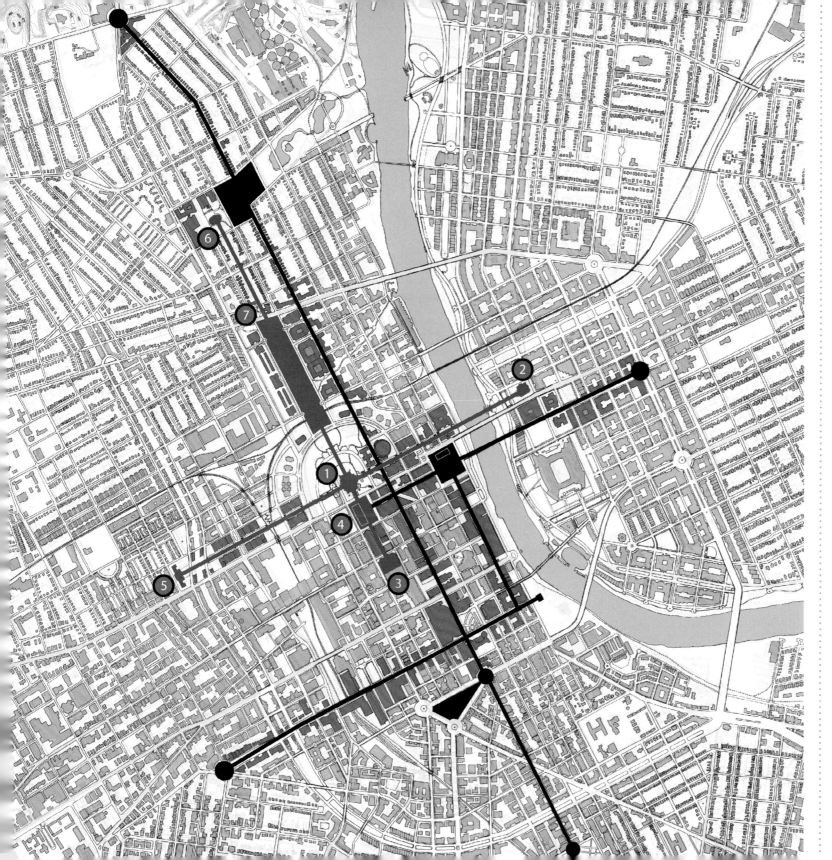

Major axes, with capitol axes highlighted in red.

(Diagram over map, 2004: NCDC, Raven Hardison)

Map Key

Proposed sites listed in bold.

1. Tennessee State Capitol
2. **East Marker**
3. Nashville Public Library
4. War Memorial and Legislative Plaza
5. **Civic Building**
6. **Marker in Werthan Bag Complex**
7. Bicentennial Mall

Archives, as well as the Tennessee State Museum to be placed directly on the Mall's eastern flank. This design closely echoes the Mall in Washington, D.C., which is also lined with educational and cultural venues.

In the Plan, the north axis is the "front porch" of the state, connecting through the Bicentennial Mall to the new Governor House and Green near the nineteenth-century Werthan Bag and Cotton Mill complex (see "Nashville and Its Neighborhoods," River District, pages 152–53). The Plan proposes a vertical marker at Werthan to denote the location of the Green and to punctuate the view from the Capitol.

South Capitol Axis

The short length of the south axis is no constraint to its significance as a bridge between city and state. The Nashville Public Library

WERTHAN

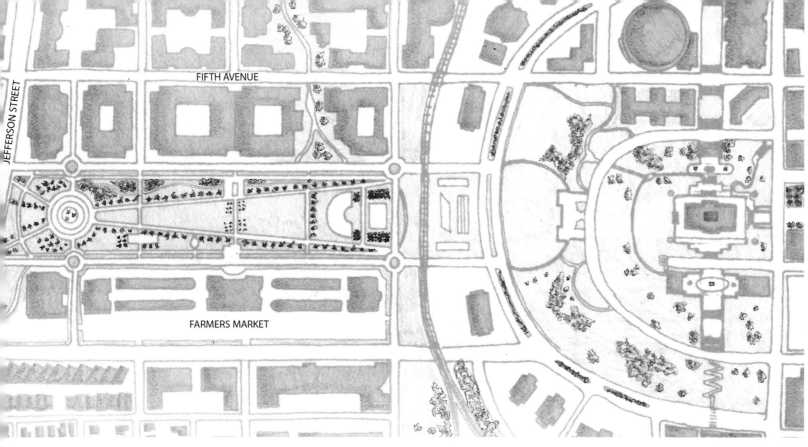

FIFTH AVENUE

JEFFERSON STREET

FARMERS MARKET

Plan of the north Capitol axis. Note its extension northward to a point within the Werthan Bag Complex.

(Drawing, 2003: NCDC [after *The Bicentennial Mall Master Plan: The Making of a District*, 1996, by Earl Swensson Associates and *Tennessee Capitol Bicentennial Mall Master Plan*, 1992, led by Tuck Hinton Architects])

Left: View from Capitol to north when this area was dominated by industrial uses.

(Photograph, ca. 1955: Metro Archives)

Center: View from Capitol to north with Bicentennial Mall; this transformation suggests the latent potential of all of the Capitol axes.

(Photograph, 2003: NCDC, Andrea Gaffney)

Right: View of Capitol to south from Bicentennial Mall; preservation of this sightline affirms the Capitol's symbolic significance to the capital city.

(Photograph, 2000: Gary Layda)

Nashville Public Library

Sectional drawing showing the relationship of the Capitol, Capitol Boulevard, and Nashville Public Library.
(Drawing, 2001: NCDC, Blythe Bailey)

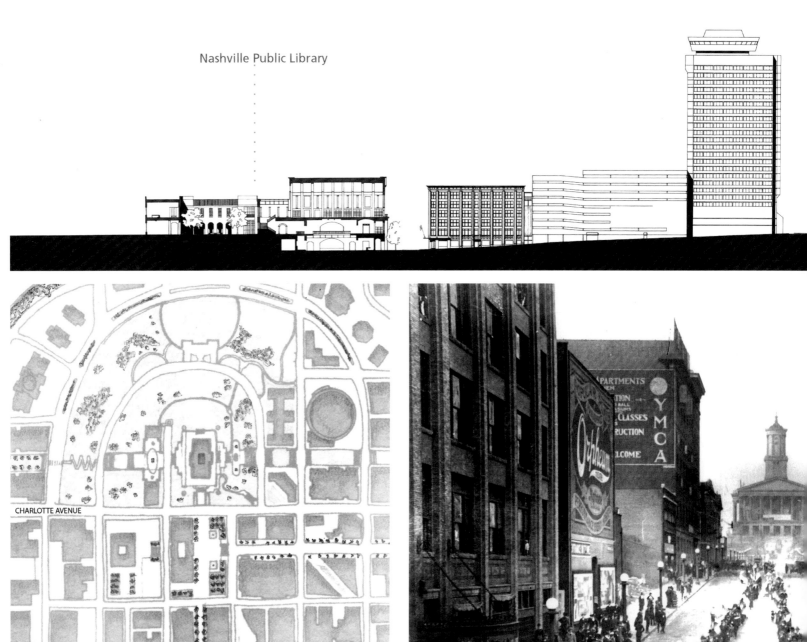

Plan of the south axis.
(Drawing, 2004: NCDC)

CHARLOTTE AVENUE

NASHVILLE PUBLIC LIBRARY

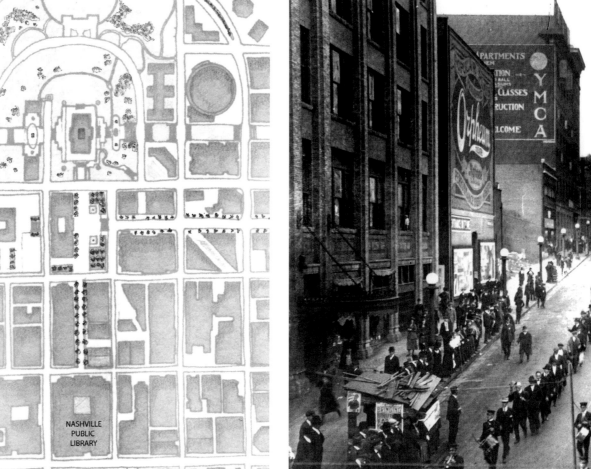

War Memorial Building and
Legislative Plaza

State Capitol

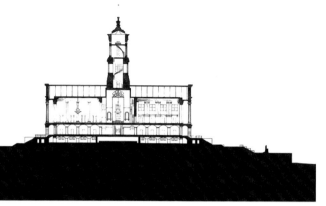

Capitol Boulevard looking
north.

Center: Victory parade after
World War I.

(Photograph, ca. 1915: Gilman Brothers)

Right top: Current conditions,
with curvilinear configuration
that blurs the axiality of
the boulevard and parking
garage facade that forms an
inhospitable street wall.

(Photograph, 2004: NCDC)

Right bottom: Proposed return
to rectilinear configuration for
right-of-way.

(Drawing, 2003: NCDC, Jason Hill and
Amanda Posch)

looks up the slope of Capitol Boulevard to the Capitol as if acknowledging the superior powers of state government. The library's quiet classicism echoes Strickland's more ornate classicism of 150 years earlier.

Capitol Boulevard is in the process of reconfiguration as a simple, elegant, tree-lined street. Once this occurs, the flanking buildings should be programmed with uses to enliven the streetscape.

East Capitol Axis

William Strickland intended the east facade—facing the Cumberland River and thus visitors to the city arriving by boat—to serve as the Capitol's ceremonial entrance. The main entrance to the grounds by carriage was from Park Place, a one-block residential street bordering the east side of the property. And a large terrace was constructed in 1880 on the eastern slope of the hill for the placement of Clark Mills's bronze equestrian statue of Andrew Jackson, further emphasizing the primacy of this face of the Capitol.[3]

Today the impact of the eastern facade is blunted by structures that unfortunately block the view corridor to it. Even more unfortunately, Metro's new Beverly Briley building, to house the city's criminal courts, is currently under construction directly within the east axis. In ensuing decades, when these buildings have served their useful lives, they should be removed to open up this historically weighted sightline from the Capitol.

The Plan of Nashville presents the east axis as a series of stepped plazas—linked by a continuous water feature—cascading all the way to the Cumberland and terminating in a vertical marker on the river's east bank. Distinct from the cultural and education theme of buildings on the north axis, the walls of the east axis are formed by new government buildings to meet future needs of Metro and state. Following the precedent of the Jackson sculpture, this civic theme finds further expression in the placement within the axis of memorials to leaders in the history of the city's public life.

Plan of east axis. Note the intersection of James Robertson Parkway has been changed from curvilinear to orthogonal, better integrating with the city grid.

(Drawing, 2004: NCDC, Gary Gaston)

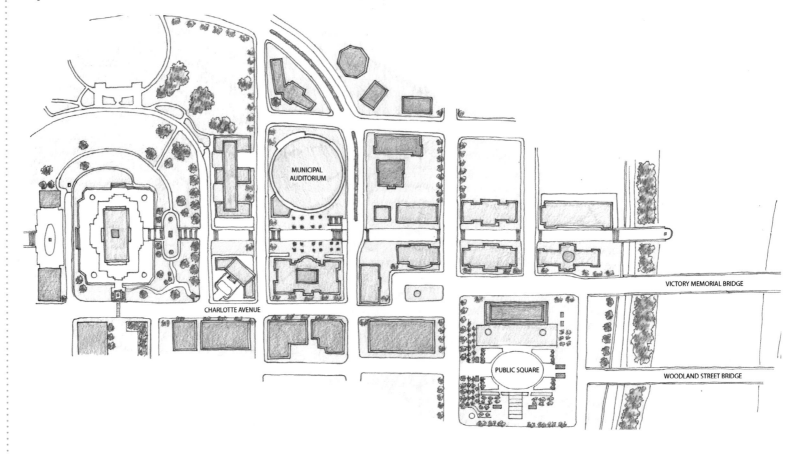

MUNICIPAL AUDITORIUM

CHARLOTTE AVENUE

PUBLIC SQUARE

VICTORY MEMORIAL BRIDGE

WOODLAND STREET BRIDGE

Left: East axis as proposed in *Central Loop Plan*, with a series of discrete plazas asymmetrically linked by terraced steps. This treatment of the axis, unlike the Plan of Nashville, does not extend to the Cumberland River.

(Drawing, 1963: MDHA, Clarke and Rapuano, Inc., for Nashville Housing Authority)

Right: View to Capitol from east, with axis occupied by garage and surface parking.

(Photograph, 2004: NCDC, Raven Hardison)

Left: Current view from Capitol to east, with sightline blocked by Criminal Justice Center.

(Photograph, 2003: NCDC, Amanda Posch and Matt Gregg)

Right: Proposed east axis extending from the Capitol steps to the river.

(Drawing, 2003: Ryan Moss)

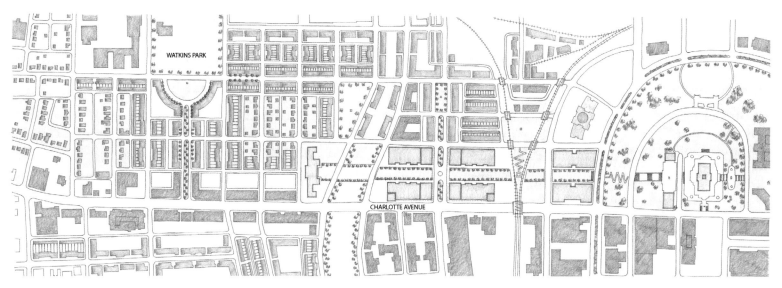

Plan of west axis. Reconfigures James Robertson Parkway to a more pedestrian-friendly design by raising it from its high-speed trench to connect with the city street system. Note how the axis forms a lawn, framed by mixed-use structures and terminated by a civic structure.

(Drawing, 2003: NCDC)

Left: View of Capitol along west axis before urban renewal.

(Photograph, ca. 1952: Metro Archives)

Right: Current view of Capitol along west axis. Note how the view is marred by warehouse storage and the blank rear wall of the Tennessee State Library and Archives.

(Photograph, 2003: NCDC, Andrea Gaffney)

West Capitol Axis

In the nineteenth century, the west axis was residential, with many elegant town houses lying near the Capitol. But as their owners abandoned these dwellings—and downtown living entirely— the neighborhood deteriorated. By the 1940s, the area immediately adjacent to the Capitol property contained dilapidated rooming houses, shacks, and outdoor privies. All this housing—and several historic African American churches—was demolished for the Capitol Hill redevelopment in the 1950s, the first urban renewal project funded by the U.S. Congress.

The major element in the redevelopment was a large, radial road, subsequently named James Robertson Parkway, which replaced the rectangular street grid. For most of its path, which loops around the base of Capitol Hill, the parkway lies at grade level. But to the west the parkway devolves into a series of elevated ramps and submerged roadways that form a barricade to the

land beyond. And, the construction of the State Library and Archives building in 1952 blocked the sightline to all but the Capitol's tower from the west.

In the Plan of Nashville the west axis is restored as an urban avenue with a tree-lined grass median, flanked by streets with parallel parking. The edges of the axis are defined by midrise, mixed-use buildings with a heavy emphasis on residential use. The terminus is a new civic structure, preferably to serve state government.

The central greenspace will serve as an amenity for people living and working in the surrounding buildings as well as infuse much-needed civic dignity into an area now dominated by metal sheds, surface parking, and chain-link fencing.

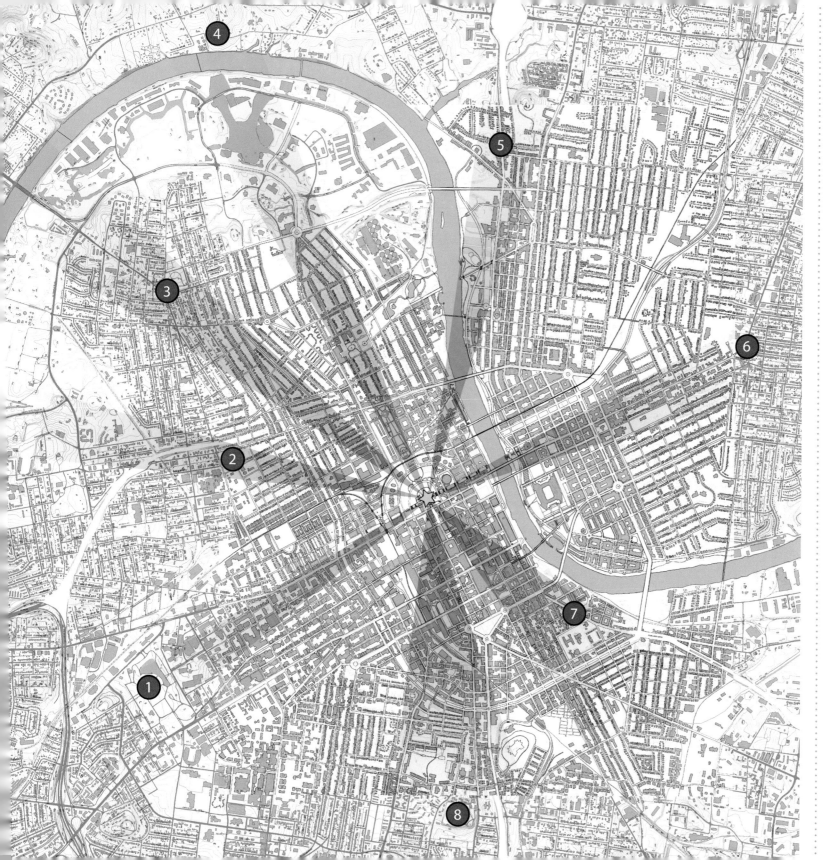

The Capitol vistas.
(Diagram over map, 2004: NCDC, Raven Hardison and Kem Hinton)

Map Key

1. Centennial Park, The Parthenon

2. Fisk University Campus

3. Bordeaux, Temple Jewish Cemetery

4. Across river from Metro Center

5. Schwab Hill

6. East Nashville, Carnegie Library

7. Rutledge Hill and Rolling Mill Hill

8. Eighth Avenue Reservoir and Rose Hill

Capitol Vistas

These view corridors are less formally defined than the axes, establishing a picturesque relationship between the city and the State Capitol. The vistas from the Capitol extend to topographical high points or visually prominent buildings.

In the Plan of Nashville, eight vistas are maintained, with future development respecting these sightlines.

Cardo and Decumanus

One way to create focus within a grid plan is to have two axes, north-south and east-west, intersect at the center, with a public square to mark the crossing. The Romans used this device in their new town planning, with the forum and other public buildings at or near the crossing. The *cardo* is the north-south street and *decumanus* the east-west street.

In the Plan of Nashville, Fifth Avenue is the *cardo* and Demonbreun Street the *decumanus*, which together form the axes of the cultural arts. As in the Roman model, significant public buildings and open space lie in the vicinity of the crossing: the Country Music Hall of Fame and Museum, the Gaylord Entertainment Center, the Schermerhorn Symphony Center, and Hall of Fame Park. (See map page 112.)

Demonbreun currently terminates at the former location of the thermal plant. Proposals for the thermal site include a baseball stadium as well as a hotel and mixed-use development. Whatever the nature of new development, it should include public access to the riverbank in the form of an extension of Riverfront Park, as well as the creation of strong sightlines to the river from Demonbreun and other east-west streets. The Plan provides a visual termination for the street with a vertical marker on the west bank.

The Importance of Civic Space

Over the history of our city, the most important public projects have been attempts to give Nashvillians engaging, stimulating, and safe places to come together.

From greenway to stadium, from community center to concert hall, from sidewalks to schools to the Sportsplex, the city's leaders have grasped the wisdom of providing Nashvillians with inviting and welcoming spaces to meet for education, enlightenment, conversation, entertainment, and the simple enjoyment of unstructured leisure time.

As a native Nashvillian, I have observed that we learn about our community first and best through the "civic spaces" we experience in the city. I grew up spending summer days on the baseball diamonds of Shelby Park, feeding the ducks in Watauga Lake on Sunday afternoons with my mom and dad, shopping at the Farmers Market with my grandfather, and watching local democracy unfold at the county courthouse.

Each venue served its own programmatic objectives, but what happened in them all was the building of community. We all work out our own sense of the community in these mundane but essential ways. People come together to meet and know their neighbors.

We see this phenomenon at work in other cities. The pocket parks of Washington, D.C., and Chicago's Civic Center—with its broad Richard J. Daley Plaza and Picasso sculpture—enrich human interaction in busy urban places.

In our town, in 1993, in a process similar to the Plan of Nashville exercise, several thousand citizens participated in the citywide goal-setting called Nashville's Agenda. They identified twenty-one goals for the future to make our city "the best it can be." An ambitious goal for the arts was for Nashville to be "a cultural center with excellent facilities for the visual and performing arts and diverse opportunities accessible to all Nashvillians and visitors alike."

Eleven years later, much progress has been made—with the advent of the Frist Center, Country Music Hall of Fame and Museum, and the emerging Schermerhorn Symphony Center—and all share the notion of providing civic space.

The symphony hall project leaders considered twenty-two different sites and selected the old Haymarket Square in the central city for its accessibility and potential for synergy with other activities in the neighborhood. A hundred years earlier, the Haymarket itself was a civic space where Nashvillians sold hay, bought horses, heard speeches, and no doubt shared the news of the day.

While the new concert hall will provide world-class acoustics for the enjoyment of music, it was also designed to enhance the day-to-day human activity in the area. The entrances oriented to the west will contribute to more daytime activity in the park across Fourth Avenue. Programmatically, the new center will be convenient for children in art and music classes at the Frist Center and Hall of Fame buildings.

These spectacular new venues will introduce more humanity to the central city, and that is a good thing. In my lifetime, the awakening area south of Broadway has been transformed from "a place nobody goes" to a network of vibrant civic spaces—all drawing more Nashvillians to a greater sense of community.

Keel Hunt
Former city editor of the Tennessean,
staff director of the Nashville Area Chamber of Commerce 1987–90, and president of The Strategy Group

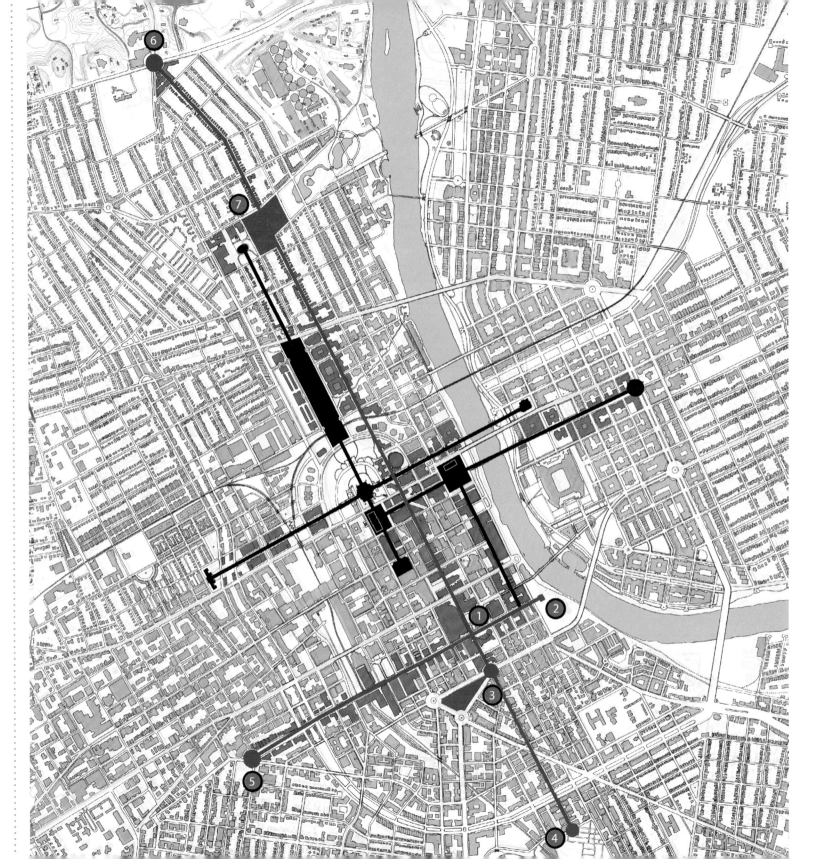

Diagram of major axes with Cardo and Decumanus of the Arts highlighted in red. The Plan's focus on a formal relationship between Fifth Avenue and Demonbreun Street capitalizes on the cultural facilities on or near these streets. Currently at the crossing of Fifth and Demonbreun are the Gaylord Entertainment Center, Country Music Hall of Fame and Park, and the new Schermerhorn Symphony Center.

(Diagram over map, 2004: NCDC, Raven Hardison)

Map Key

Proposed sites listed in bold.

1. Crossing of the two axes. Crossing occurs at the Country Music Hall of Fame Park, Schermerhorn Symphony Center, the Country Music Hall of Fame, and Gaylord Entertainment Center.

2. **River Lawn**

3. **Gateway Park**

4. Nashville City Cemetery

5. *Musica* by Alan LeQuire

6. **Marker**

7. **Governor House and Green**

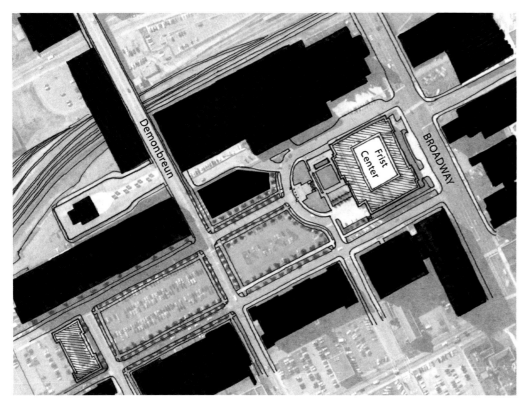

The Plan replaces the surface parking lots of the Frist Center for the Visual Arts and Cummins Station with Frist Gardens. This parking is relocated below grade or to a garage shared by both facilities. The gardens will supply the western edge of SoBro with civic space that the district notably lacks, except for the Hall of Fame Park between Fourth and Fifth Avenues.

There is some historic precedent for gardens—of a sort—in this area. In 1827 Vauxhall Garden opened to the public immediately south of Demonbreun Street at Ninth Avenue. This early amusement park was several acres and featured a large hall for assemblies and dining modeled after its London predecessor of the same name, surrounded by what were described in contemporary advertisements as "green groves and a wilderness of lamps." A miniature railroad inside the hall moved visitors around in cars propelled by hand cranks. The park operated for more than a decade.

Plan for Frist Gardens.
(Drawing, 2003: NCDC, Gary Gaston)

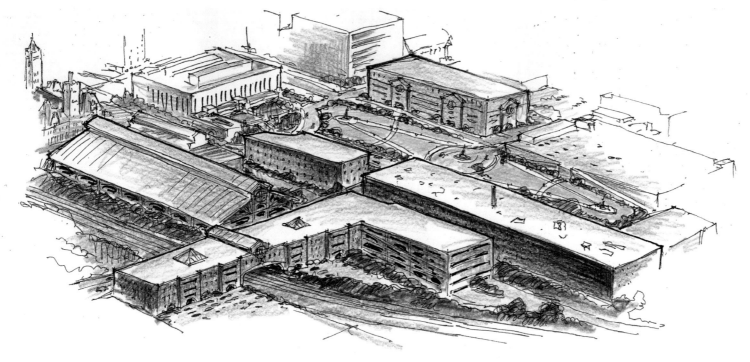

Perspective view from southwest. The Plan envisions this area as a transportation hub. Note that the shed of Union Station has been rebuilt as civic space.
(Drawing, 2004: Frank Orr)

Map Key

Proposed sites listed in bold.

1. Public Square and Metro
   Courthouse

2. War Memorial and Legislative Plaza

3. Rutledge Hill terminates
   axis visually

4. **Marker**

"People . . .
spend more per
square foot on
their kitchens
than they would
ever put into
an open public
space. The
problem is that
our notion of
quality of life
ends at our front
door."

Martha Schwartz,
New York Times Magazine
(May 16, 2004)

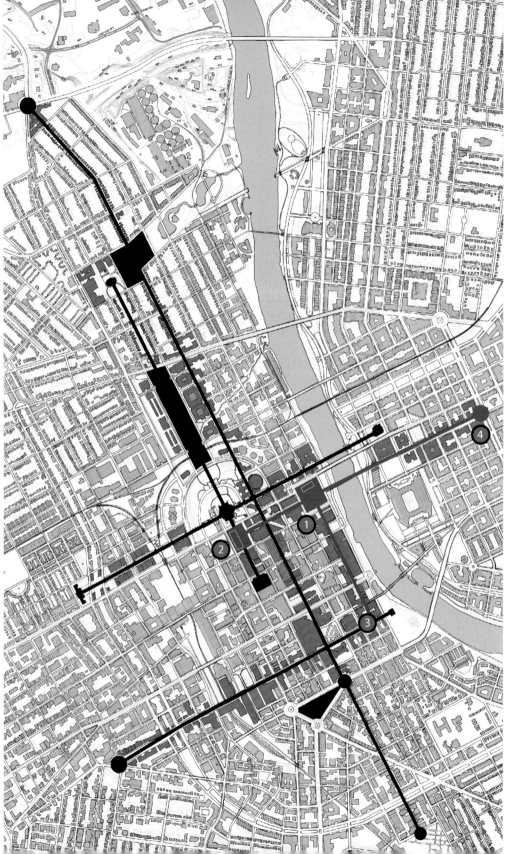

The City-State Axis

As the avenue between the major monuments of Metro and state government, it would be hard to equal Deaderick Street for symbolic value. The east end terminates in the public square-in-the-making in front of the Metro Courthouse, the west in Legislative Plaza and the War Memorial, which lie before the State Capitol.

The importance of the relationship between the architecture of city and state was recognized by Emmons Woolwine and Frederick C. Hirons, the designers of what was originally called the Davidson County Public Building and Courthouse. According to a *Tennessean* article by Rufus Jarman in May of 1935, when the result of the design competition for the Courthouse was announced, the winning design placed the building on the site "so that its entrance will fall in line with the general effect produced by the Capitol and War Memorial. The base of the columns is approximately on a level with the entrance to the Capitol grounds" from what was then called Cedar Street (now Charlotte Avenue). The visual relationship between Courthouse and Capitol that the architects sought was later obscured by the construction of large office buildings on the northern side of Deaderick Street.

The urban renewal plan for downtown Nashville by the New York firm of Clarke and Rapuano emphasized the significance of Deaderick Street as a boulevard lined with broad sidewalks shaded by double rows of trees. (See next page, center.) Note, however, that the buildings flanking the street in this plan stand as individual entities surrounded by open space, thus violating the Baroque tradition of continuous planes of architecture that give strong walls to the street.

With the *Central Loop Plan* in hand, city officials used federal funds to demolish existing structures along Deaderick in the 1960s. The

Left: Deaderick Street, pre-urban renewal, looking towards War Memorial, and Deaderick Street today.

(Top photograph, ca. 1960: Metro Archives; bottom photograph, 2003: NCDC)

Center: Public Square and Deaderick Street as proposed in the *Central Loop Plan*, with formal promenades lining the street.

(Aerial rendering, 1963: MDHA, Clarke and Rapuano for Nashville Housing Authority; perspective sketch, 1963: MDHA, McBurney, Clarke and Rapuano for Nashville Housing Authority)

Right: Deaderick Street ca. 1980 and 2004. Although the allées of trees envisioned in the urban renewal plan were realized, today the pedestrian path is cluttered with street signs and the Metro Transit Authority's Bus Transfer Station.

(Top photograph, ca. 1980: MDHA, Clarke and Rapuano, Inc.; bottom photograph, 2004: NCDC, Raven Hardison)

vacant sites were then sold to the state and private developers for new construction, most of which occurred in the 1970s. While the plan was not followed literally for the redevelopment of the city-state axis, its influence on the form of Legislative Plaza and the way the buildings fail to relate to Deaderick Street is clear.

The physical character of Deaderick Street established by this so-called urban renewal does not encourage the use of this significant public space. The facades of buildings at street level lack transparency; many feature high, blank

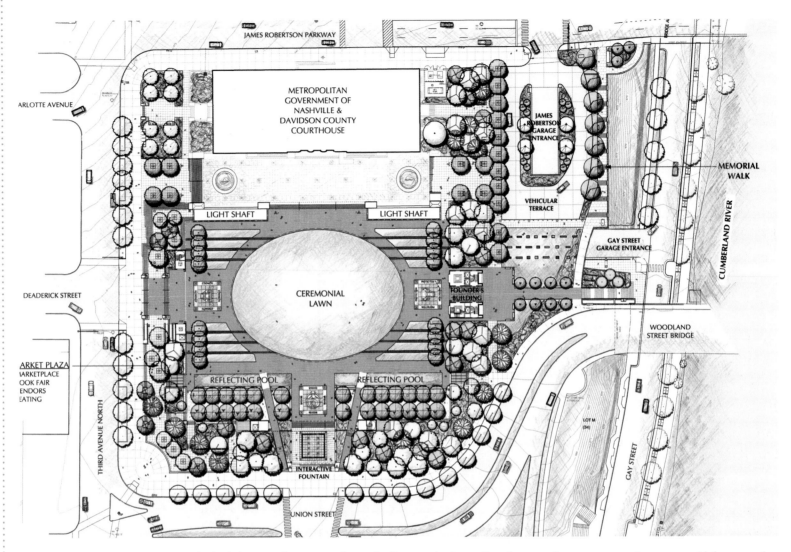

Plan for new Public Square, scheduled for completion in 2006.

(Drawing, 2004: Hawkins Partners, Elizabeth Graham and Chris Whitis)

podiums on which the towers rest. And while the sidewalks are generous, many sections are obstructed by signage and inappropriately placed street furniture and bus shelters serving the city's transit mall. The Plan recommends that this clutter be removed or repositioned to open up the sidewalks for promenading, and that activity be added to the ground floors of the buildings to socialize the street.

The Metro Transit Authority is currently looking for a site for a new bus transfer station. The authority intends to construct an indoor facility in order to protect waiting riders from in-

clement weather and offer some basic retail and services—sandwich and coffee shop, a day care center, etc.—to make mass transit a more appealing option. This relocation, which is scheduled for 2007, creates a prime opportunity for the rehab of the Deaderick Street right-of-way.

The terminus of Legislative Plaza is also unsuccessful as social space, except for the occasions when the plaza hosts the Southern Festival of Books. What the festival brings to the plaza is what it lacks the rest of the year: a reason to be there. The placement on the plaza of opportunities for daily social life—food and drink

vendors, a newsstand, etc.—would draw people working in the surrounding buildings, as well as patrons of the performing arts center, to the plaza.

At the eastern end of Deaderick Street, the remaking of the public square is the most important urban design project this community will undertake for a long time. In the process, Nashville can reclaim its civic heart, lost when the historic square—which dates to the original platting of the city—and the nineteenth-century buildings that gave human-scaled walls to the space were annihilated by urban

Bryant Park in New York City, a large lawn surrounded by trees, was one of the inspirations for the design for the new Public Square.

(Photograph, 1997: Project for Public Spaces, Inc.)

renewal for a surface parking lot and wide roads.

The design of the new square features a large lawn and water features, and relies for its sense of enclosure on groves of trees. The Founders' Building—actually two buildings connected by a bridge—punctuates the axis from War Memorial and tells the story of the square. Plaques will memorialize the original settlers led by James Robertson and John Donelson. An observation deck will contain a visual history of the square in fifty-year increments engraved in granite panels, while providing an overlook to the Cumberland River.

These gestures to infuse content into the square are admirable. The square, however, will remain isolated until the streets around square and courthouse are rationalized—right angles instead of curves, for example—to slow traffic and make pedestrian crossings easier. The four-acre square would also be improved by defining the edges with architecture whose functions—coffee shop, restaurant, etc.—would bring people to the square beyond the limits of the eight-to-five workday.

The city-state axis as it exists today illustrates the fallacy of land use monoculture—no matter how grand the scale—in creating a civic realm. The Plan of Nashville calls on both city and state government officials to consider, for future government buildings, the relation of building to street. The incorporation of general public uses at street level, and the replacement of concrete barriers with more attractive perimeter security design, would enable government to contribute to the city as social neighborhood.

Second Avenue in downtown Nashville.

(Photograph, 2003: Vanderbilt University)

"A Central Business District that lives up to its name and is truly described by it, is a dud."

Jane Jacobs,
The Death and Life of Great American Cities (1961)

DOWNTOWN AS NEIGHBORHOOD

As JANE JACOBS began pointing out in the 1960s, a city center needs an intricately woven diversity of uses that reinforce each other economically and socially if it is to succeed. This mixture of uses—office and residential, retail and service, entertainment and recreation—in a fine-grained pattern is the opposite of suburban planning, which arranges uses in self-contained pods. Cool Springs, with its segregation of dwellings from offices from retail is a good example of this phenomenon, and is why Cool Springs, which has most of the elements of a town, fails to cohere as one.

The citizens who participated in the Plan of Nashville process registered a particular concern that downtown is too devoted to work and needs more housing. To these Nashvillians, more people on the streets for more hours of the day

and night would make the city feel safer. These streets should be pedestrian-friendly, beautiful—free of utility wires and poles—and lined with buildings that enliven sidewalks rather than turn their backs to them. Downtown also needs a public transit system to circulate people efficiently. Workshop participants concluded that the revival of downtown had been focused too much on marketing to tourists and weekend visitors. If we make a downtown that is good for the natives, for the people who live there—or would like to—and work and play there, the tourists will follow.

In responding to these concerns, the Plan of Nashville concentrates on two strategies: promoting a more dense fabric of mixed-use buildings and enhancing the urban character of the streets.

Density is Destiny

In city planning, the term "density" refers to the average number of individuals or units per space unit, for example, a population density of five hundred people per square mile or a housing density of ten dwellings per acre. Synonyms for "density" are more revealing for our purposes here: "solidity" and "strength" are just what density can deliver to a city.

A strong downtown for Nashville—defined as the area bounded by the Cumberland River, the Gulch, Gateway Boulevard, and the railroad tracks immediately north of the State Capitol—is dependent on achieving higher levels of density in units and individuals. One of a city's greatest assets is bringing together people into communities of needs and interests. The more people, the larger these communities, be they

those needing mass transit or groceries or clothing or dry cleaning, or those interested in music or movies, books or newspapers, a glass of wine or a good meal. For downtown Nashville to succeed as a neighborhood, the central city must have a sufficient number of people in it to demand the necessities, and some of the luxuries, of daily life—which the market will then supply.

A larger downtown population would provide the critical mass necessary to sustain public transit, groceries and pharmacies, bars and restaurants, retail shops and services. Much of this commerce would logically locate in the ground levels of buildings, which would bring a higher level of activity and visual interest to the street.

The work force in the area bounded by Jefferson Street, the river, and the interstates to the south and west numbers almost 45,000, according to a 2003 survey by the Nashville Downtown Partnership. Of these, approximately 14,500 are in the numerically stable category of government workers. Indeed, the state, Metro, and federal governments are the top three employers in downtown, in that order. Of the surveyed employees, only 3 percent also live in downtown and 90 percent drive to work alone.

Aside from lunch, these workers typically satisfy their need for goods, services, and entertainment closer to their place of residence and demand little from the city except car storage during working hours and transportation infrastructure to get them in and out of downtown. In the Partnership survey, respondents said that the downtown elements most in need of improvement were: cost and availability of parking, the high numbers of panhandlers and transients, and the variety of retail offerings.

The possibility of adding significant numbers to the downtown work force is bleak. The market for downtown office space is stagnant; vacancy rates have hovered in the 10 percent and

This block on Fifth Avenue North in Germantown has a density of eight dwelling units to the acre.

(Photograph, 2004: Germantown Partners, Scott Chambers)

Hyde Park, Cincinnati. This neighborhood achieves densities of fifty units to the acre while defining a public realm of high quality.

(Photograph, 2004: Metro Planning Department, Keith Covington)

You Can't Get There from Here

Embedded in the current Metro zoning and tax codes are disincentives to the Plan's mid-rise strategy for increasing density and reweaving the city fabric.

The 1974 zoning code for Metro—following the lead of the New York City code—encouraged the building of tall, slender towers surrounded by open space in the downtown core. While the code was revised in 1998, the current zoning code still gives height bonuses to developers who construct plazas adjacent to their buildings, even though these plazas erode the street wall. And because Metro lacks a master plan for the location of downtown plazas, and design guidelines to make them successful, these developer-plazas—such as the "porch" behind the Commerce Center—are not integrated into the civic space and are not used as gathering points. Developing a plaza master plan, and requiring developers to build to the sidewalk for the first five to seven stories—unless a plaza corresponded to this master plan—would reinstate the street wall with new construction.

Land values also play a role in building height. The current floor-area-ratio (FAR) for the central core is 15/1, which means that for every square foot of land in the parcel, a developer can construct fifteen square feet of building—a minimum of fifteen stories if built to the property line and no bonus is invoked. A developer can, of course, build taller—for example, the Bell South tower—if a building footprint occupies only part of a site. In any case, this FAR ratio is a major determinant of the price of land. For a developer to pay for a site on which he/she can construct fifteen or more stories and then build fewer, he/she must receive some other incentive to hold the height.

The decay and demolition of older mid-rise buildings and their replacement with surface parking—a phenomenon that has blighted Church Street in particular—is fostered by the Metro tax code. Property taxes are calculated from the value of the property, reflecting both the land and structure value as determined by Metro property assessors. These appraisals are based on sales of comparable properties and/or revenue generated by the property. The assessment ratio of taxes for land and building is the same—40 percent of appraised value for commercial properties, 25 percent for residential.

The rehabilitation of older structures results in higher appraised values and thus higher taxes. (Metro does have a program that defers taxes on the post-improved value of the property for seven years, if the upper floors are rehabbed for residential use.) If property decays through lack of maintenance, however, the value goes down and the owner is "rewarded" with reduced taxes. Land without a structure is assessed at the value of the land plus improvements; in the case of surface parking these improvements are the paving and lighting.

A property owner with a building whose floors are not fully occupied—in many cases because these floors need remodeling and rehabilitation—can reduce the tax burden by tearing the building down and paving the land for surface parking. Developers consider surface parking an interim—and very low maintenance—use, in which the land produces an income to pay the (lower) taxes while the owner withholds the land from higher utilization—new construction—creating an artificial scarcity of land, which drives up the value.

One strategy to combat demolition for surface parking and the consequent underutilization of land in the heart of the city is to tax land more heavily than buildings, according to land tax advocate Pam Neary. "Pittsburgh has used a two-tiered system since 1913, when the land portion of property value was taxed at twice the rate of buildings," Neary reports. In 1979 the city increased its tax on land to almost five times the rate on structures in order to induce reinvestment in the city. During the 1980s, "the value of Pittsburgh's building permits rose by over 70 percent relative to the two decades that preceded the tax reform."[4]

Parts of Canada and Australia also employ variations of the land tax approach, assessing land value based on the property's highest and best use—i.e., the highest potential use, not the current use. Such a taxation system encourages reinvestment in property and higher densities because underutilized land is taxed as if it were more fully utilized. A property owner, therefore, is encouraged to develop vacant parcels to get the maximum yield in rent, because the owner is paying taxes as if receiving this revenue stream.

Metro's current zoning and tax codes have produced some unintended consequences: the demolition of older urban fabric and the warehousing of land in the form of surface parking.

City officials should reconsider these policies to support an increase in downtown density.

Christine Kreyling

higher range for some years now. If we are to grow the density of the downtown population—and animate the daily life of its public spaces—we must look elsewhere.

In the Plan of Nashville, the key strategy for achieving greater density is more residential development. As Memphis developer Henry Turley stated during the "Housing Summit" at the Nashville Civic Design Center (January 29, 2002): "Downtown Nashville needs only three things to turn itself around: housing, housing, and more housing. Everything else will follow." One thing that would undoubtedly follow when the downtown population reaches a certain size is an increase in consumer goods and services available in downtown, which would make the central city more attractive to workers, their employers, and potential residents as well.

The average density of housing in the rectangle formed by Charlotte and First Avenues, Gateway Boulevard, and Ninth Avenue is very low: 2.8 units to the acre (687 units in 244 acres) according to August 2003 statistics supplied by the Nashville Downtown Living Initiative. Even a typical first-ring suburb with a diverse mix of single and multifamily dwellings—such as East Nashville's Edgefield or Lockeland Springs—averages about eight units per acre. Cities such as San Diego, Cincinnati, and Indianapolis are building housing to achieve fifty units or more to the acre in their downtowns. If downtown Nashville were to reach a similar level of housing density, the number of residential units would be 12,200.

In the Plan of Nashville, density of building fabric is increased by an infill of mixed-use mid-rise buildings constructed to the edge of property lines. The idea is to limit verticality, like Washington, D.C., or Paris, to get greater horizontal density—the same number of apartments will occupy a larger foot-print in a lower

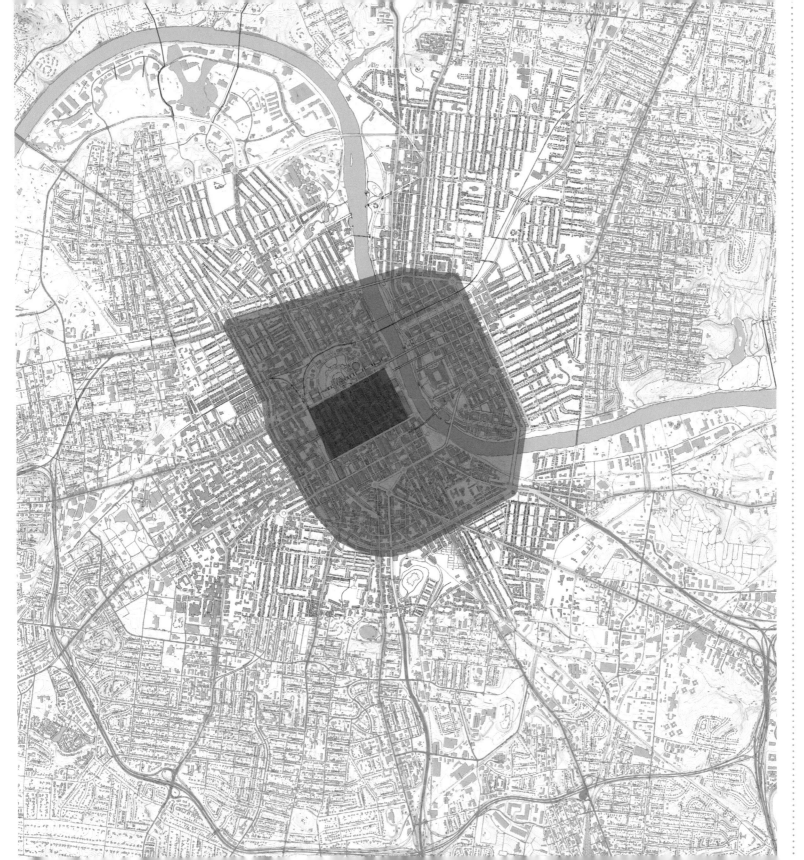

Building heights diagram showing the relationship among the central core, the enframing area, and the historic pikes and main streets.

(Diagram over map, 2004: NCDC, Raven Hardison)

Map Key

- No Limit
- 8–12 levels
- 3–5 levels

121

"No wonder
the streets
had seemed
so empty. The
city had gone
somewhere else
and cunningly
hidden itself
inside its own
facade."

Jonathan Raban,
Old Glory
(1981)

building, for example, and foster the formation of continuous planes or walls along the street.

Streets and a Network of Public Spaces

As social space, a city is a connected series of outdoor rooms. The buildings are the walls; the sidewalks and streets are the living space of public life. Enhancing the charater of these "rooms" enhances the quality of the life within them.

The paramount issue in the cultivation of urban character is spatial enclosure. The Plan of Nashville calls for buildings to be placed at the sidewalk, not set back. The uses of the build-

ings at street level, and the transparency of the facade, should encourage public interaction between inside and outside to reinforce the sociability of the space. The sidewalk should be wide enough to accommodate sitting and strolling as well as brisker paces. In other words, the success of the urban street has less to do with the materials and street furniture in the right-of-way, and more to do with the buildings that compose the edge.

The Plan also recognizes two other forms of spatial enclosure to add variety to the grid. Streets with terminated vistas supply visual

punctuation and hierarchy to public space. Looking north up Second Avenue to the Metro courthouse, for example, we see commerce crowned by government. On the non-monumental scale we have the Nashville Arcade: a room within the rooms.

Just as grand axial relationships help define the Capital City, so the secondary or not-so-grand axes help define the downtown neighborhood. These streets form a tight, interlaced web that ties the downtown together, adding much to its sense of place and feeling of cohesion.

Existing secondary axes.

(Drawing over map, 2004: NCDC, Raven Hardison)

These secondary axes supply a sense of drama to the urban landscape.

(Photographs, 2004: NCDC, Brian Christens and Nekya Young)

Left: Church Street looking east to the Coliseum.

Center: Seventh Avenue looking south to First Baptist Church.

Right: Tenth Avenue looking south to Frist Center for the Visual Arts.

Right (small): Commerce Street, looking west. Commerce Street is a wide roadway, much of it lined with the sides of parking garages, huge curb cuts, and blank building facades that span up to a block without a single transparent (non-reflective) window. This is not the form of a successful social space. The Plan recommends that Commerce Street should be redeveloped with a significant street-level presence to the buildings. Lying in the heart of the central business district, the street is an ideal location for banks, offices, and daytime shops that cater to the area's office workers.

(Photograph, 2004: NCDC, Gary Gaston)

Bottom: The plan for Church Street. Church Street's central location and narrow right-of-way make the street the logical candidate for the main street of the downtown neighborhood. Everything that one needs for living downtown—actual living quarters as well as locally-focused retail—should be found along its length or on the intersecting cross-streets. There are approximately seven hundred residential units existing and planned for Church Street. If the vacant upper levels of existing buildings and the surface parking lots were redeveloped for residential, this number could double.

(Drawing, 2004: Barge Waggoner Sumner and Cannon, Inc.)

Left: Towers on Broadway.
Broadway is the historic terminus of the spoke roads or pikes that tied Nashville to the Middle Tennessee region. Broadway is also the "High Street" bisecting downtown. In response to this dual identity, the Plan recommends that Broadway present attractions for locals as well as visitors, with music venues encouraged to support the Music City USA theme and Broadway's traditional personality. The upper levels of the buildings along lower Broad should have residential or live/work uses. The importance of Broadway is signified by the fact that the street serves as the address of many of the city's most prominent buildings: Union Station, the Post Office (now Frist Center for the Visual Arts), Christ Church Cathedral, the Customs House, First Baptist Church, the Gaylord Entertainment Center, and the Nashville Convention Center. Many of these buildings are vertically punctuated by towers, which defines a unique architectural character for the street. To preserve and enhance this character, these towers and the sightlines to them should be maintained, and future development should consider the "tower" theme when the scale and massing of new construction supports it. The east end of Broadway terminates at Riverfront Park. While care should be taken to preserve the vista to the Cumberland River, the Plan recommends placing a vertical marker at the terminus at a scale commensurate with Broadway's right-of-way and place within the hierarchy of streets.

(Photograph, 2004: NCDC, Mark Schimmenti)

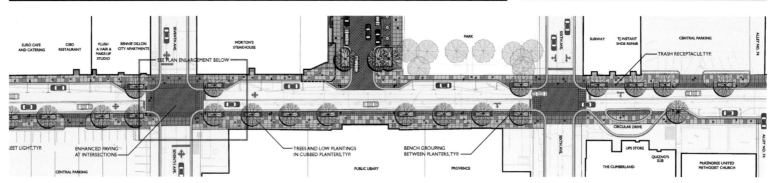

The Secondary Axes

The Plan presents improvements to the existing streets of downtown organized by their orientation: "East-West" and "North-South."

East-West Streets

Generally wider than the streets that run north-south, the east-west streets should be enhanced as Nashville's major downtown avenues.

North-South Streets

Downtown Nashville's north-south streets are generally of smaller width—and often feature shorter building heights—than the east-west streets. While the north-south streets are the address for much of the city's historic party wall architecture, they are rarely the address for significant structures and offer few connections between downtown and the neighborhoods to the north.

In the blocks where the historic architecture prevails—such as Fifth Avenue between Church and Union Streets—the street walls are characterized by two-to-three-story masonry buildings with a high degree of transparency at the ground floor. The future of these streets lies in the preservation of existing buildings and the creative emulation of the historic, fine-grained character.

The Car in the City

Given that one definition of "street" is that part of a thoroughfare reserved for vehicles, it may seem myopic for the Plan of Nashville to put so much emphasis on the pedestrian portion of the thoroughfare—the sidewalk and crosswalks—and so little on the car as user of public space.

This emphasis, however, is a necessary form of vision correction. As early as the 1920s and '30s, international "seers" like the architect Le Corbusier concluded that cities would have to be totally redesigned for the automobile. A 1928

Left top: Union Street, looking east. Union Street was called the "Wall Street of the South" before the Depression and is still commercially active. Numerous banks, offices, hotels, and several residential buildings are located here, and there are only two small surface parking lots. The edges, therefore, are well defined by structures. The major urban design flaw of the street is the Tennessee Performing Arts Center's rear facade. The massive blank wall and furtive doorways should be redesigned as a complement to the more user-friendly entrance to TPAC at Sixth Avenue and Deaderick Street.

(Photograph, 2004: NCDC, Raven Hardison)

Right top: Contrast this street of similar size in Chattanooga with Union Street. Trees form a pleasant canopy and the sidewalks are activated by lively and transparent storefronts.

(Photograph, 2004: NCDC, Gary Gaston)

Bottom: Recent remodeling of entrance to Tennessee Performing Arts Center at the corner of Deaderick Street and Sixth Avenue North.

(Photograph, 2004: Scott McDonald © Hedrich Blessing, courtesy of Earl Swensson Associates)

The Nashville Convention Center: Where To Put a New One and What To Do with the Old One

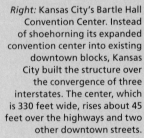

To build or not to build a new convention center for Nashville is an open question. Those who make their livings attracting visitors to town— or selling tourists something once they've arrived— are obviously in favor. Those who think that the city has invested quite enough in big boxes—arena, stadium—for the foreseeable future, or who question the cost/benefit ratio, are opposed, or at least skeptical.

From an urban design standpoint, the prime consideration is: If the city builds a new convention center, where will it go?

Convention center boosters say Nashville needs a structure with a minimum of 400,000 square feet of contiguous floor exhibition space, a minimum of 1.1 million square feet of gross space, and an adjacent 1,000-room hotel to stay in the game of competing for conventioneers. That translates to a fifteen-acre footprint, with another fifteen acres reserved for expansion. That's a big building. By way of comparison, the Gaylord Entertainment Center site is seven acres.

Placing such a widescraper within the city street grid—south of the Gaylord Entertainment Center is one such proposal—would obliterate the block structure of a big chunk of SoBro, thus concentrating traffic on the remaining streets and setting up a massive obstacle for pedestrians to negotiate. A convention center is also by its very function inward looking and therefore adds nothing to the streetscape unless wrapped with other uses, making the footprint larger still.

Locating a convention center on the former site of the thermal plant has also been proposed. But this placement would block public views and access to the Cumberland River by an intermittent land use whose building envelope is, as already stated, inward looking and therefore not functionally en-

hanced by a river view.

At an October 2001 urban design forum on the subject, one participant suggested that the best strategy would be to bury the convention center underground. The Plan of Nashville suggests a similar strategy.

The Plan proposes that the new convention center be placed spanning the railroad gulch, flanking what is now the Church Street viaduct. Railroad and automobile traffic can pass underneath the convention center. Messy issues such as loading and unloading can also be accomplished in an "out of sight" area that does not conflict with pedestrian or automobile traffic. At street level, the convention center can be designed in a way that engages the pedestrian, with storefront shops and spaces that open onto the viaduct.

At present this placement may seem remote. But as the anchor to the western end of downtown Church Street, the convention center would actually be integral to the redevelopment of this reviving part of the city. Convention patrons would have an

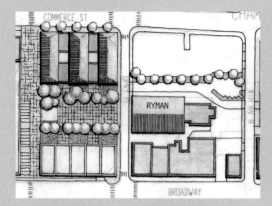

easy stroll along the street to restaurants and entertainment venues to the east, such as found in Printers Alley and on Second Avenue.

The current convention center stands on prime real estate. If the city builds a new center, the old one will be demolished. In this proposed redevelopment site plan, the Renaissance Hotel retains a portion of the old convention center immediately behind the hotel tower for smaller hotel functions.

The plan is oriented around a public plaza in front of the Ryman Auditorium, allowing the facade of the historic building to be viewed from a distance and providing a gathering place for natives as well as tourists. The plaza is flanked by mixed-use—commercial and residential—buildings.

The Broadway facade of the new development extends the urban character and the entertainment district of lower Broad one block west. The upper levels of these buildings fronting the plaza have retail and commercial space to bring activity to the open space. Buildings facing Commerce Street feature residential uses, for which the plaza will serve as an amenity.

Christine Kreyling

Left: Current convention center site showing proposed redevelopment. Note the plaza in front of the Ryman Auditorium.

(Drawing, 2002: NCDC, Jason Hill)

Redeveloped site looking toward Ryman Auditorium.

(Drawing, 2002: NCDC, Jason Hill)

Corbusier diagram of the city of the future looks much like the 1963 *Central Loop Plan* for Nashville by Clarke and Rapuano—and the suburbia of today: wide arterials going directly into a pod of land use. The fine-grain network of the city disappears. Also absent in these diagrams is any traffic congestion on these arterials, and a storage place for all the vehicles once they stop moving. Now who's nearsighted?

Fortunately, Paris was not remade to Corbusier's plan, nor Nashville to Clarke and Rapuano's. But enough damage was done to Nashville to raise the question, as Lewis Mumford puts it, "of whether any city dedicated wholeheartedly to traffic could sufficiently survive for any other purposes."[5]

Downtown Nashville has survived. But for it

to prosper the internal combustion engines must be relegated to their proper place: as one user of space, but not the prime determinant of form and function in the downtown neighborhood.

The emphasis on moving as many vehicles as possible in the shortest time into and out of downtown has resulted in the widening of streets, the conversion of two-way streets to one-way corridors, and the elimination of on-street parking to increase the number of travel lanes. The right angles of the corners at many intersections were also reformed into swoopy curves to increase the turning radii, especially for trucks. All these accommodations to vehicles encourage higher speeds and thus have a negative impact on the pedestrian environment.

Privileging the private vehicle as the user

of public space, in addition to eroding the pedestrian space, actually intensifies the need for more accommodation to vehicles. In 1955, Ft. Worth planner Victor Gruen tried to calculate how much road space would be needed for cars in the downtown of 1970. He predicted the amount of future economic development, translated that into individual users of the economic activities, and then into the number of cars the individuals would be driving. The resulting amount of road space he arrived at was three times the existing roadbed.

Gruen then realized that the downtown would have to spread out physically to supply the acreage for new road capacity, thus spreading thinner the economic activities the roads were intended to support. To take advantage of the new economic development—banks and legal offices, retail and restaurants, culture and entertainment—in lower density patterns, people would have to depend more on driving and less on walking. Public transportation would quickly become inefficient for both rider and operator. The downtown would thus need even more road space for cars traveling from venue to venue, and for parking once they got there. Gruen's conclusion was that "the more space that is provided cars in cities, the greater becomes the need for the use of cars, and hence for still more space for them."[6]

Given this automotive logic, the Plan of Nashville calls for a freeze on the addition of road capacity to downtown. The Plan also recommends strategies for streets that would balance the needs of vehicles with the other users competing for this public space.

The Plan recommends that downtown be subjected to a program of traffic calming—return to two-way movement, on-street parking, and crosswalks signalized to allow walkers to get from curb to curb at a reasonable pace, not a trot. To eliminate potential conflicts between cars and pedestrians on sidewalks, curb cuts should be reduced to a minimum and alleys used to bring vehicles within blocks. Pedestrian safety would also be improved by banning right-turns-on-red by vehicles at intersections. Many drivers don't even bother to pause, much less make the supposedly mandatory stop, before entering the crosswalk—even when the pedestrian has the green light.

In addition to the demands on public space made by vehicles in motion are the demands made by cars when they are idle and must be stored.

Downtown Nashville currently has approximately 30,000 off-street parking spaces—excluding private garages—and 900 on-street metered spaces. Of the 30,000 off-street spaces, 16,700 are in 94 surface lots and 13,200 are in 33 garages.

Surface parking is the bane of a downtown—gaps in the smile of the city. The lots erode the street wall, bring pedestrians into conflict with cars crossing sidewalks via curb cuts to access the lots, and contribute nothing but ugliness to the streetscape. The Plan of Nashville calls for the phasing out of surface parking in downtown.

The alternative is structured parking. The limestone on which Nashville rests makes underground garages costly. Above-grade garages are expensive because of the high land values in downtown. The market unaided will not support either option.

City governments such as that of Bethesda, Maryland, have built garages and then used the revenue they generate to pay off the construction costs. Metro Nashville should do the same after developing a downtown parking master plan that determines feasible locations that are convenient for the bulk of users.

This structured parking should be of good urban character: first-floor retail, architectural cladding of the upper levels, and accessed from alleys rather than the street proper. Placement at the center of blocks would allow the structure to be embedded within the architectural fabric so that higher and better land uses could directly address the street. Reduced fees, or no fees, for short-term parkers (up to two hours) would make downtown more attractive to visit for meals and entertainment and could provide a crucial support for the development of retail.

The long-range vision in the Plan is a vastly improved public transit system that will make driving and parking less attractive (see "Mass Transit for Local Circulation," pages 87–91). But in the short term we must live with the car.

Art as Civic Enterprise

Art keeps awake the sense of wonder in the world, to paraphrase British essayist G. K. Chesterton. And there are no places more deserving of such wakefulness than the public realm of the city.

Weaving art into the urban fabric demonstrates that the citizens consider the city itself to be a work of art, a vessel of expression capable of being shaped by their collective vision and will. Art becomes, not a special event, but a gesture of respect to the spaces of daily life, embodying our human potential as creative animals.

For art to express the public's vision and will, however, it must be the result of the same kind of community-based planning process that has produced the Plan of Nashville. Such artworks are a relatively recent addition to the American civic experience—Seattle and Portland pioneered the practice. But public art has ancient roots in the art-as-memorial tradition.

The Athenians erected votives on their most sacred public space—the Acropolis—commemorating citizens whose lives, and sometimes deaths, epitomized civic behavior. Nashville's most effective commemorative is also its largest—the Parthenon, which has evolved from a symbol of the aspirations of 1897 into a symbol for the entire city. Not much smaller, the War Memorial (1925)—with its bronze Spirit of Youth holding in his palm a Nike, the Greek symbol of victory—is a tribute to the "Sons of Tennessee who gave their lives in the Great War, 1914–1918." These combinations of architecture and sculpture in the classical style express a sense of civic destiny: the glory that was Greece is now ours.

During the Depression, art not specifically commemorative arrived in the public realm, funded by government—primarily federal—sources. The primary goal of the art programs

"When traffic takes precedence over all other urban functions, [the city] can no longer perform its own role, that of facilitating meeting and intercourse. The assumed right of the private motor car to go to any place in the city and park anywhere is nothing less than a license to destroy the city."

Lewis Mumford,
The City in History
(1961)

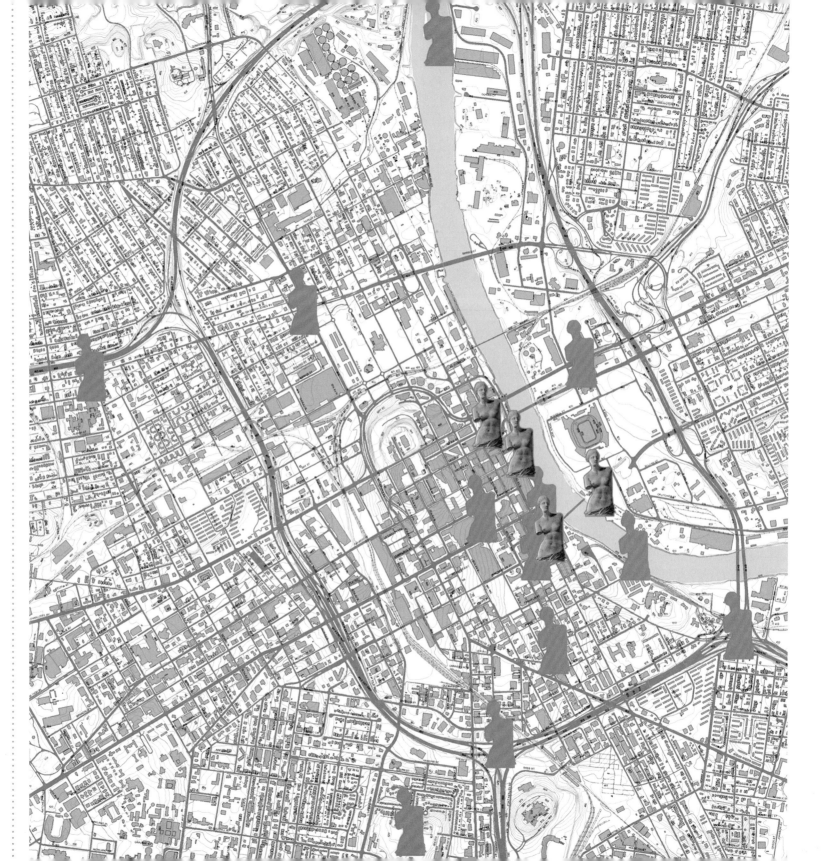

Sites for public art, identified during a series of Plan of Nashville Public Art workshops conducted by Seattle public artist Jack Mackie for the Metro Arts Commission.

(Diagram over map, 2004: NCDC, Raven Hardison)

Map Key

Top sites for public art indicated by detailed icon.

1. East and west termination of Shelby Street Pedestrian Bridge
2. Riverfront Park
3. Public Square

Putting the Public in Public Art

Left: Public artist Jack Mackie's cast bronze inlaid *Dance Steps on Broadway,* integrated into a neighborhood streetscape revitalization project funded through the Seattle Arts Commission and Seattle Engineering Department.

(Photograph: Art on File)

Center and top right: The Prince, a mobile by Nashville artist Adrienne Outlaw, is in the children's area of the Main Library downtown on Church Street.

(Center photograph, 2004: NCDC, Raven Hardison; top right photograph, 2001: Gary Layda, courtesy of the Metro Arts Commission)

Bottom right: Alexander Calder, *Flamingo,* 1974, Federal Plaza, Chicago. An example of the genre of individual expression in a public space, where the organic profile and vermilion color of the steel sculpture serve as a counterfoil to the black geometries of buildings by Mies van der Rohe.

(Photograph: commissioned by the U.S. General Services Administration, Art in Architecture Program)

Public art is a new phenomenon in modern terms. To achieve truly "public art" we must understand how it differs from "art in public places."

Since the early twentieth century, "art" has been defined as self-assertion by an artist—the individual's inquiry as sculptor or painter. These artist's inquiries, thrust into the public realm, are what most of the public refer to as public art.

Alexander Calder's *Flamingo* and other art like it are often large-scale sculptures—gallery or museum pieces simply too big to fit inside—that have little or no relationship to their location. More problematic is that such works have little relevance to or understanding by the public for whose benefit they have been so placed.

Created by the artist and solely expressing the artist's voice and intent, these works come with their meaning predetermined, and thus suffer no loss of meaning if moved to another site. These private works in our plazas are "art in public places." But it takes more than a public location to make "public art."

Thoughtful community involvement precedes, accompanies, and follows all public artwork. The citizens participate in the selection of the project and the artist. And the artist consults directly and frequently with the "owners" or users of a public space during development of the artwork. Such a process is inclusive and empowers voices in a community not otherwise heard.

The product is art whose content and context cross generational, ethnic, and class lines, and thus communicates with a broad audience. The artwork does not speak solely in the artist's voice, but translates into its audience's language. While the community does not say specifically what the art will be, their voices about a site—their experience of place—inspire the images and content of the artwork.

A particularly public avenue for public art is that which meets a public infrastructure need. Artists now design highway soundwalls and airport pavers, transit station canopies and tree grates, utility hatchcovers and screening for garages, gates and railings that reference local legends and histories, fauna and flora, symbols and aspirations. Such art thus presents a voice of local place, local experience, and local vision.

Jack Mackie, public artist, Seattle, Washington
Jerry Allen, art administrator, San Jose, California

> "I think the center is going to hold. I think it is going to hold because of the way people demonstrate by their actions how vital is centrality. The street rituals and encounters that seem so casual, the prolonged good-byes, the 100 percent conversations—these are not at all trivial. They are manifestations of one of the most powerful of impulses: the impulse to the center."
>
> William H. Whyte,
> *City: Rediscovering the Center* (1990)

was to put artists to work. While the community was not directly consulted on the nature of the projects or the selection of artists, the art produced was inspired by local history and culture. The Davidson County Public Building and Courthouse (1938), for example, features murals depicting allegorical interpretations of the themes of Industry, Agriculture, Commerce, and Statesmanship in Middle Tennessee in the person of Andrew Jackson.

After World War II, however, art and civic expression parted company. Commemoration became mere naming—witness the Victory Memorial and Jubilee Singers bridges, whose designs are indistinguishable from non-honorific public works. And "art" became embedded in the concept of individual self-expression and formal exploration, even when works of art were sited in civic spaces.

The most notorious example of individual self-expression in a public place is Richard Serra's *Tilted Arc*, a curved wall of rusted steel commissioned for New York's Federal Plaza in 1981. People who worked nearby, calling the sculpture an eyesore and an obstruction, campaigned successfully for its removal in 1989. The validity of the citizens' aesthetic judgment is irrelevant for our purpose here. What is relevant is that the public recognized that artwork, commissioned without their involvement and thus essentially a vehicle of private expression, had been placed in their space.

Metro Nashville's Public Art Program brings art and the citizenry back together. In 2000, the Metro Council passed an ordinance that sets aside 1 percent of the value of general obligation bonds issued for Metro construction projects—both new and major renovations—for public art. Community representatives work with the relevant government agencies to identify the site for and nature of each project, and select the art-

ist. The artist then engages in an ongoing dialogue with the community—in the form of public workshops—to develop the artwork.

The Metro Arts Commission saw the Plan of Nashville as an opportunity to plan for public art. To this end, the Commission staff teamed with the Nashville Civic Design Center to sponsor two workshops conducted by Seattle artist Jack Mackie. The workshops explored ways that public art can serve as a tool of urban design—both as functional elements of the public infrastructure and as artwork that will enhance the city's sense of place.

Using the principles of the Plan of Nashville (see "Avenues to a Great City," Ten Principles, page 44), workshop participants studied the city and located areas and specific places where public art could help to achieve these goals. The participants ultimately produced a priority list for public art sites and identified the East Bank near the Shelby Street Pedestrian Bridge as a primary area for one of the Public Art Program's initial projects.

To help the center hold, the Plan of Nashville addresses the two interlocking roles that Nashville's downtown plays. In presenting strategies for enabling the central city to become a self-sustaining neighborhood, the Plan is occupied by how downtown works as social space. The strategies for accentuating Nashville as the capital of Tennessee focus on the creation of a visual orientation for the city intended to satisfy the human need for beauty.

It is unfashionable to talk about beauty today, whether the subject be a painting or a sculpture—or a city. "Form follows function," which was the mantra of modernist architects and city planners, eroded our level of visual expectation. Some modernist designers—acutely sensitive to formal properties such as harmony and

clarity—made beautiful objects. In the hands of less talented followers, their design philosophy devolved into a relentless focus on practical function for its own sake. The result is a landscape of increasing ugliness and a citizenry that has suspended its ability to see because the sights are so unlovely.

Beauty and functionality are not mutually exclusive properties, as long as function is defined in the broadest possible sense. "The beautiful rests on the foundations of the necessary," writes Ralph Waldo Emerson in his essay "The Poet." So the success of Nashville as capital city rests on the footings of the downtown neighborhood. A downtown may have vitality without being a capital. But a capital—no matter how grand a work of art—may falter if the daily life of the city is inanimate.

NEIGHBORHOODS

NASHVILLE AND ITS NEIGHBORHOODS: FANNING THE FLAMES OF PLACE

It is at the level of the neighborhood that a child first becomes conscious of the building blocks of place. Colin Powell—the U.S. general-turned-Secretary of State—describes this dawning consciousness in *My American Journey*, when he writes about growing up in the Hunts Point section of the South Bronx.

When I stepped out the door onto Kelly Street, I saw my whole world. You went left three blocks to my grade school, one more block to my junior high school; between the two was a sliver of land where stood St. Margaret's Episcopal Church, our church. A few blocks in the opposite direction was the high school I would later attend. Across the street from us, at number 957, lived my Aunt Gytha and Uncle Alfred Coote. On my way to

school, I passed 935 Kelly, where Aunt Laurice and Uncle Vic and their children lived. Farther down, at 932, my godmother, Mabel Evadne Brash, called Aunt Vads, and her family lived. And at 867 were Amy and Norman Brash, friends so close they were considered relatives…

The block of Kelly next to ours was slightly curved, and the neighborhood had for years been known as "Banana Kelly"… Outsiders often have a sense of New York as big, overwhelming, impersonal, anonymous. Actually, even now it's a collection of neighborhoods where everybody knows everybody's business, the same as in a small town. Banana Kelly was like that.

There was a repeating pattern to the avenues that connected our streets. On almost

every block you would find a candy store… selling the *Daily News* and the *Post* and the *Mirror*. No one in my neighborhood read the *New York Times*. These little stores also carried school supplies, penny candy, ice cream and soft drinks…Every few blocks you found a Jewish bakery and a Puerto Rican grocery store. Italians ran the shoe repair shops. Every ten blocks were big chain stores, clothing and appliance merchants, and movie houses…The south Bronx was an exciting place when I was growing up, and I have never longed for elms and picket fences.[1]

Powell's recollection is telling for our purposes here because it touches precisely on the basic elements of neighborhood: housing, shops, communal institutions, the streets that bind the

"A place that ever was lived in is like a fire that never goes out. It flares up, it smolders for a time, it is fanned or smothered by circumstance, but its being is intact, forever fluttering within it, the result of some original ignition."

Eudora Welty,
Notes on River Country
(1943)

"A neighborhood is where, when you go out of it, you get beat up."

Murray Kempton, quoting Puerto Rican office worker, "Group Dynamics," *America Comes of Middle Age* (1963)

other elements together—and, of course, neighbors. The details of his description—Jewish bakery, Puerto Rican grocery, no elms or picket fences—also suggest that the specific attributes of these basic elements determine the neighborhood's physical character and social identity. A neighborhood's age, types of housing, kinds and quality of goods and services, the nature of its institutions, the architectural style and materials of its buildings, the design and functionality of streets and sidewalks and other transportation infrastructure, amount and types of landscaping, number and nature of parks, as well as the demographics and ethnicities of its residents, all work together to create a distinctive sense of place—and shape the self that grows up in it.

The Ideal Neighborhood

Underlying a neighborhood's distinctive attributes, like the skeleton beneath the skin, are organizational patterns that vary little from place to place. These patterns repeat the logic of the city in miniature.

Each neighborhood has a center and edges.[2] The center—which does not necessarily lie at the

geographical middle but is the physical and social focal point—may be marked by a square or green or an important intersection. At or near the center are typically clustered the civic buildings. The focal point for the Edgefield neighborhood, for example, is East Park and Warner School.

The edges are the neighborhood's limits, which are important in establishing the social sense of belonging to a somewhere. In *The City in History,* Lewis Mumford writes of the psychological importance of the wall—the epitome of the edge—to the medieval town in creating "a feeling of unity as well as security."[3]

Among the residents of a neighborhood, those who have the most unerring sense of its boundaries are the children. That's because children define the limits of place by walking—to school, to a friend's house, to the Sno-Cone stand. And, according to the *Charter of the New Urbanism,* walking is the instrument of measurement for the ideal neighborhood: a ten-minute walk (approximately a half-mile) from edge to edge. A bus stop located within this walking distance increases the probability that residents will use mass transit.

A neighborhood's children also function like the canary in the mineshaft, because they are the most vulnerable to adverse conditions. If a child cannot easily and safely navigate through the neighborhood, then that neighborhood does not perform well and lacks a sense of security.

Commerce is often associated with the neighborhood center. But in urban areas, in which the aggregation of neighborhoods forms towns and cities, commercial buildings often lie at the edges, along high streets or main streets that serve as the "zipper" between neighborhoods. The Hillsboro Village area along Twenty-first Avenue South is a good example of this phenomenon in Nashville, pulling together the Belmont-Hillsboro and Hillsboro-West End neighborhoods.

The neighborhood street system is a network of connectivity organized into a clear hierarchy. The hierarchy includes alleys, local streets primarily designed for use by residents of the neighborhood, and connector streets—principal streets and avenues—that serve adjoining neighborhoods. Boulevards and pikes accommodate many neighborhoods, are used for longer-distance travel—such as the commute from home to downtown—and connect entire communities.

A fine grain of blocks—a block of approximately 240 feet by 450 feet is optimal—enables more direct travel between home and daily destinations for pedestrians as well as vehicles. This network also provides a variety of routes, thus dispersing traffic and keeping local traffic off the boulevards. While the local street system within the neighborhood is used primarily by insiders who already know their way, the pattern of organization has enough predictability for outsiders to navigate without major confusion. Each street within this system is designed to balance the needs of pedestrians, bicyclists,

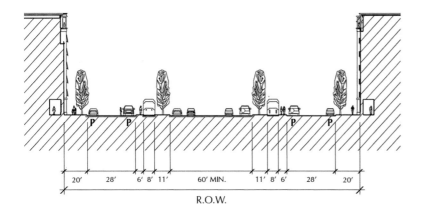

20' 28' 6' 8' 11' 60' MIN. 11' 8' 6' 28' 20'

R.O.W.

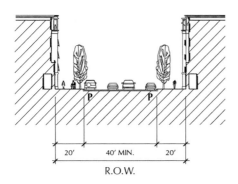

20' 40' MIN. 20'

R.O.W.

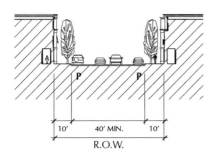

10' 40' MIN. 10'

R.O.W.

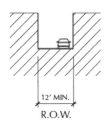

12' MIN.

R.O.W.

and drivers—sidewalks, on-street parking, and rights-of-way narrow enough to calm traffic—enabling the casual encounters among neighbors that help form the social bonds of the community.

Land uses in the neighborhood reflect a balanced mixture in close proximity: office and retail, schooling and recreation, and a variety of housing—rental and owner-occupied, single and multifamily—for a range of ages and incomes. Development opportunities in small increments, rather than the assemblage of parcels for big-box retail and large housing tracts, reflect the traditional pattern of neighborhood building and contribute to the organic, fine-grained character.

Like the city as a whole, the neighborhood's architectural fabric is composed primarily of background buildings—solid citizens that establish a basic character but don't call attention to themselves. These buildings are placed on the blocks to define the street walls—either built to the sidewalk, which is standard for commercial and mixed-use structures, or with the consistent setbacks more typical of residential areas. At selected places in this fabric—a central location or the terminus to a sightline—stand the architectural special events, such as a school, library, or church. These are the community's monuments. Such buildings add ceremony and dignity to the streetscape and give the neighborhood a collective sense of pride, whether individual residents actually use them or not.

The Not-So-Ideal Neighborhood

The insistence of the Plan of Nashville on the form of the traditional neighborhood as the ideal building block of the city may be more fully understood by considering its less than ideal opposite: post–World War II suburbia. Crucial distinctions are found in street and land use patterns.

According to traffic engineer Walter Kulash,

Sample sections that illustrate the street hierarchy. From top to bottom: boulevard/pike; connector/principal street; local street; alley.

(Drawings, 2004: Earl Swensson Associates, Corey Little after Graphic Standards)

"Streetscape is not just some abstract notion of quaintness. It is the self-reinforcing quality of liveliness that causes people to want to walk."

Justin Davidson,
Newsday
(August 5, 2004)

Aerial of Bellevue, exemplifying post–WWII suburban development patterns.
(Photograph, 2002: Metro Planning Department)

planning regulations established during the post-war suburban building boom "called for street systems deliberately designed to keep through traffic off residential streets, and they specified the antithesis of connected streets: isolated pods of development connected only to a sparse system of arterial highways. Street layouts were no longer networks, but instead became 'dendritic' in nature, with all streets branching from a single connection to the regional arterial road system. The conventional suburban hierarchy was designed to consist of local streets ending in cul-de-sacs and collector streets"[4] that feed vehicles into major arterials.

Kulash points out that this suburban logic

Development Patterns and the Environment

Many otherwise intelligent people have somehow gotten the idea that living at low density is good for the environment. Many cringe at the idea of living even at American small-town densities that average between six and ten units per acre. They see all the green of suburbia and think this must be better ecologically. Additionally, they like the idea of having a yard for the pets and for the kids to play in, and perhaps even a pool.

In the typical suburb, what once was a beautiful meadow or forest has now been replaced by an incompetently managed and over-fertilized lawn, with exotic vegetation supporting swarms of equally exotic insects and birds that would never naturally occur within the area. In many parts of the country the whole-sale replacement of native plant species with exotic ornamental plants imported from other parts of the world has facilitated the establishment of large populations of alien insect and animal populations, sometimes completely displacing native species. A recent careful and extensive study of habitats in England concludes that we are entering a period of massive species extinction, all thanks to our naïve management of the environment.

Although the impacts of suburbia on the ecology of the land are large, the worst environmental impacts of suburbia and low-density living are the result of having to drive long distances for every purpose, burning up fossil fuels and filling the air with greenhouse gases on our way to the playground five miles away.

With the advent and popularity of car-dependent forms of development, the portion of typical American family expenditures allocated for transportation steadily rose from less than 2 percent in 1900 to nearly 30 percent today—excluding the portion of income taxes that supports transportation, the portion of your house that stores the car, and private sector costs associated with providing parking lots and access roads. Increases in transportation costs are directly related to the suburbanization that took place after World War II and the deliberate destruction of our nation's public transportation systems, and reflect the dependency of our nation on automobile ownership and use.

Suburban patterns of development increase the number of vehicle trips per household and the length of each trip. Average trip length is approximately four times longer in suburbs than in traditional American towns. It would be absolutely impossible for people to live within most suburban communities without the use of an automobile. This makes our economy entirely vulnerable to any significant disruption in the flow of energy that could result from the instability of the Middle East, terrorism, and the increasing global demands on oil reserves. Sadly, the increased energy use, air pollution, and global warming have not provided a higher quality of life. For the elderly, children, and those hard pressed to afford an automobile, the promise of the green suburb was a lie, leaving this large segment of the population dependent on relatives or friends to shuttle them to and from basic services.

In contrast, the compactness of traditional development patterns minimizes use of land and impacts on natural systems, and results in reductions in energy and water use, reductions in air pollution, and more efficient handling of all forms of waste. Traditional patterns of development provide a diversity of housing types in close proximity to places of work and shopping, and even to schools. Yards exist, but are smaller, requiring less water use, and less displacement of native systems per capita, and less chemical support. Instead of every home having a second-rate playground, small parks exist in close proximity to many houses and many children, where they have the opportunity to play together without being shuttled there by car. Because of the compactness, it is also possible to economically provide efficient water, wastewater, and solid waste collection, treatment, and disposal systems.

The suburb is an experiment that has failed society. Given its inefficiency and its environmental impacts, the car-dependent suburb is an experiment that may prove fatal.

Dan Cary, environmental planner

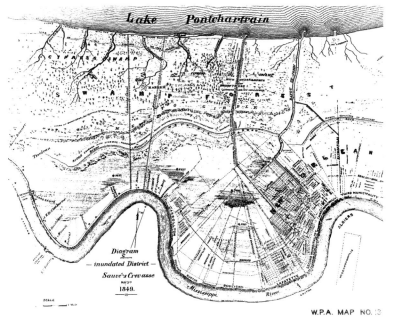

compels all drivers onto the arterial, producing intersection congestion even in low-density developments: "Attempting to accommodate short, local, daily trips is an abuse of the intended function of arterial streets and fuels much of the demand for more and wider highways." In addition to producing needless congestion, Kulash says, the suburban street layout "is the worst possible environment for pedestrian travel. Access between people's homes and their destinations is seldom direct and usually requires travel through hostile environments such as major arterial streets and parking lots." Few trips are within walking distance. "And walking or biking is often dangerous and unpleasant because there are no sidewalks, or they may exist only on the multi-lane arterial road where traffic is heavier and faster, with much greater noise and fumes."

Isolated pods of a single land use—such as are found at Cool Springs, Nashville's so-called "edge city," where residential, office, retail, and entertainment are segregated—require people to drive to each destination and attempt to park there, in-creasing the number of vehicles on the road and the amount of asphalt on the ground. And the typical subdivision contains a solitary housing type—single or multi-family, rental or owner-occupied—with same-size units on same-size lots, thus enforcing segregation by economic class and often by age. This is the recipe for an assortment of monocultures, not a city.

The City of Neighborhoods

If neighborhoods are to mass together to form a city they must be closely linked, without losing individual identity. Methods of linkage include streets and sidewalks, bike paths, mass transit, and even linear parks or greenways. A good example of the phenomenon of a city of neighborhoods is New Orleans, a place that, in the words of Peirce F. Lewis, "occupies a special niche in America's small chamber of urban delights."[5]

The neighborhoods of New Orleans built prior to 1940 exhibit the characteristics delineated in the section above. Each is of walkable size, with a center, clearly defined edges, and a tight network of streets laid out in a grid plan skewed in response to the broad bends of the Mississippi River. These neighborhoods are linked by a system of avenues and boulevards that either parallel the path of the river or lie perpendicular to the waterfront. Because of the minimal intrusion of the interstate—protests blocked a riverfront expressway in the 1960s—the historic neighborhoods fanning back from the river still exhibit classic neighborhood form.

Most of the characteristics of the ideal neighborhood were once present in Nashville's first-ring neighborhoods. These earliest of Nashville's suburbs—enabled by the advent of the streetcar—originally had natural edges, such as the Cumberland River and its flood plains, the Gulch, and other topographic features. The bridges across these natural barriers are woven into the city's history. While these neighborhoods exhibit less density of building fabric than downtown proper, they are nevertheless urban in character due to their network of streets, the preponderance of buildings oriented to the

"I have an affection for a great city. I feel safe in the neighborhood of man, and enjoy the sweet security of streets."

Henry Wadsworth Longfellow, "The Great Metropolis," *Driftwood* (1857)

Historic neighborhoods of Nashville.

(Map, 1860: Tennessee State Library and Archives)

Aerial view. Note the fracturing of the traditional neighborhood form by the interstates, and the gaps caused by surface parking.

(Photograph, 2003: Metro Planning Department)

cial strips has sucked mercantile life out of the neighborhoods. The aggregation of big-box retail at the interchanges of interstates has destroyed downtown shopping and pulls customers to the perimeter. Both developments have eliminated the multiple layers of retail found in vital neighborhoods.

Beginning in the 1970s, urban pioneers joined forces with long-time residents in the protracted process of reclaiming the first-ring neighborhoods, primarily by a rehabilitation of the housing stock. They received support from some shifts in public policy. Historic and conservation zoning overlays administered by the Metro Historic Zoning Commission have been crucial tools of preservation and restoration. The Metro Development and Housing Agency's redevelopment districts—some with design guidelines—provide economic incentives for new development. In 2000 the Metro Planning Department established an urban zoning overlay to enable new construction of urban character. Mayor Bill Purcell's initiative to build more affordable housing in the city will help to sustain the first ring's diverse population. Today these neighborhoods are experiencing reinvestment in the form of infill housing and new small businesses.

The strongest influence on the quality of life in these neighborhoods, however, is the caliber of the public spaces. And the most pervasive public space is the system of streets, over which the individual developer, home or business owner has little control. It is the streets that bind neighborhoods together and to each other, that prevent a city of neighborhoods from being a city in pieces. The Plan of Nashville's major focus in the first-ring neighborhoods, therefore, is on improvements to the public realm.

public right-of-way, and residential population densities of six to ten units to the acre.

Since the 1940s, however, the first-ring neighborhoods—and their links to each other—have been compromised by government policies hostile to neighborhood form. Public housing projects replaced traditional building fabric with housing blocks oriented away from the street that have devolved into islands of poverty and crime. The building of wide roads without suitable provisions for pedestrians, and the intrusion of limited access highways—the interstates and "parkways"—have fragmented the neighborhoods and isolated them from each other and the downtown. This isolation is compounded by the limited nature of public transit.

The zoning of the historic pikes-turned-commuter-corridors for continuous commer-

Nashville's first-ring
neighborhoods.
(Map, 2004: NCDC)

Existing conditions of the River District. Note how the district is enscribed by the river on three sides.

(Map, 2002: Metro Planning Department)

THE RIVER DISTRICT

THE TERM "RIVER DISTRICT" was suggested for the area inscribed by the Cumberland River north of Jefferson Street by citizens who participated in the Plan of Nashville community workshops. These citizens felt that the traditional name, "North Nashville," had become identified with the area's problems rather than its positive attributes.

Then and Now

The most venerable of the district's neighborhoods are those described as Old North Nashville and New North Nashville in the Metro Historical Commission's study of 1977, *Nashville: Conserving a Heritage*.[6] Old North Nashville lies east and south of the interstate loop and was originally part of a 960-acre tract owned by land baron David McGavock. In the 1830s and '40s, agriculture gave way to residential development occupied largely by German families—hence "Germantown." Prominent among these immigrants were the Neuhoffs, meat packers; the Gersts, brewers; and architect Adolphus Heiman.

Travel to and from downtown was traditionally along what are now Fourth and Fifth Avenues; avenues closer to the river were avoided as thoroughfares due to the industries—especially the smelly stockyards and slaughterhouses—located along them. The northern edge of this neighborhood was, beginning in the latter decades of the nineteenth century, the site of large cotton and textile mills whose workers lived nearby—many from DeKalb County, thus the nickname "Kalb Hollow"—due to limited transportation options at the time. In 1938 several blocks of worker housing were replaced by Cheatham Place, a small-scale public housing complex.

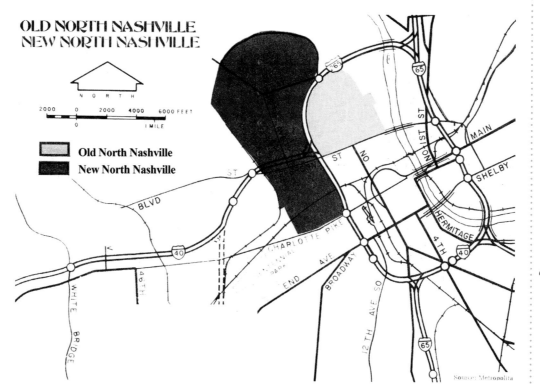

OLD NORTH NASHVILLE
NEW NORTH NASHVILLE

Old North Nashville
New North Nashville

Old and New North Nashville, from *Nashville: Conserving a Heritage*.

(Map, 1977: Historical Commission of Nashville-Davidson County)

"You've got to recognize the heritage, but you've got to move on."

Reverend John Beach, community workshop participant

Aerial of Old North Nashville looking toward the Werthan Bag complex. Note how Eighth Avenue North ended at St. Cecilia Academy. Across from the Werthan complex is now the location of Cheatham Place Homes.

(Photograph, 1934: Metro Planning Department)

Existing conditions of the eastern portion of the River District. Compare with the Plan's treatment of the same area on page 144.

(Map, 2002: Metro Planning Department)

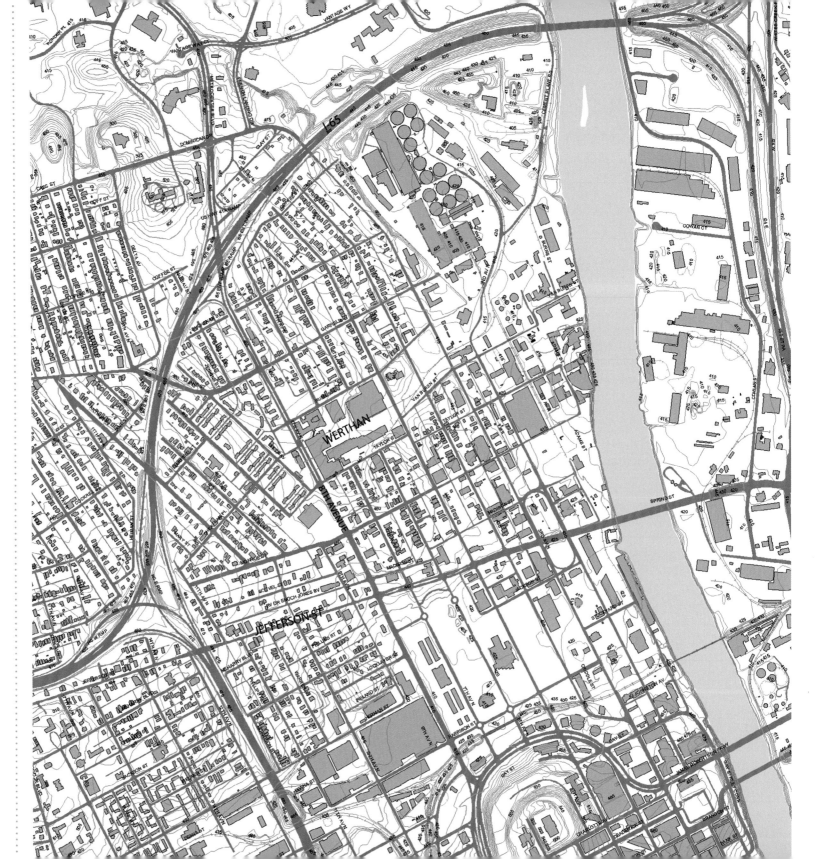

The physical character of Old North Nashville is defined by this history: compact blocks of primarily modest homes mixed with the occasional grander structure, corner stores and the small warehouses of light industry. The Roman Catholic Church of the Assumption (constructed between 1856 and 1859), the Carnegie Library (1915) on Monroe Street, Morgan Park (1909) and Elliott School (now Centerstone's Ella Hayes Center) are the neighborhood's landmarks.

North and east lie larger warehouses, many of which are undergoing rehabilitation for offices and residences. One of the first such conversions was Riverfront Apartments (1986), which incorporated the skeleton of Kerrigan Ironworks. The interstate and chain stores built to suburban design—such as Kroger and Eckerd—are unfortunate incursions; more recent residential and commercial infill has respected the traditional urban fabric. Demographically this neighborhood is racially mixed.

New North Nashville lies west of the interstate and east of the railroad tracks, north of Charlotte Avenue and south of Ted Rhodes Park and Golf Course and Metro Center. The neighborhood's history as a center of the city's African American life goes back to the first "contraband" camp for fugitive slaves, established just west of the Nashville-Chattanooga Railroad depot by the Union army in 1863. According to historian Bobby Lovett, the tent camp started with 150 inhabitants and grew to nearly 2,000 refugees who worked on military projects in return for minimal food, lodging, and wages. Vast railroad yards and military barracks were located between the camp and what was then the city's western edge.[7]

The founding of Fisk University in 1866 for the education of the emancipated slaves—utilizing some of the former Union barracks—transformed a temporary encampment into a permanent African American settlement. The subsequent relocation of Meharry Medical College and Pearl High School to the area, as well as the establishment of what became Tennessee State University, confirmed the neighborhood as the hub of black culture. Housing patterns reflect this history, with larger residences for wealthier families—now sadly decaying—near the Fisk and Meharry campuses surrounded by housing for those with lower incomes.

Jefferson Street is the traditional "main street" of New North Nashville, D. B. Todd Jr. Boulevard the primary north-south street. The neighborhood is home to the city's first public park, Watkins Park, which was transferred to the Parks Board at its first meeting in 1901 after having been given to the city by Samuel Watkins in 1870.[8] Watkins, a construction contractor who founded the Watkins Institute, quarried the stone for the State Capitol in the vicinity of the park; Confederate soldiers captured during the Battle of Nashville in 1864 were interned in the quarry. Farther to the west, near the TSU campus is Hadley Park, which in 1912 became the city's first public park for black citizens. Buena Vista Park (1934), whose springs were a popular source of mineral water in the nineteenth century, lies to the north, as does the old St. Cecilia Academy, whose main building dates to 1862, and the Temple (Jewish) Cemetery.

This neighborhood has good urban bones, housing dominated by the traditional detached single-family residence, and major landmarks such as Fisk's Jubilee Hall—the first building in the United States constructed for the higher education of blacks. But several public housing projects violate the traditional urban character. And the construction of I-40 without regard to the geometry of the street system or the natural boundaries of the neighborhoods was a serious blow to New North Nashville, limiting access to Jefferson Street from the residential areas to the north.

The Plan

The overall concept of the Plan for the River District is to focus on prominent natural and manmade features to develop a new internal and external identity that builds on the solid foundations of the past. The urban fabric is strengthened through the restoration of the network of streets. Neighborhood centers are emphasized through the redevelopment of "high streets" and public spaces. While the most important long-term goal is the restoration of the local street system through the removal of I-40 (see "Four-Step Program," page 77), interim strategies such as more frequent links over the interstate could go a long way to heal the district.

Natural Features

The Cumberland River is the most prominent topographical feature, defining the district's edges on three sides. It is logical, therefore, that participants in the community workshops, frustrated by the association of "North Nashville" with poverty and crime, should choose the term "River District" to name the area.

The land adjacent to the Cumberland is natural floodplain, which has historically hindered its development. Metro government stepped in to replace a former detention home with Ted Rhodes Park and Golf Course in 1954. To create Metro Center on top of a former landfill in the 1970s, a levee was built along the river's south bank, existing wetlands were drained or condensed into lakes, fill dirt added, and presto: office buildings in a "park-like" setting.

Today environmental laws would not permit this high degree of manipulation. In the Plan, park returns to wetland, albeit a managed one, using Shelby Bottoms—with its walking

The Plan for the River District.
(Drawing, 2003: NCDC)

8TH AVENUE

5TH AVENUE

JEFFERSON STREET

trails and wildlife habitat—as a model.

Industrial uses and warehouses relocate to more appropriate settings, such as near interstate interchanges. The office buildings remain, but the surrounding grounds are restored to a much more naturalistic and sustainable landscape for public use, with water as the theme.

Existing water features, as well as wetland conditions and habitat are preserved, and new ones created. Native species replace non-native plants, and high maintenance lawns and exotics are eliminated. Much of the surface parking is replaced with structured parking—with architectural cladding and first-floor retail or office uses—shared among various buildings. Dense tree plantings form a buffer between buildings and park land, and streets are lined with allées of trees. The overall effect is of architecture floating in a sea of green. (See "Embracing the

Looking south down the Cumberland from the River District.

(Photograph, 2004: NCDC, Gary Gaston)

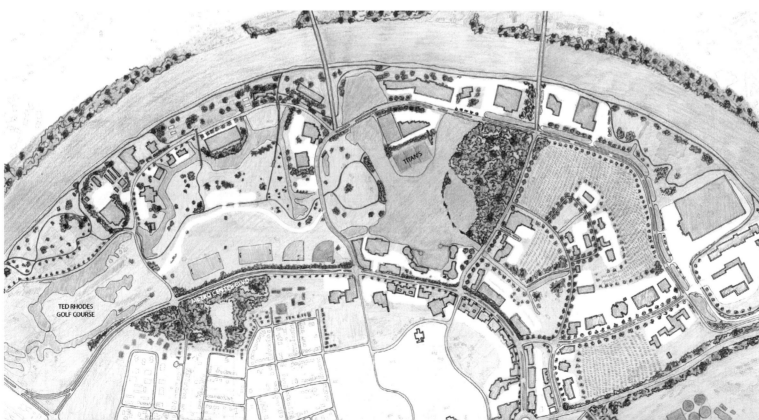

Plan of Buena Vista Bottoms. Metro Center is re-envisioned as a mixed-use neighborhood set within a natural oasis.

(Drawing, 2004: NCDC, Raven Hardison and Matthew Champion)

TED RHODES GOLF COURSE

TITANS

145

Trails along Metro Center Lake and the Cumberland River indicate how parts of the office park retain their naturalistic landscape.

(Photograph, 2004: NCDC, Raven Hardison)

Right: Metro Center Lake. In the Plan, the naturalistic landscape, shown on the far side of the lake, is encouraged; less sustainable lawn, in foreground, is discouraged.

(Photograph, 2004: NCDC, Raven Hardison)

Looking to the downtown skyline from Thirty-fifth and Clare Avenues near the TSU campus; modest suburban ranch houses with a spectacular view.

(Photograph, 2004: NCDC, Gary Gaston)

Cumberland River," pages 58–71, for further information about treatment of river banks.)

Away from the river's floodplains, the River District is characterized by notable gullies and hills. This topography should be protected—steep slopes should remain undeveloped—and vistas exploited in enhancing the district's unique character.

Hierarchy of Streets

Principal Streets act as connectors between neighborhoods and to other parts of the city. A principal street can take the form of a boulevard, avenue, street, or parkway. These streets should feature mixed-use buildings—such as residential over retail—and travel lanes that also carry mass transit.

Diagram of streets and
neighborhood centers.
(Map with drawing, 2004: NCDC)

Map Key

Solid black lines: principal
streets

Dashed black lines: local streets

Dashed red lines: centers

147

Eighth Avenue looking north. Beautiful landscaping would transform the character of this major street. Note the Werthan Complex in the distance to the right of the roadway.
(Photograph, 2004: NCDC, Randy Hutcheson)

Metro Center Boulevard has the potential to become a grand avenue; the introduction of mixed-use building types that add definition to the right-of-way is a critical step in the street's evolution.
(Photograph, 2004: NCDC, Raven Hardison)

Designing the principal streets to a higher urban standard indicates the street's importance, and helps people find their way to neighborhood centers, parks, and civic spaces. This higher standard includes architecture that forms consistent street walls, minimal curb cuts, good sidewalks and bike lanes as well as landscaping.

Eighth Avenue North/Metro Center Boulevard/Ed Temple Boulevard/Twenty-eighth Avenue North curves through the River District on a path that echoes the curves of the Cumberland River, passing on its circuit through historic neighborhoods and by the floodplains of Metro Center and the golf course, the agricultural fields of Tennessee State University and the campus itself. Redesigning this loop as a grand urban avenue will capitalize on its potential as the district's summary statement.

Jefferson Street, as the major avenue of commerce in the River District, functions as a "zipper" between the neighborhoods as well as the educational institutions. Street walls need reinforcing and major intersections should be of strongly urban character. Both eastern and western ends of the street should be defined as termini or gateways by an artistic or architectural gesture.

A master plan to return Jefferson Street to its prior status as the community's "main street" was developed with federal funds by the North Nashville Community Development Corporation in 2002. The intent is for the master plan to serve as a road map for future development on the street.

Other principal streets in the River District that require the restoration of good urban design include D. B. Todd Jr. Boulevard and Clarksville Highway, which link Bordeaux across the river to the north and Charlotte Avenue to the south.

Local Streets form a low-speed network within a neighborhood that provides multiple

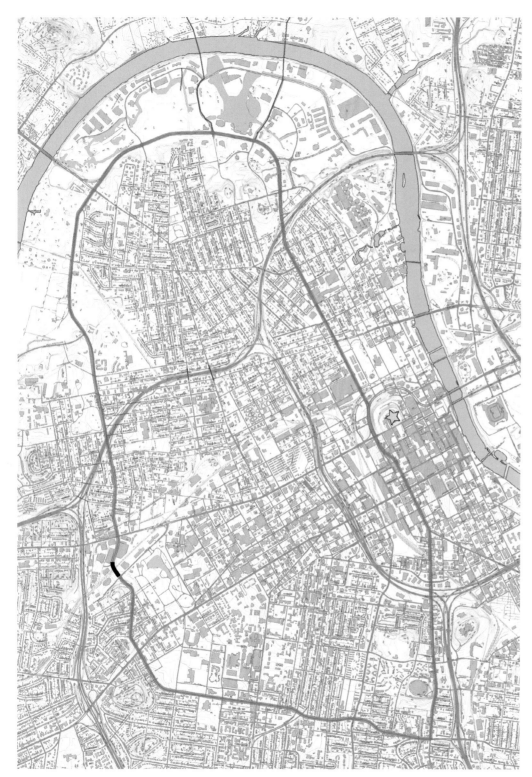

connections to the principal streets; they should feature primarily residential buildings and have no more than two travel lanes.

Neighborhood Centers

The focal points of neighborhoods within the district are sited at the intersection of important streets. The treatment of the center at Monroe Street and Eighth Avenue North is presented as a re-formation case study whose strategies can be applied to others.

Traveling north on Eighth Avenue one passes from downtown through the zone of the Bicentennial Mall and Farmers' Market to the first-ring neighborhoods. The intersection of Eighth Avenue and Monroe Street announces the transition from town to neighborhood. To reinforce the physical character of this intersection, now eroded by suburban-style setbacks, buildings are placed at the edges of the right-of-way with parking in the rear. A high level of streetscaping—trees lining the right-of-way and medians—continues to the hill at Dominican Avenue.

Clockwise from top left:

In this section of Jefferson Street, mixed-use buildings with entrances from the sidewalk and transparent windows welcome the pedestrian.

(Photograph, 2004: NCDC, Gary Gaston)

North Nashville Community Development Corporation plan for the intersection of Eighth Avenue North and Jefferson Street. A new African American Museum to be located on the southeast corner of this intersection is currently in the planning stages; this institution should be designed so that it contributes to the urban character of the street.

(Drawing, 2002: Moody Nolan/Hawkins Partners)

Monroe Street, looking west. Note that while the sidewalk needs repair, it is buffered from the street by a generous planting strip whose mature trees provide shade for pedestrians and add aesthetic quality to the streetscape. Nashville once had many of these planting strips, but they have gradually been eliminated by Metro Public Works due to the maintenance they require.

(Photograph, 2004: NCDC, Raven Hardison)

Carnegie Library on Monroe Street, constructed in 1915 and still a neighborhood landmark that adds ceremony and dignity to the streetscape and gives the neighborhood a collective sense of pride.

(Photograph, 2004: NCDC, Gary Gaston)

Quick idea sketch done during community vision workshop.

(Sketch, 2003)

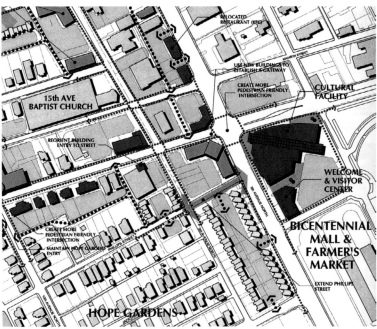

Of particular importance is the treatment of the Kroger and its surface parking. The big-box retailer—important to the commerce of the area—is retained, but new buildings fill in the edges of the overly large parking lot. These new structures—which could be occupied by supporting commercial services such as dry cleaner, copy shop, etc.—have a dual focus, with entrances at front and back, forming a courtyard that the grocery anchors.

Other intersections in need of transformation to centers include (see map, page 147): Jefferson Street and D. B. Todd Jr. Boulevard, Jefferson Street and Eighth Avenue North, Monroe Street and D. B. Todd Jr. Boulevard, Jefferson Street and Twenty-eighth Avenue North, D. B. Todd Jr. Boulevard between Buchanan and where D. B. Todd becomes Clarksville Highway at Clay Street, and Metro Center Boulevard and Dominican Drive—this latter becomes a center when the intersection is converted to a roundabout. The motel disappears, the Maxwell House Hotel parking lot and empty lot diagonally across from the hotel are developed.

Plan for intersection of Monroe Street and Eighth Avenue North; note how Monroe and Eighth are redesigned with streetscaping and buildings that grow to the public right-of-way.

(Drawing, 2003: NCDC, Gary Gaston)

Perspective view of proposed intersection of Eighth Avenue North and Monroe Street. The buildings along the street screen the big-box retail behind.

(Drawing, 2003: NCDC, Jason Hill)

Plan of Governor House and Green.

(Drawing, 2003: NCDC, Gary Gaston)

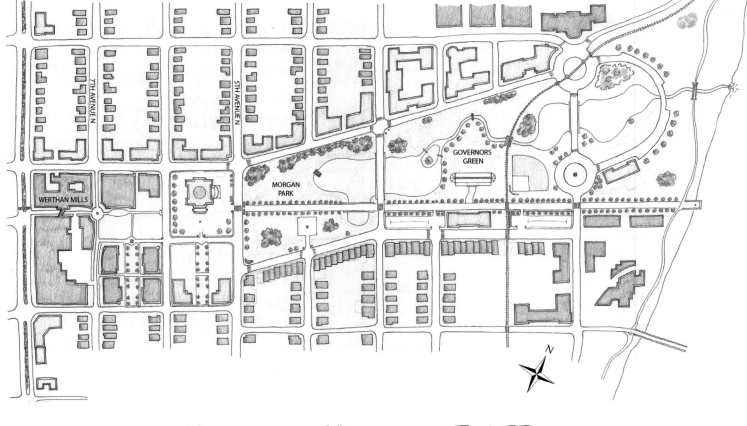

Perspective of Governor House and Green looking from the north.

(Drawing, 2004: Gary Everton)

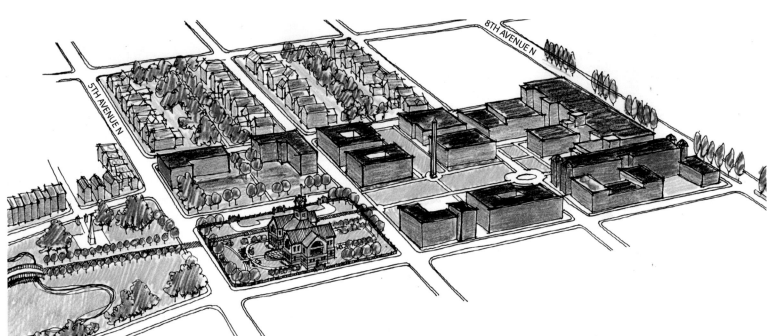

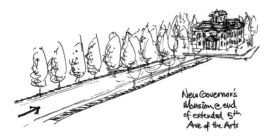

New Governor's Mansion @ end of extended 5th Ave of the Arts

Civic Space: Governor House and Green

During the community workshops, citizens lamented that Tennessee's governor lives in "hiding" in a suburban villa and has no specific architectural presence near the State Capitol. They proposed to rectify this absence with a new residence that contributes to the built metaphor of an accessible state government.

Governor House is to be used, not necessarily as personal living quarters, but as the place where the chief executive stages official functions and entertains guests and visitors to the capital. Citizens noted that the current executive residence lacks the space to present large gatherings, and temporary tents must be set up on the surrounding lawn for this purpose.

The proposal for this new civic building represents the elaboration of a theme presented more fully in the "Downtown" section of the Plan, to reassert Nashville's status as state capital by strengthening the sightlines to and from the Capitol (see "Capitol Axes," pages 98–108). The north axis of the Capitol is the State Axis, with the Bicentennial Mall, the proposed site of the State Museum and other state government structures. Governor House extends the north axis into a first-ring neighborhood; immediately to the west of the building is a vertical marker directly on axis with Mall and Capitol.

Governor House is set one block to the west of Morgan Park, on what is currently the site of the still operational section of the Werthan Bag and Cotton Mill complex. (Note that Gov-

ernor House does not impinge on the historic Werthan buildings.) A grand lawn—Governor Green— represents an expansion of historic Morgan Park, whose recreational fields will be reincorporated into the larger Green. The model for Governor Green is London's St. James Park, with its mixture of formal and informal gardens and stately tree-lined promenade.

To the east the Green stretches all the way to the river and terminates in an overlook for viewing the river, the east bank of the Cumberland, and downtown. Adjacent is a small boat dock. To the west, the Green continues through the Werthan complex to Cheatham Place and the neighborhood center that includes the Kroger, providing residents across Eighth Avenue with a pleasant and easy path to Green and river. Residential development forms a border around the Green.

Housing

The River District housing stock is dominated by single-family detached homes of good urban design. Major efforts should be taken to preserve this housing through better codes enforcement and the development of financing mechanisms for rehabilitation. Vacant lots should be redeveloped with new infill that respects the district's traditional urban character; good examples of one kind of infill can be found in Hope Gardens. Metro Center Boulevard and the Metro Center campus, on the other hand, should feature new development of larger scale and mixed-use building types, to bring a residential component to the area.

One of the sites most in need of redevelopment in the River District is John Henry Hale Homes, located along Charlotte Avenue between I-40 and Seventeenth Avenue North.

HENRY HALE NEIGHBORHOOD

EXISTING

PARKING LANES
(could serve as alleys with rear access to duplexes)

DUPLEXES
(Located within interior or property and along areas of topography)

LINEAR GREEN
(Connecting Watkins Park to Edmondson Park)

FUTURE CIVIC BUILDING
(On Axis with Capitol)

Named for an early black physician, this public housing project, built in 1951, consists of 498 units on the 32.4-acre site. In spring 2004, MDHA announced that the agency had received a federal Hope VI grant for $20 million to fund demolition of the existing housing blocks, infrastructure reorientation, and reconstruction of housing in a style more in keeping with that of the surrounding neighborhoods. The replacement plan calls for 180 affordable units, 40 market-rate units, and 40 single-family units as infill in the surrounding neighborhood. It is important that all new construction be consistent with the principles of urban design presented in the Plan.

The Neuhoff complex is a former slaughterhouse and meat packing plant located on eighteen acres six blocks north of the Metro Courthouse and flanking the Cumberland River. A master plan developed by the owners features adaptive reuse of the industrial structures, with multi-family housing as the center of the plan. Cultural organizations also find homes here. New construction is guided by sustainable building practices. The proposed greenway connecting Metro Center with downtown passes through the site; this greenway is enhanced by additional open space with direct access to the river.

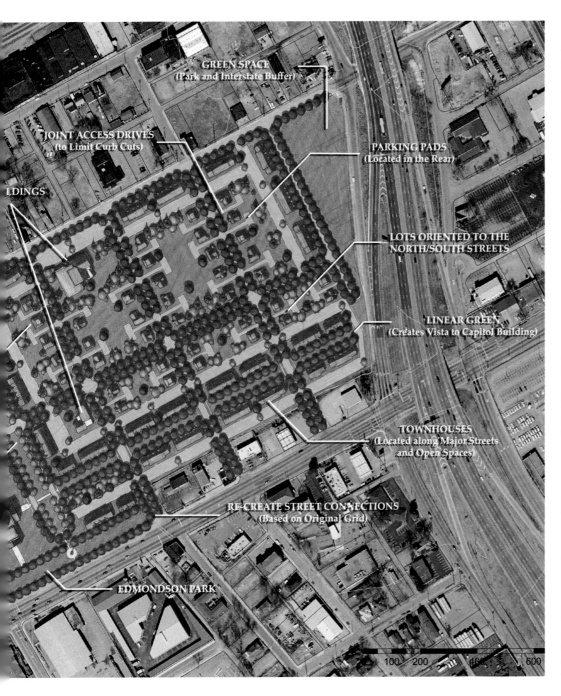

GREEN SPACE
(Park and Interstate Buffer)

JOINT ACCESS DRIVES
(to Limit Curb Cuts)

PARKING PADS
(Located in the Rear)

LDINGS

LOTS ORIENTED TO THE
NORTH/SOUTH STREETS

LINEAR GREEN
(Creates Vista to Capitol Building)

TOWNHOUSES
(Located along Major Streets
and Open Spaces)

RE-CREATE STREET CONNECTIONS
(Based on Original Grid)

EDMONDSON PARK

100   200   400   600

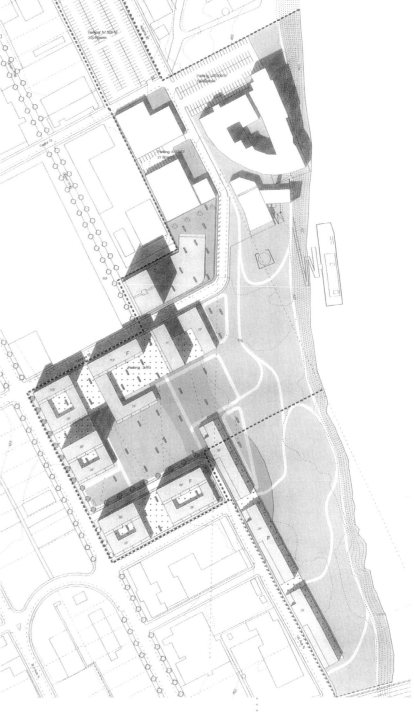

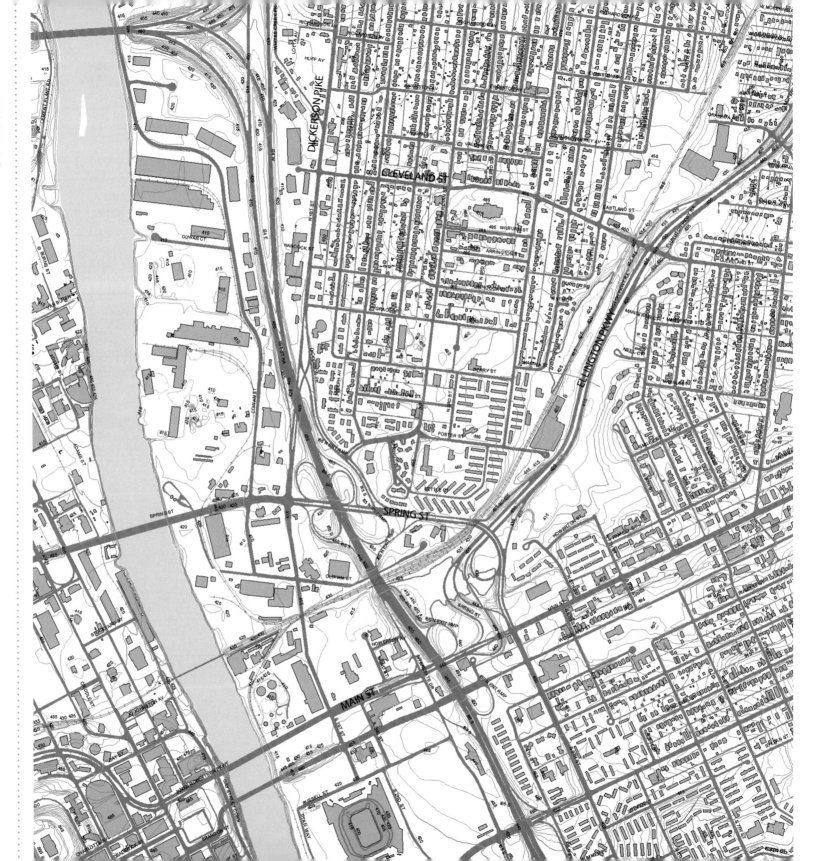

Map showing existing conditions of the Northeast Nashville District. Compare with the Plan's map of the same area on page 159.

(Map, 2002: Metro Planning Department)

NORTHEAST NASHVILLE

Then and Now

When Edgefield was incorporated as a separate city in 1869, the area north of the railroad tracks was called North Edgefield, according to the Metro Historical Commission's *Nashville: Conserving a Heritage*.[9] The area's history as an African American enclave began with the second contraband camp established by the federal troops in 1864. Without a bridge across the Cumberland—destroyed by retreating Confederates in 1862—the river was a barrier preventing thousands of fugitive slaves from reaching Nashville itself. "Because a major railroad ran through the community," writes historian Bobby Lovett, "the Union army used the contraband slaves there to build repair shops and warehouses on the eastern side of the river."[10]

In 1880 Edgefield was annexed into Nashville; by 1908 the city limits had reached what is now Douglas Avenue. Rapid growth was delivered by the streetcars; the main line traveled along First Street and Dickerson Pike, another drove through the neighborhood via Meridian Street and Lischey Avenue before reaching Douglas.

The McFerrin Park neighborhood is south of Cleveland Street, its focal point the park that began as the Meridian Street playground at Meridian Street and Grace Avenue in 1909. The park moved to its present location on what had once been the farm of John B. McFerrin, a Methodist Church leader, in 1920.[11] The Cleveland Park neighborhood is north of Cleveland Street and takes its name from the park that was part of the Nashville Housing Authority's urban renewal program in East Nashville, and was given to the Park Board to administer in 1963. Between Douglas Avenue and Trinity Lane are the Highland Heights and Avondale neighborhoods. Trinity Lane forms the northern edge of Northeast Nashville and lies in the midst of what was the plantation of Thomas Talbot, an early settler and innkeeper whose family cemetery is now in the interstate right-of-way.

The historic "main street" of these neighborhoods is Dickerson Pike, which dates to the late 1700s when Robert Cartwright, a Revolutionary War soldier, was appointed by the Davidson County Court to build a road from Nashville to Mansker's Station in Goodlettsville along what had been a buffalo trail. The Dickerson name came from a misspelling of the last name of Jacob Dickinson, who founded the Dickinson Meeting House, a primitive Baptist Church, on the route. As the main road into the city from the north—some nineteenth-century maps refer to it as Louisville Branch Pike—the street developed with suburban villas and motels, as well as mixed-use and commercial buildings. Many workers at the lumber mills on the East Bank lived in frequently flooded bottomlands at the southern end of the pike, in a black shantytown whose colloquial name—"Crappy Shoot"—is a good indicator of the living conditions.

Large blocks of public housing replaced shanties in 1953, but failed to improve the public perception of the area. In the 1960s the interstate severed Northeast Nashville from the river,

> "We have isolated communities. Let's make them whole."
>
> Raymond Thomas, community workshop participant

Meridian Street in the Cleveland Park neighborhood; lush street trees, sidewalks, on-street parking, and narrow travel lanes create a high-quality streetscape.

(Photograph, 2004: NCDC, Gary Gaston)

Aerial of Northeast Nashville showing how the area is isolated by interstate and Ellington Parkway; dashed marks show the locations of vehicular access. The "spaghetti junction" where Ellington Parkway, Spring Street, Dickerson Pike, and the interstate intertwine is a pedestrian no-man's land in which walkers teeter precariously on the sides of roads to access East Nashville and the bus route on Main Street.

(Diagram over photograph, 2004: NCDC, Gary Gaston)

DOUGLAS AVENUE

CLEVELAND STREET

BRICK CHURCH PIKE

DICKERSON PIKE

ELLINGTON PARKWAY

SPRING STREET

Map showing the proposed
changes in the Plan of Nashville.
(Drawing, 2003: NCDC)

> "The Cumberland River needs to be clean on both sides. You don't wash one ear and leave the other one dirty."

Ray Dayal, community workshop participant

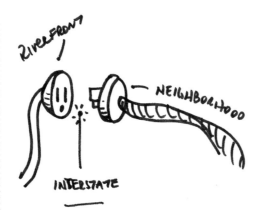

and Ellington Parkway superseded the railroad tracks as the barrier to the rest of East Nashville. Today Northeast Nashville is as effectively barricaded from the rest of the city as a walled medieval town.

This isolation has made Northeast Nashville the city's undiscovered country. The basic neighborhood fabric is of good urban design: a regular grid system with alleys. Most of the streets—especially those south of Douglas Avenue—have sidewalks, mature trees, and on-street parking. The housing stock is generally of good quality, though much is in need of moderate repair, and there are few vacant lots. The area is scattered with churches, schools, community centers, and small commercial centers. Historic structures still standing include the McGavock-Gatewood-Webb Home (early 1800s), the White-Joy home (early 1800s with 1890s addition), the Tony Sudekum home (1890s), Joy's Greenhouse (1879), and the Trinity United Methodist Church (1852). A higher percentage of owner-occupied homes and strong neighborhood organizations would be major aids to revitalization.

The close proximity to downtown and the river, as well as the affordability of the real estate, make Northeast Nashville a prime candidate for preservation, restoration, and redevelopment.

The Plan

The Plan for Northeast Nashville concentrates on establishing a network of connections to the river and East Nashville. The long-term goal is the transformation of the interstate into an urban boulevard (see "Four-Step Program," page 77) that would provide new investment opportunities for the district. More immediate strategies capitalize on the area's adjacency to the Cumberland and create new civic space at the terminus of Ellington Parkway as a focal point for the district.

Natural Features

The Cumberland River forms the natural western edge of the Northeast Nashville neighborhoods. The Plan transforms the layer of industry and interstate that segregates these neighborhoods from the riverfront into a mixed-use neighborhood and public park. Industrial uses

CLEVELAND ST

CUMBERLAND
NE PARK

BRICK CHURCH PIKE

and warehouses, which are not dependent on access to the river, relocate to more appropriate settings. The new development connects to the existing neighborhoods of McFerrin Park and Cleveland Park by streets with generous sidewalks and bikeways.

Cumberland Northeast Park features playing fields as well as non-programmed open space for more informal recreation. The park is traversed by Cumberland Drive, a low-speed pedestrian-and-bike-friendly street that echoes the course of the river and connects to the East Bank greenway to the south. The park is designed to serve not merely as an amenity for local residents, but as an attraction for the larger community in the manner of Shelby, Centennial, and Warner parks. Cumberland NE Park also has a pedestrian bridge to the west that connects to the Neuhoff complex (see "River District," page 155), home of the Nashville Cultural Arts Project, and the East Germantown mixed-use neighborhood. (For further information on linking east and west banks, see "Embracing the Cumberland River," pages 58–71.)

The creation of the Cumberland NE neighborhood is enabled by the transformation of the I-24 right-of-way in Northeast Nashville into an urban boulevard (see "Four-Step Program," page 77). This neighborhood is of medium density—appropriate because of the large amount of public open space nearby for the use of the residents—forming a transition zone between the high density of downtown and the lower densities of the traditional fabric east to Dickerson Pike. The walkability index of the neighborhood is high and there are easy and efficient connections to the public transit system. Cumberland NE also benefits from the revitalization of Dickerson Pike (see "Neighborhood Centers," pages 165–68), which serves as the zipper street

Enlargement of the plan for Cumberland Northeast Park. Note Cumberland Drive, the winding road along the edge of the park.

(Drawing, 2003: NCDC, Gary Gaston)

Illustration of Cumberland
Drive. The top image is a
section through the drive;
lower portion is the plan.

(Drawing, 2004: NCDC, Jason Hill,
Gary Gaston)

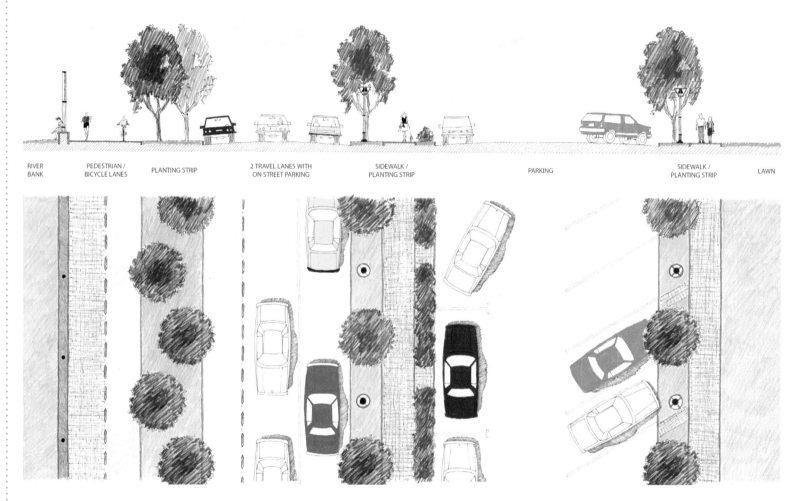

| RIVER BANK | PEDESTRIAN / BICYCLE LANES | PLANTING STRIP | 2 TRAVEL LANES WITH ON STREET PARKING | SIDEWALK / PLANTING STRIP | PARKING | SIDEWALK / PLANTING STRIP | LAWN |

connecting the existing neighborhoods with park and river.

The Ellington neighborhood lies at the new terminus of Ellington Parkway (see "Neighborhood Centers," pages 165–68); its character is mixed-use with a higher preponderance of commercial uses than Cumberland NE. The neighborhood is home to East Station, a multimodal transit hub.

To the interior of the district, heading north, the topography features increasingly rolling terrain, which provides beautiful vistas of downtown. The views of the skyline along Dickerson Pike are some of the best in the city. As with the River District, this topography should be protected—steep slopes should remain undeveloped—and vistas considered when planning new development.

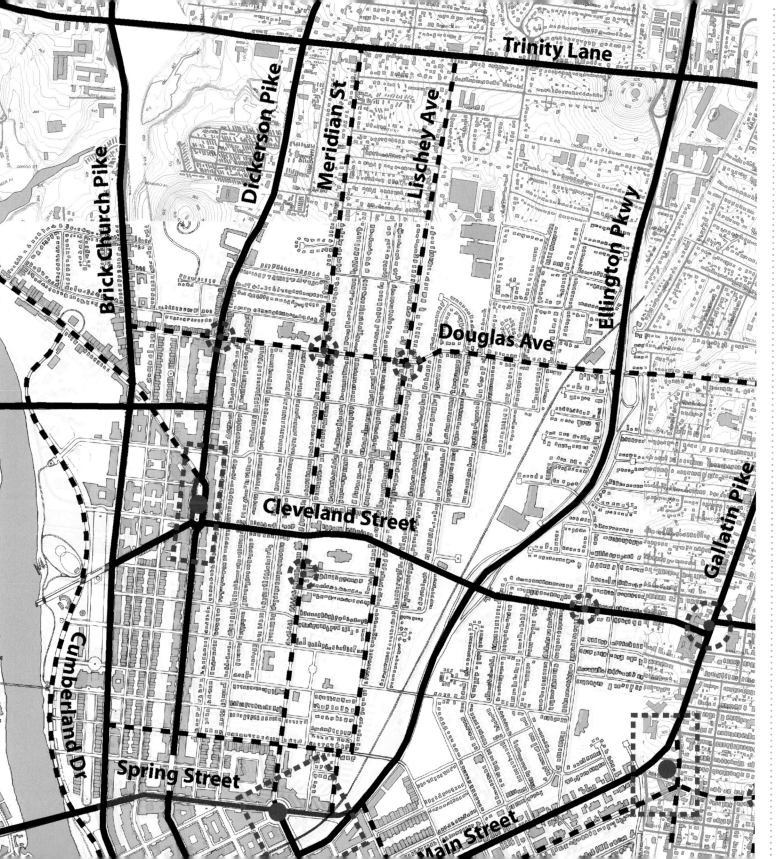

Diagram of streets and centers.
(Diagram, 2004: NCDC)

Map Key

Solid black line: principal streets

Dashed black lines: local streets

Dashed red lines: centers

163

Hierarchy of Streets
Principal Streets

Dickerson Pike as the northern gateway into the
city for commuters as well as for long-distance
travel was replaced in the 1960s by the interstate. The commercial and social life of the pike
rapidly declined, becoming infamous for its
prostitutes and drug dealers. Today the Metro
Development and Housing Agency is targeting
Dickerson Pike with grants to create jobs and
expand business opportunities (see "Neighborhood Centers," pages 165–68).

Numerous impediments to developing the
urban character of Dickerson Pike include deteriorated sidewalks, fences running to the edge
of sidewalks, front-loaded parking with frequent
curb cuts, and vacant lots littered with debris.
These conditions create a visually dishearten-

ing and pedestrian-unfriendly atmosphere. For
those who rely on mass transit, the situation on
Dickerson is even worse. There are only three
bus stops between Douglas Avenue and the
southern terminus, and no bus shelters.

Existing buildings vary widely, from structures in good repair to demolition-ready. Yet
the pike's excellent sightlines to the downtown
skyline and its under-utilized capacity suggest
that the street's value as a gateway into the city
makes it worthy of major redevelopment efforts.

development to Dickerson Pike, the Metropolitan Development and Housing Agency commissioned the Dickerson Pike streetscape plan to address the street's negative elements. The plan has three focal points or centers: Dickerson/Spring Street, Dickerson/Cleveland, Dickerson/Douglas Street.

Brick Church Pike closely parallels the interstate in Northeast Nashville, which severely limits the street's commercial viability and potential as public space. In the Plan for the Cumberland NE and Ellington neighborhoods, the historic pike becomes an urban avenue parallel to Dickerson Pike and a link to the East Bank.

Cleveland Avenue, a major link to East Nashville across Ellington Parkway, is extended to Cumberland NE Park and neighborhood in the Plan.

Local Streets

Among the local streets that feature sections of good urban design and sections in need of restoration are Douglas Avenue, which runs east-west, and Lischey Avenue and Meridian Street, both running north-south and traversing the McFerrin and Cleveland Park neighborhoods.

Neighborhood Centers

Ellington Parkway at its southern terminus is currently a tangle of ramps that participants in the community workshops referred to as "concrete spaghetti" (see "Spaghetti Junction," page 85). The citizens overwhelmingly demanded that this area be reclaimed with a pedestrian-friendly design of urban character. Participants also expressed grave concern about Tennessee Department of Transportation plans to convert the parkway from four to six lanes for the purpose of diverting traffic from the overloaded interstate. The citizen vision for the terminus was that of a traditional urban surface street, and for

This section of Dickerson Pike illustrates the street's problems: continuous curb cuts, eroded sidewalks, hostile environment for mass transit users, and landscape dominated by utility poles and wires.

(Photograph, 2004: NCDC, Gary Gaston)

Plan for Ellington terminus; a triangular green space and roundabout transform the terminus of the parkway. Note the commuter rail line, elevated above the intersection in the same manner as the trestle at Bicentennial Mall.

(Drawing, 2003: NCDC, Gary Gaston)

Perspective sketch of the Ellington Parkway terminus roundabout and transit hub. To the south, the commuter railway is integrated into the design of the triangular green space.

(Drawing, 2004: Frank Orr)

Perspective of Ellington Boulevard, with a linear park or green space almost a block wide that links the river with the proposed transit hub.

(Drawing, 2003: Metro Planning Department, Jerry Fawcett)

Historical image of Dickerson Pike at Cleveland Street.

(Photograph, 1950: Metro Archives)

Existing conditions of Dickerson Pike.

(Photograph, 2003: NCDC)

View of proposed changes to Dickerson Pike.

(Drawing, 2004: NCDC, Gary Gaston)

This intersection was identified in the community workshops as a major focal point for the McFerrin Park and Cleveland Park neighborhoods. The Plan strengthens this intersection as a commercial center for the district, transforming pike into urban boulevard.

Intersection of Wilburn and Meridian Streets; note that while the storefronts have been modified in a way that is hostile to the street, they could easily be returned to their traditional transparency to enhance the good urban design of the building form.

(Photograph, 2004: NCDC, Gary Gaston)

Intersection of Lischey and Douglas Avenues; signage and surface parking are of suburban rather than urban form and erode the quality of the streetscape.

(Photograph, 2004: NCDC, Gary Gaston)

the rest of the road a true "parkway" in the manner of the thoroughfare through Washington, D.C.'s Rock Creek Park, with picturesque landscaping and paths for walking and biking.

The Plan endorses the "Rock Creek" vision, suggesting limits on development and lighting levels flanking the roadway to enhance a park-like atmosphere and the addition of a commuter rail line in the right-of-way (see "Regional Transit," pages 90–91). In addition, the parkway should be bridged in many more locations to create better connections with East Nashville.

For the southern terminus of Ellington Parkway the Plan presents an urban avenue that connects to Spring Street and East Boulevard (which replaces the interstate; see "Four-Step Program," page 77) via a roundabout. East Station, a multi-modal transit hub, is located adjacent to the roundabout, making this intersection a major activity center—"Midtown East." The station is the first city stop for commuter and intercity trains approaching Nashville from the north (Hendersonville, Gallatin, Bowling Green, Louisville); passengers can transfer to local public transit or exit and walk to home or office—or to a Titans game at the stadium.

Housing

Existing private housing in Northeast Nashville is predominantly single-family detached homes of good urban design. Because this housing defines the district's basic physical character, the fact that much of it is rental property and in need of repair is a cause for concern. As with the River District, major efforts should be taken to preserve housing stock through better codes enforcement and the development of financing mechanisms for rehabilitation. Vacant parcels should be redeveloped with new infill that respects the district's traditional urban character. These goals could be more easily accomplished

with the formation of active neighborhood associations.

Constructed in 1953, the public housing of Sam Levy Homes—480 units on thirty acres—had devolved into a chronic source of crime and violence in Northeast Nashville. In response, the Metro Development and Housing Agency sought and received a federal Hope VI grant for the transformation of this housing project, to be replaced with more traditional housing types of lower density—226 duplexes and townhomes—and to include 45 market-rate units to bring

more economic diversity to the site. Demolition began in July 2004 and new construction will be completed in late 2005.

The MDHA plan for Sam Levy Homes is a tremendous improvement over the former housing project and will ultimately have great positive effects on the rest of the neighborhood. But the site's lack of connection to the adjacent neighborhood was outside the scope of MDHA's plan. Until the surrounding street system is reformed, to calm traffic and enable better pedestrian access to the site, the area will remain

isolated. This reformation is an issue for the Tennessee Department of Transportation and the Metro Public Works Department. TDOT's plans to add more lanes to Ellington Parkway have been halted in the wake of citizen protests, but new plans have yet to be revealed.

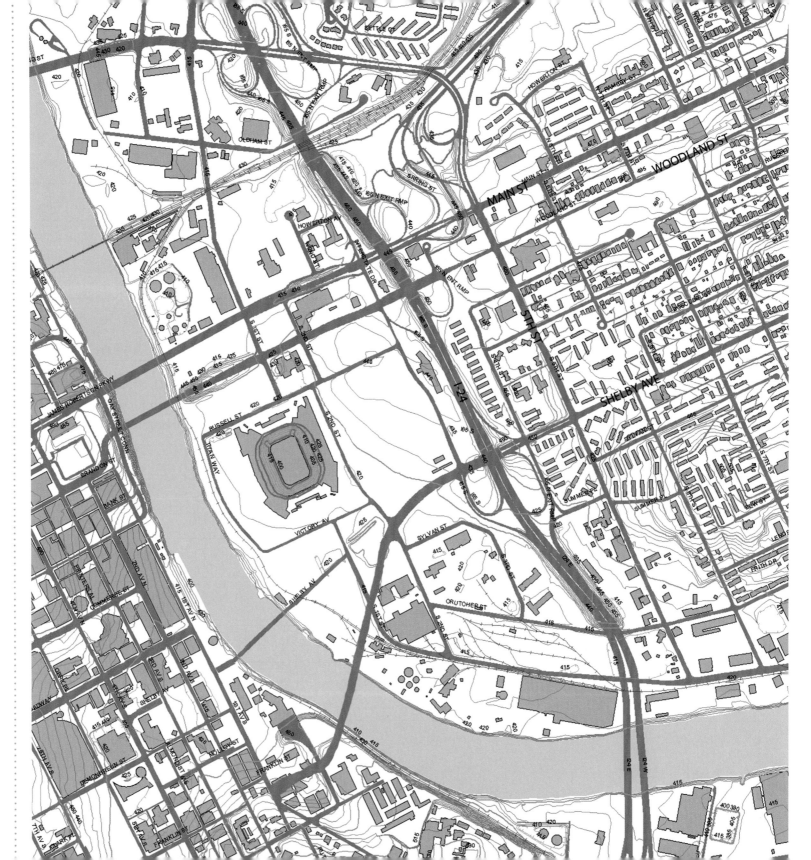

Map showing existing conditions of the East Nashville District. Compare with the Plan's version of the same area on page 175.

(Map, 2002: Metro Planning Department)

EAST NASHVILLE

Then and Now

The river's course has shaped in East Nashville what Michael Fleenor describes (in his introduction to a book of historic images of the district) as "a somewhat separate identity from the city across the Cumberland River, of which it is a part."[12] This perception of separateness—which was real until 1880, when the city of Edgefield was annexed by Nashville—has at times posed problems for the area, but it has also engendered a feeling of community perhaps unmatched in any other part of Nashville.

As with most of Nashville outside the central city, the earliest land use was agricultural. On the first map of Nashville in 1786, what is now Edgefield was the plantation of James Shaw, who was granted the land for service in the Revolutionary War.[13] Ferries were the original means of crossing the Cumberland, until the first bridge was constructed in 1823.

Cultivated land was gradually sold for large estates and "country homes." Dr. John Shelby—whose name adorns park and street—built several of these villas, including "Fatherland" and "Boscobel." The wealthy migrated east seeking cleaner air and more bucolic conditions than downtown provided. With the coming of the mule-drawn streetcar in 1872, estates and farms began to be subdivided into building lots along a traditional grid of streets. Bishop Holland McTyeire first searched for a site for Vanderbilt University in East Nashville, before choosing cheaper land to the west.

By the latter decades of the nineteenth century, the proliferation of industry on the East Bank made the atmosphere of East Nashville less pastoral. Between 1880 and the 1920s, Nashville was a leading market for hardwood,

The Fatherland Estate, built by John Shelby in 1855. Demolished in 1952 for the construction of James A. Cayce Homes.

(Photograph, ca. 1895: Nashville Public Library, The Nashville Room)

> "Let's cross the river."
>
> Jack Cawthon,
> community workshop
> participant

East Nashville after the fire of 1916.

(Photograph, 1916: Tennessee State Library and Archives)

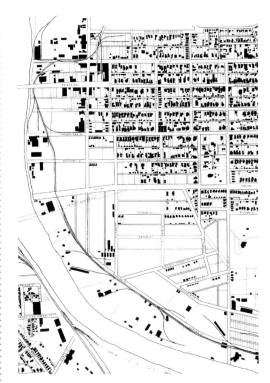

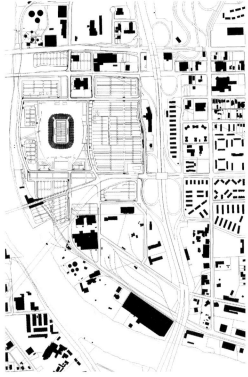

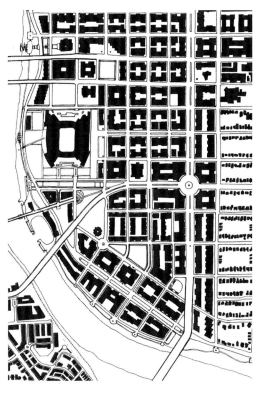

which was felled on the Cumberland Plateau and then floated on the river to the city. Many of the sawmills and furniture factories were on the East Bank, and the prevailing winds blew the noise and dirt to the east.

On March 22, 1916, those same winds blew a fire that had started in the Seagraves Planing Mill into Edgefield, destroying 648 homes; one life was lost and 3,000 people were left homeless. The rubble-strewn empty lots remained through the building slump of World War I, accelerating the migration to newer suburbs opening in the West End.[14] The eventual replacements were more modest cottages and bungalows. Other natural disasters include a flood that covered the East Bank in the winter of 1926–27, and the tornado of 1933 which came to ground in East Nashville, cutting a path of

destruction all the way to Inglewood.

But the calamities with the longest lasting impact were manmade: urban renewal and the interstate. Built in three stages in the 1940s and '50s, James A. Cayce Homes is, at 738 units, the city's largest public housing project. Demolished for Cayce were the historic Shelby Williams mansion, which formed part of Boscobel College, and the "Fatherland" estate, as well as dozens of less grand structures. In their place appeared large housing blocks that turned away from the surrounding streets. The impact was not merely architectural. Such a centralization of poverty bred a culture of crime and violence that leached into the adjacent neighborhoods of Edgefield and Boscobel Heights and beyond.

Urban renewal also delivered the demolition of many other homes and stores and their

replacement with cheaper structures. The interstate blasted through the East Bank in the 1960s; its influence extended beyond the road's right-of-way into nearby residential neighborhoods that became undesirable due to the noise and air pollution. Streets providing access to the interstate were widened. Rezoning enabled the break-up of larger homes into apartments. The percentage of owner-occupied housing declined and absentee landlords arrived. Banks redlined the district with lending policies that restricted the renovation and rehab of the older homes.

In the 1970s, East Nashville began its long slow climb back to respectability. Urban pioneers renovated houses, formed activist neighborhood associations, and recruited individuals who would represent neighborhood interests—rather than those of the slumlords—in the

Metro Council. Neighborhood leaders lobbied for down zoning to duplex maximum in residential areas and historic and conservation zoning overlays administered by the Metro Historic Zoning Commission to guide the preservation of the existing architecture. The Metro Development and Housing Agency offered low-interest loans for facade renovations and established the Five Points Redevelopment District—its first outside downtown—to encourage commercial reinvestment. The location of the football stadium on the East Bank created new bonds between east and west.

When the tornado roared through in 1998, East Nashville was prepared to turn disaster into a great leap forward. In the aftermath, widespread community collaboration with a team of design professionals supplied by the American Institute of Architects produced the R/UDAT (Rural/Urban Design Assistance Team) *Plan for East Nashville.*[15] This plan assessed the area's strengths and weaknesses and created a vision for the future that led to the ReDiscover East district association and design guidelines for the MDHA redevelopment districts to control infill development.

Today East Nashville, one of the most economically and ethnically diverse districts in the city, is seeing increased reinvestment that builds on the footings of the past. The district is composed of many neighborhoods: Edgefield, Douglas Park, East End, Lockeland Springs, Maxwell, Eastwood, Rolling Acres, Rosebank, and East Hill are those with active associations. The street system is a fine-grained network, with alleys, sidewalks, on-street parking, and good access to public transit. The area is dotted with churches, schools, and community centers; Shelby Park and Bottoms, as well as smaller parks, provide recreation and more passive greenspace.

Boscobel Street in Edgefield.
(Photograph, 2004: NCDC, Gary Gaston)

Phoenix Rising

On a cold Sunday afternoon in December 1976, more than two thousand people from all over Middle Tennessee lined up in the rain for the opportunity to go inside two houses and three churches in an East Nashville neighborhood. We had not been sure anyone would come. The east side of the river was perceived to be crime-ridden and derelict, a place to avoid. Indeed, many Nashvillians from other parts of town went from birth to death without ever venturing across the Cumberland into the residential areas there. But the Victorian-era buildings on tour that day, and the stories of the people associated with them, had captured the attention of the media, and people crossed the river.

Identified in a 1975 Metropolitan Historical Commission study of neighborhoods as a top priority because of its concentration of Victorian and early-twentieth-century architecture, Edgefield had just been nominated to the National Register of Historic Places. A neighborhood association was organizing, choosing the phoenix rising from the ashes as its symbol. By 1978, Edgefield had become the city's first historic zoning district, choosing to abide by restrictions to the treatment of building exteriors in exchange for the halting of demolitions and guidance in the design of restoration and new construction.

The Edgefield model of listing in the National Register, marketing itself as a historic neighborhood, and raising awareness of that identity through the media and a public event quickly became a revitalization strategy for numerous other areas. Richland-West End was the next to host a tour and to be listed in the National Register; Germantown followed with its Oktoberfest. The early '80s brought the listing of seven more residential neighborhoods, and one of those, Woodland in Waverly, became the second historic zoning district. In 1985, Nashville became the first city in the nation to create conservation zoning as a less strict standard than that of historic zoning to protect historic neighborhoods; the East End and Lockeland Springs neighborhoods, with more than 1,200 properties, were the first to apply. Now eight conservation zoning districts have been designated, and neighborhoods continue to be added to the National Register. Longtime residents in the urban districts credit the zoning overlays with saving their neighborhoods. At no time was the value of overlays more dramatically evident than in the wake of the 1998 tornado, when East Nashville's historic architecture was protected throughout the restoration and rehabilitation efforts.

While the saving of landmarks such as the Ryman and Union Station first comes to the public mind as our greatest preservation victories, it is the preservation of neighborhoods that has had the most far-reaching impact here in Nashville. The recounting of the listings and designations, though, makes it sound deceptively simple. As recently as the 1970s, the city center was in danger of being ringed by slums; housing stock for all income levels was rapidly being lost; city and business resources were focused on new growth in the suburbs. Longtime owners who hung on and buyers who made major investments were going against the tide of decades of government and business policies. A survey of historic neighborhood residents by our office in 1984 identified their issues: absentee landlords, zoning and code violations, lack of neighborhood services, crime, and the inflexible lending policies of banks headed the list.

Interestingly, "historic preservation" was rarely mentioned by respondents. That survey made it blindingly clear to us that merely saving the buildings is not enough. True neighborhood preservation happens only when the entire environment is healthy; and that health comes through the tenacity and creativity of owners, flexibility and cooperation of the business sector, and the collaboration of government. Nashville has tapped all of those resources, literally bringing old neighborhoods back to life. And the city is infinitely richer for it.

Ann Roberts
Executive Director, Metro Historical Commission

The Plan

The district of East Nashville is inscribed on three sides by the Cumberland River. The northern edge is less easy to define—perhaps Douglas Avenue west of Gallatin Road and Cahal Avenue to the east, although Trinity Lane and McGavock Pike are also possible. The lack of an obvious edge to the north is due to the high degree of connectivity that blurs the boundary between East Nashville and Inglewood. This connectivity among neighborhoods is one of the district's strengths.

The basic concept shaping the Plan for East Nashville extends the fine-grained network of blocks west and south to the river, while reinforcing neighborhood centers and the traditional urban character of the streets.

The East Bank Neighborhood: Connecting to the Cumberland

The East Bank of the Cumberland River is in a period of transition after more than 150 years of devotion to industry. The Coliseum football stadium replaced piles of sand and gravel and decrepit industrial sheds. A link in the greenway system hugs the river bank. The Shelby Bridge has reopened as a pedestrian and bicycle connection to downtown.

But the south section of the East Bank, extending to the entrance to Shelby Park, is still home to mounds of scrap metals and under-

WOODLAND ST

MAIN ST

SHELBY AVE

EAST BLVD

CUMBERLAND DR

Map showing the proposed changes in the Plan of Nashville.
(Drawing, 2003: NCDC)

Opposite: Quick sketch of river overlook done during community vision workshop.
(Sketch, 2003)

175

Perspective view of the East Bank.

(Drawing, 2004: Earl Swensson Associates, Ken Henley)

utilized warehouses. During community workshops, citizens stated that these industrial uses make access to the river and greenway difficult and are not, in the twenty-first century, the highest and best use of land this close to downtown. They expressed similar feelings about the vast parking lot around the Coliseum which, they pointed out, lies largely vacant most days of the year.

A 2002 study of the East Bank, a collaboration between the Nashville Civic Design Center and East Nashville residents, proposed growing the neighborhood fabric into this still-industrial section, capitalizing on the views of the river and the bluffs to the west and healing the gap between greenway and park.[16] The Plan of Nashville's vision for the East Bank is based on this earlier study, but expands the field of action to include the stadium parking and the interstate right-of-way.

The Plan features a mixed-use urban village, with a large triangular civic space at the center flanked by a neighborhood school and surrounded by mixed-use buildings. A roundabout solves the intersection of a series of streets with different alignments and emphasizes the importance of the civic triangle as the symbolic heart of the new neighborhood.

Along the riverfront, industry relocates to more appropriate sites. Hotels and apartment buildings define the edge of a large expanse of riverfront greenway with numerous connections into the neighborhood. Davidson Street is reconfigured as Cumberland Drive, a low speed pedestrian-and-bike-friendly street that echoes the course of the river and runs all the way from Shelby Park to Cumberland NE Park (see "Northeast Nashville," page 161).

In the parking lot around the stadium the historic street grid is restored and the blocks

WALKING TRAILS / FLOWERS / BENCHES

are filled with mixed-use buildings and structured parking wrapped with additional mixed-use space. When the interstate is converted to a boulevard (see below) this restored grid will be fully integrated into the traditional network of East Nashville streets.

Hierarchy of Streets
Principal Streets

East Boulevard is the response to what the community workshops articulated as the district's dominant problem: the interstate as barrier between East Nashville and all the territory to the west. The Plan replaces the interstate with a surface road whose capacity is designed for large volumes of traffic at moderate speeds and is integrated into the existing street system. Roundabouts handle congestion at key intersections. Significant housing and retail of medium density can be programmed into the former interstate right-of-way. What was once a divider becomes a zipper, pulling new and old neighborhoods together. (For further information on the interstate transformation, see "Four-Step Program," page 77.)

Main Street/Gallatin Road is the traditional commuter and long-distance route through East Nashville to downtown and thus has been given the "arterial treatment": a wide road with capacious lanes for high speeds, and continuous commercial zoning at its edges.

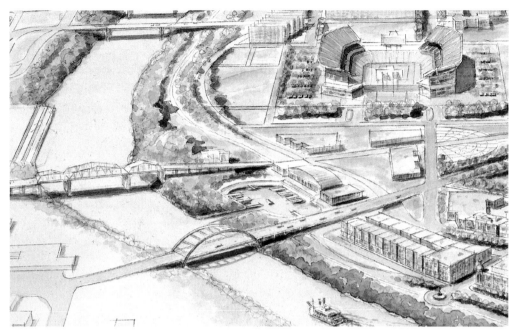

Quick idea sketch done during community vision workshop.
(Sketch, 2003)

Perspective of the East Bank Marina. The Plan features a marina between the Shelby and Gateway bridges, the logical location due to the site's proximity to pedestrian and vehicular links to downtown, the Coliseum, and new East Bank neighborhood.
(Drawing, 2004: Earl Swensson Associates, Ken Henley)

Perspective sketch of East Boulevard at Roundabout.
(Drawing, 2004: Frank Orr)

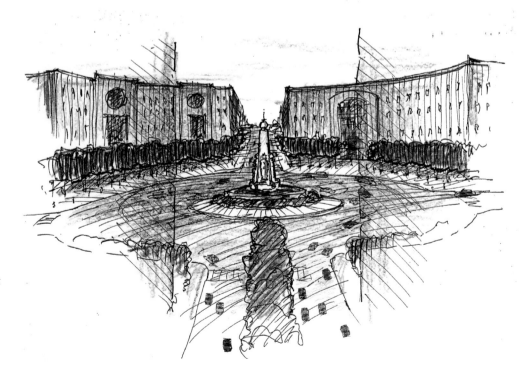

Diagram of streets and centers.
(Diagram, 2004: NCDC)

Map Key

Solid black lines: principal streets

Dashed black lines: local streets

Dashed red lines: centers

Spring Street

Main Street

Shelby Ave

East Blvd

1th St

Main Street lies within the Metro Development and Housing Agency's "East Bank Redevelopment District," which has design guidelines intended to gradually urbanize this street. The number of curb cuts are reduced, on-street parking is introduced, larger sidewalks with planting strips are created, and lighting is of a pedestrian scale. (See also "Taking the Low Road," pages 53–56 and "Reforming the Arterials," pages 74–75 for additional information on reconfiguring Main Street/Gallatin Road.)

Shelby Avenue became a major entrance from East Nashville into the central city with the construction of what was originally called the Sparkman Bridge in 1909. The street, which is the most direct route to Shelby Park, is primarily residential, with the occasional interruption for a store, gas station, or church. At the request of the Public Spaces and Transportation Committee of ReDiscover East—the East Nashville district organization—Metro Public Works recently reduced the number of car lanes in the right-of-way, adding bike lanes and on-street parking. The effect has been slower traffic and a more pedestrian-friendly street.

West of Fifth Street, however, Shelby Avenue becomes car heaven and pedestrian hell: six lanes passing over the interstate before curving into the approach to the Gateway Bridge. This wide, high-speed thoroughfare is dangerous for walkers and bicyclists trying to access the Shelby

Bridge from the east. The Urban Design Committee of ReDiscover East has recently begun to explore strategies with Metro Public Works and the Tennessee Department of Transportation to restore an avenue configuration—modeled on the Civic Design Center's East Bank study of 2002—to this segment of roadway.

Woodland Street serves as the "main street" pulling together the Edgefield, East End, and Lockeland Springs neighborhoods. The fabric lining the street is a mixture of traditional residential and commercial structures and newer, suburban-setback infill with parking out front—the result of urban renewal plans to widen the street to four lanes that were never implemented. Much of Woodland lies within the Metro Development and Housing Agency's East Bank and Five Points Redevelopment Districts, both of which have design guidelines intended to restore the street's traditional urbanism with new

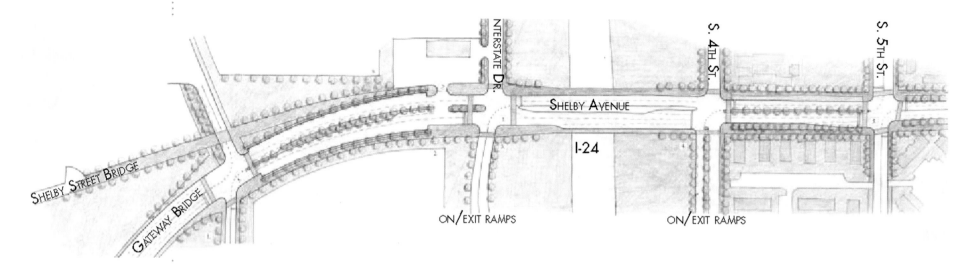

S. 5TH ST.

S. 4TH ST.

INTERSTATE DR.

SHELBY AVENUE

I-24

SHELBY STREET BRIDGE

GATEWAY BRIDGE

ON/EXIT RAMPS

ON/EXIT RAMPS

Above: Shelby Avenue and Gateway Bridge approach.

(Diagram, 2002: *East Bank of the Cumberland River: Findings and Recommendations*, Nashville Civic Design Center)

Fifth Street looking toward Ellington Parkway. The four lanes of Fifth Street currently serve as the high-volume connection between the Gateway Bridge/I-24 and Ellington Parkway; with the transformation of the interstate into East Boulevard, Fifth Street can return to its local character.

(Photograph, 2004: NCDC, Randy Hutcheson)

development that is sensitive to the residential scale of the adjacent neighborhoods.

Local Streets

Tenth Street was widened during urban renewal and the historic homes along it demolished, replaced with ranch houses and large apartment buildings that turned away from the street. The current four lanes are not needed to handle the volume of traffic; the street should therefore be narrowed by replacing the outer lanes with on-street parking and a planting strip. As the buildings along the street reach the end of their useful lives, they should be replaced with residential development more respectful of the traditional neighborhood character.

Neighborhood Centers

Five Points' history as East Nashville's commercial center is reflected in its early-twentieth-century storefronts. Newer infill is of a more suburban character. The area is currently experiencing redevelopment, with restaurants and cafes, an art gallery and garden store that are destinations for Nashvillians in general. Filling in the gaps with shops of good urban design and upper-level residential units—as the design guidelines for the Metro Development and Housing Agency's *Five Points Redevelopment*

Left: Early-twentieth-century storefronts on Woodland Street in Five Points epitomize the "neighborhood center" ideal.

Right: On the opposite side of the 1000 block of Woodland Street is the hostile makeover of the former Woodland Street Theater, totally out of character with its neighbor across the street.

(Photographs, 2004: NCDC, Gary Gaston)

Iconic buildings at the civic square site: East Library, East Literature Magnet School, and Woodland Presbyterian Church.

(Photographs, 2004: NCDC, Gary Gaston)

Plan prescribe—will complete the restoration of Five Points as the commercial centerpiece of the East Nashville community.

In addition to the centers described above, East Nashville is replete with what are called "commercial corners": small stores occupying one or more corners of an intersection in what is otherwise residential fabric. Big-box retail, chain stores, and strip malls have made such structures less viable for basic retail. But many have found new life as restaurants, bakeries, music clubs, art galleries, and boutiques. These corners illustrate how commercial and residential can be successfully integrated if the scale and design of each is compatible.

Civic Space

One of the major recommendations to emerge from the post-tornado R/UDAT study of East Nashville was for the creation of a central public space at the point where Main Street pivots

Corner of Thirteenth and Holly Streets.

(Photograph, 2004: NCDC, Gary Gaston)

to become Gallatin Road. This topographical high point, with splendid views of the downtown skyline, features several buildings of strong civic presence and dignity: East Carnegie Library, which dominates the site and is flanked by East Literature Magnet School, and the Woodland Presbyterian Church. The adjacency to Five Points, and the need to heal the great divide made by the width and fast traffic of Gallatin Road, also recommend this as the location of complementary public space that showcases East Nashville's cultural life. Metro government has recently provided funds for the development of a landscape master plan for the East Civic Square.

Housing

East Nashville housing stock is largely single-family detached homes of good urban design and represents the highest concentration of Victorian architecture in the city. Great strides have been made in the restoration and rehabilitation of this residential fabric. New infill, including some scattered site affordable housing, generally respects the architectural character of the district. Problem sites—and inadequate codes enforcement—persist, but are gradually being eliminated due to the rise in real estate values.

The biggest remaining housing challenge in East Nashville is found south of Shelby Avenue: James A. Cayce Homes, the largest public housing project in the city. Federal Hope VI grants have enabled the Metro Development and Housing Agency to replace similar public housing at several sites around Nashville with a less dense fabric of affordable and market-rate residences. The size of Cayce, however, will require a much larger infusion of federal dollars. When they are secured, the site should be redeveloped with architecture of good urban design in a manner that reknits the traditional street network and takes advantage of river views from the hillcrests.

Aerial view of James A. Cayce Homes.

(Photograph, 2003: Metro Planning Department)

SHELBY AVE

5TH ST

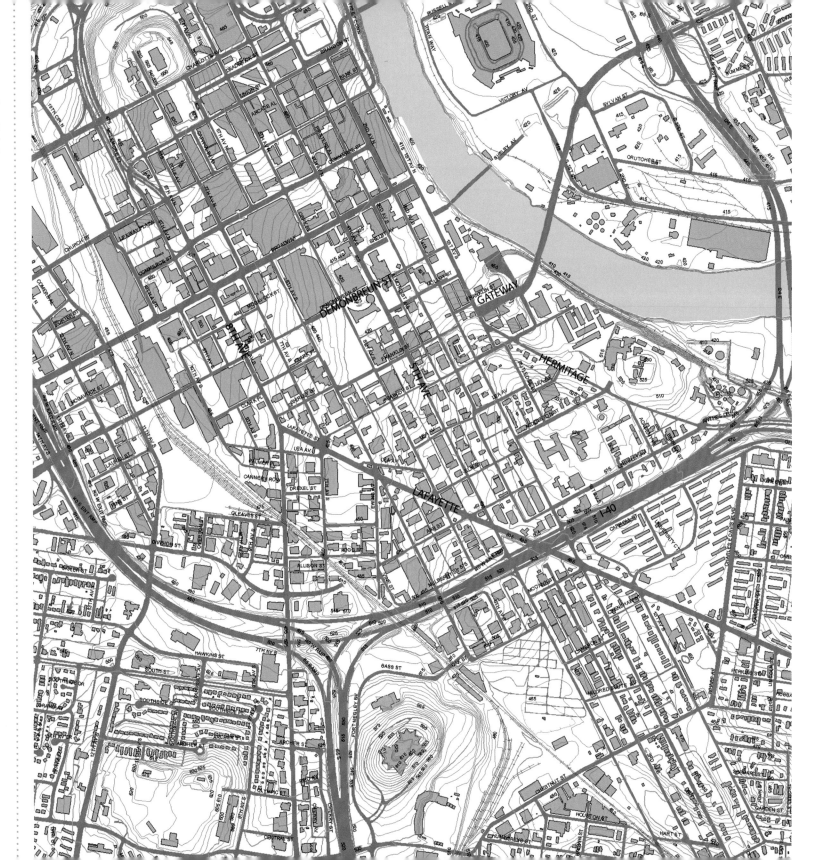

Map showing existing
conditions of the SoBro District.
Compare with the Plan's version
of the same area on page 189.

(Map, 2002: Metro Planning Department)

184

SOBRO

Then and Now

"SoBro" is a relatively new name for the district of Nashville that stretches south of Broadway to the interstate and west to the Gulch. The designation was coined by the *Nashville Scene* in the mid 1990s, during the controversy over state and local government plans to build a six-lane corridor through the area, bridging the Cumberland to connect I-24 to the east with I-40 to the west.

Historically, the district was rarely considered as a whole, perhaps due to the striking changes in topography, land use, and social geography among the floodplain near the river, the hill to the south, and gradually rising ground to the west. The lowland to approximately Fifth Avenue emerged after the Civil War as "Black Bottom," not because its population was largely African American—although it subsequently became so—but because of "frequent flooding and the ever-present black mud and stagnant pools of filthy water," according to historian Bobby Lovett.[17] The neighborhood was first home to poor white immigrants, soon joined by working class freedmen, who together supplied the labor for the growing industries to the south. By 1870 Black Bottom had more than three thousand residents crowded into 741 tenements.

As the white immigrants increasingly occupied the higher-rent properties on the slope up to the west, the Bottom became overwhelmingly black, and African American institutions appeared to serve them. St. Paul, the second oldest African Methodist Episcopal Church, still stands on the southeast corner of Fourth Avenue and Franklin Street (now occupied by Everton Oglesby Architects). The Pearl School was founded in Black Bottom in 1883, subsequently relocating to North Nashville in 1917 at the re-

Downtown and South Nashville, with Black Bottom indicated.

(Map, ca. 1900: Tennessee State Library and Archives)

"Make the politicians come across Broadway."

Zach Liff, community workshop participant

quest of middle-class blacks distressed by the surrounding shanties, saloons, and brothels.

Equally distressed were white Nashvillians who proposed various "urban renewal" schemes—the first, in 1888, a park—to obliterate the slum. In 1893 the city condemned some tenements for construction of the Hay Market, where farmers migrated from the public square to sell hay and swap horses. In 1907 the South Nashville Women's Federation lobbied for a city bond issue for the park, as well as a bridge across the river, to eliminate Black Bottom. The Sparkman Street Bridge (now Shelby Bridge) was constructed in 1909 to terminate near the Hay

Market, displacing some shanties as industrial warehouses located nearby. But the park bond issue failed in 1910, in part, according to historian Don Doyle, "because of fears that slum dwellers would only migrate to middle-class neighborhoods."[18]

The industries utilizing Black Bottom's labor pool were largely devoted to grain. The Gerst brewery was located in South Nashville, as were mills for the processing of flour and meal, which by the turn of the last century were Nashville's leading wholesale products. Large roller mills were constructed on the river bluffs, leading to the name "Roller Mill Hill" (now called "Rolling Mill Hill").[19]

Slightly to the west, Rutledge Hill had a different tone entirely. The name derives from one of South Nashville's first families, Henry Middleton and Septima Sexta—"76"—Rutledge, South Carolina natives whose fathers had both signed the Declaration of Independence.[20] In 1814 the Rutledges constructed a large villa with elaborate terraced gardens on the slope leading to the hill's crest which they called "Rose Hill." (Portions of the villa were incorporated into the house that still stands at 101 Lea Avenue).

The Rutledges and other early residents were attracted by what crowned the hill: Davidson College (1803–6), which became Cumberland College (1806–26) and then the University of Nashville (1826–75). The campus, known as College Hill, which also served as the early meeting place of what became the Vanderbilt Medical School, ultimately featured several distinguished buildings, including the central Gothic Revival structure designed by Adolphus Heiman (1853) that is now occupied by the Metro Planning Department. Surrounding this collegiate center were fashionable townhouses. South Nashville was the first Nashville suburb to be incorporated as a separate city in 1850; in

1854 it was annexed by Nashville proper. But after the University of Nashville became Peabody College and went west along with the medical school, Rutledge Hill was gradually abandoned as a residential neighborhood.

The river bluffs east of Rutledge Hill have been occupied by government services since the location of the first reservoir there in 1833. The Tennessee School for the Blind opened nearby in 1872 (razed in 1959). Nashville General Hospital followed in 1890, to take advantage of the proximity to the medical school, occupying the

first building of what would become a sprawling complex.

The arrival of the electric streetcar in Nashville in 1888 opened up land to the southwest and west of the city for suburban development. Inscribed by railroad tracks and yards, South Nashville, with the exception of Rutledge Hill, was increasingly dominated by industrial uses. Residents who could afford to leave did so. By 1920, those who remained composed a racial crazy quilt of mill hands, carpenters, coal haulers, and common laborers living in poor working-class residences interspersed among warehouses and factories.[21]

As heavy industry peaked and declined in South Nashville, replaced by the smaller sheds of light industry, South Nashville became increasingly depopulated. Many residences were demolished, and those remaining were taken over by businesses. To the south, public housing projects were constructed in the Cameron-Trimble neighborhoods in the 1940s and '50s; in the 1960s the interstate created one-way high-speed

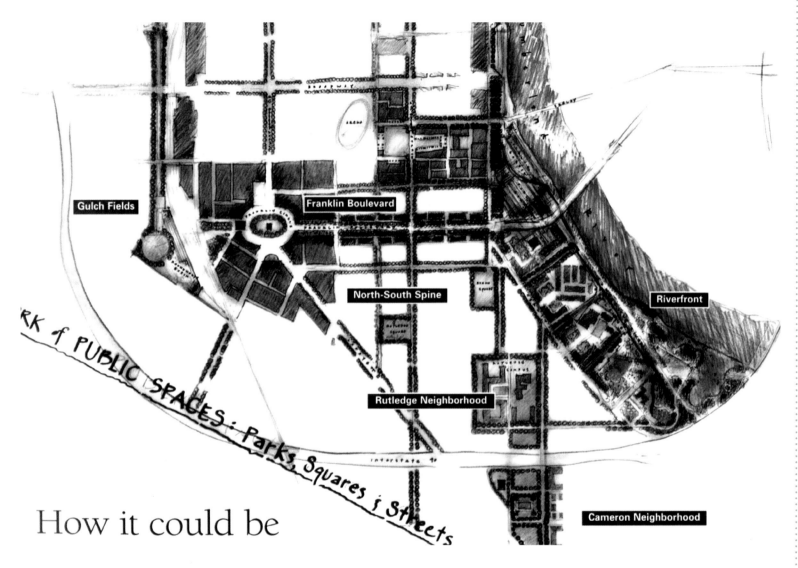

"How it could be," *The Plan for SoBro.*

(Drawing, 1997: Warren Byrd for *Nashville Scene*, City Press Publishing)

Map labels: Gulch Fields · Franklin Boulevard · North-South Spine · Rutledge Neighborhood · Riverfront · Cameron Neighborhood · RK of PUBLIC SPACES: Parks, Squares ; Streets · Interstate 4º · BROADWAY

How it could be

access routes on Second and Fourth Avenues. The Nashville Thermal Plant began to burn garbage on the riverbanks in 1972 and Metro government offices took over the College Hill campus.

So much of the historic architectural fabric was replaced by incompatible infill that the National Park Service rejected the nomination of Rutledge Hill to the National Register of Historic Places in 1976 on the grounds that

too many structures had already been lost. (A smaller district consisting of eleven structures was listed in 1980.) New apartment construction flanking the hill was largely on the suburban model and contributed little to the streetscape. Vacant and underutilized parcels littered the landscape. Adult entertainment businesses and homeless shelters moved in.

In 1995, when Metro's Planning and Pub-

lic Works departments announced plans to construct a seven-lane high-speed corridor through the area roughly on the irregular path of the much smaller Franklin Street, it seemed that the sacking of South Nashville was about to be complete. The battle to tame the corridor into an avenue took almost five years to win. In the process, however, the focus on the area south of Broadway, now called SoBro, created a new

James Geddes Engine Company
Number 6, historic firehall
converted to office use on
Second Avenue South in
Rutledge Hill.

(Photograph, 2004: NCDC, Raven Hardison)

SoBro's warehouse buildings,
like this one on Eighth Avenue
South, offer excellent potential
for loft housing development.

(Photograph, 2004: NCDC, Raven Hardison)

Quick idea sketch done during
community vision workshop.

(Sketch, 2003)

awareness of the area's latent promise, a promise articulated in *The Plan for SoBro,* published by the *Nashville Scene* in 1997, and reaffirmed by The Subarea 9 Master Plan Update later in the same year.[22]

Despite all the demolition, SoBro is still home to significant architecture of diverse styles. On the south side of Broadway are Union Station, the Frist Center in the old Post Office, and the Customs House. The industrial monuments of Cummins Station and the Cannery line the eastern side of the Gulch, and other warehouses worthy of rehabilitation are scattered throughout the district. On Rutledge Hill, landmarks include Lindsley Hall, Litterer Laboratories, James Geddes Engine Company Number 6—the last firehall in the city to use horse-drawn equipment—and the Lindsley Avenue Church of Christ and other historic churches, as well as a number of late-nineteenth-century homes. On the river bluffs, the historic segments of General Hospital as well as the 1930s Metro car barns are to be incorporated into new development planned for Rolling Mill Hill (see below).

New architecture of distinction includes the Nashville Arena (now Gaylord Entertainment Center) and the Country Music Hall of Fame and Museum. Construction began on the Schermerhorn Symphony Center in 2003, the same year that the undistinguished architecture of the Thermal Plant began to be demolished. The city is currently studying options for the redevelopment of the Thermal site.

New and rehabilitated transportation infrastructure will supply better connectivity to and

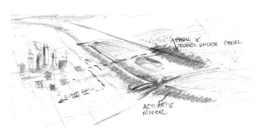

within the district. The Gateway Bridge and Shelby Pedestrian Bridge provide access across the river from the east; the Demonbreun viaduct—under reconstruction—is a major entrance across the Gulch from the west. The future Franklin Corridor-turned-Gateway Boulevard will furnish better east/west circulation.

Perhaps the most important step in realizing the potential of SoBro was taken when Metro government began to explore the creation of a mixed-use neighborhood on the river bluffs formerly occupied by the roller mills and General Hospital. The Metro Development and Housing Agency subsequently commissioned a master plan for the thirty-four-acre site and has commenced installing the infrastructure—streets, sidewalks, water and sewer lines—necessary for redevelopment.

Today SoBro, with its acres of surface parking, is wide open and waiting for redevelopment.

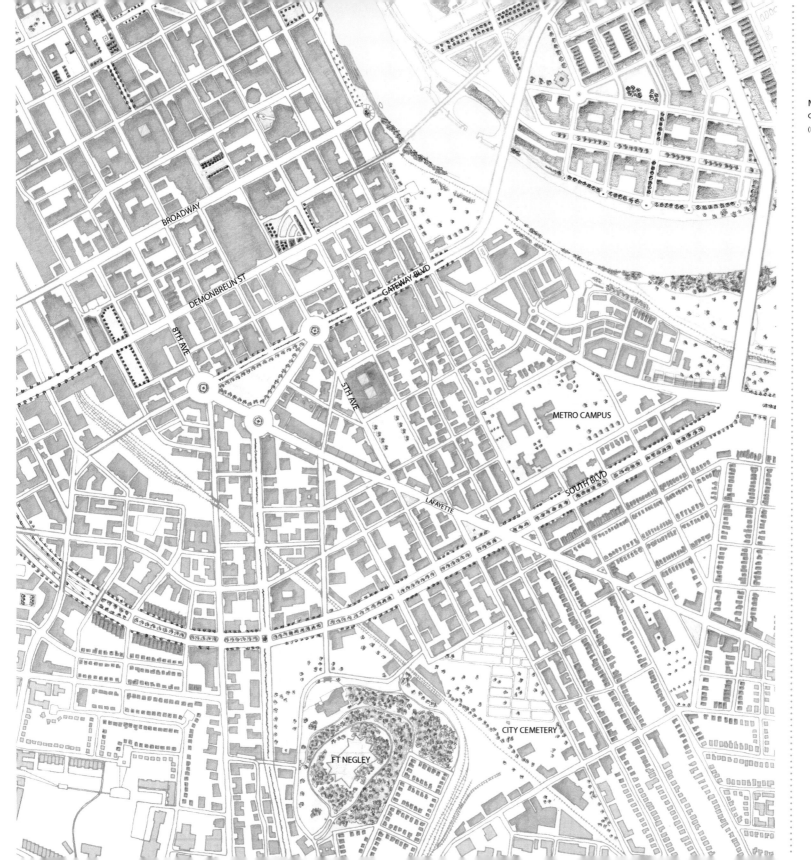

Map showing the proposed
changes in the Plan of Nashville.
(Drawing, 2003: NCDC)

BROADWAY

DEMONBREUN ST

8TH AVE

GATEWAY BLVD

5TH AVE

METRO CAMPUS

SOUTH BLVD

LAFAYETTE

CITY CEMETERY

FT NEGLEY

The Plan

The Plan of Nashville's vision for SoBro builds on that of the 1997 community charrette that produced *The Plan for SoBro*. The latter assessed the strengths and weaknesses of the district, proposed that the Franklin Corridor plan be modified to the design of an urban avenue, and in general called for the redevelopment of the district into a mixed-use neighborhood of a more dense urban character than is found in East Nashville or the River District, yet of a lesser scale—mid-rise not high-rise—than is found in downtown. The Plan of Nashville endorses these basic concepts, and expands upon them.

Natural Features

The topographical variety of SoBro—river banks and river bluffs, bottomland and hills, rising ground to the west abruptly terminating in the Gulch—gives the district its unique character. In response to this topography, the orthogonal grid is skewed to accommodate the historic pikes that pass between the hills to the southwest. As a result, the texture of SoBro's streets—their irregular frequency, length, and termination; intersections where more than two streets cross; triangular lots; diagonal sightlines—is distinct from that of downtown. This pattern should be emphasized by better definition of the street walls as consistent planes of architecture.

On one of the hills to the southwest lies the ruins of Fort Negley, constructed in 1862 by fugitive slaves overseen by the occupying Union troops and reconstructed under the federal Works Progress Administration during the 1930s. After years of neglect, the fort is currently being reconfigured as an educational venue to interpret the city's Civil War history and will serve, along with the historic City Cemetery on the hill's flank, as a green buffer at the edge of the SoBro district.

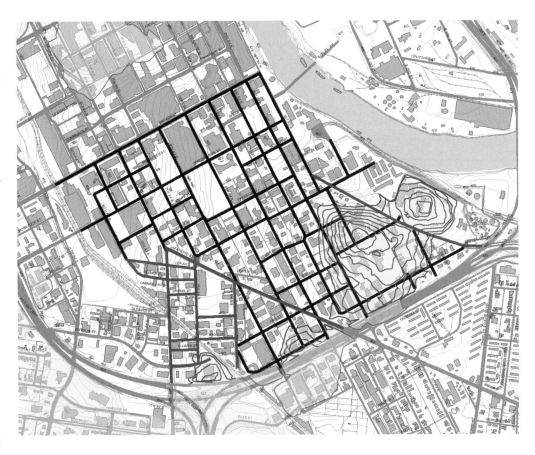

The most obvious strategy to capitalize on the river edge of SoBro is to develop it with uses for which a river view is an amenity: public greenspace and mixed-use structures featuring retail—such as restaurants and cafes—at first level and residences above. This is already in the works on the bluffs of Rolling Mill Hill, where the Metro Development and Housing Agency is in the preliminary stages of plotting a new urban neighborhood.

The clearing of the Thermal site in 2004 also opened up valuable river real estate for redevelopment; the fact that the eleven acres are Metro-owned enables the city to dictate its highest and best use in a way that advances the public interest. Current discussion centers on a baseball stadium for the Nashville Sounds, surrounded by mixed-use buildings.

For thirty years Nashvillians have looked away from this section of the riverfront because of the ugliness of what it contained. Even before the land was cleared and its dimensions and contours visually apprehended, however, citizens in the community workshops suggested that a park would provide a welcome amenity for a district conspicuously lacking in civic and park space. In determining the future of the site, the analysis should consider what SoBro needs for the district to become a quarter of neighborhoods that serve as a strong support to downtown.

Whatever proposal is realized, care should be taken to enable public access to the Cumberland River in the form of a greenway along the edge and the creation of strong sightlines to the river from east/west streets. The treatment of First

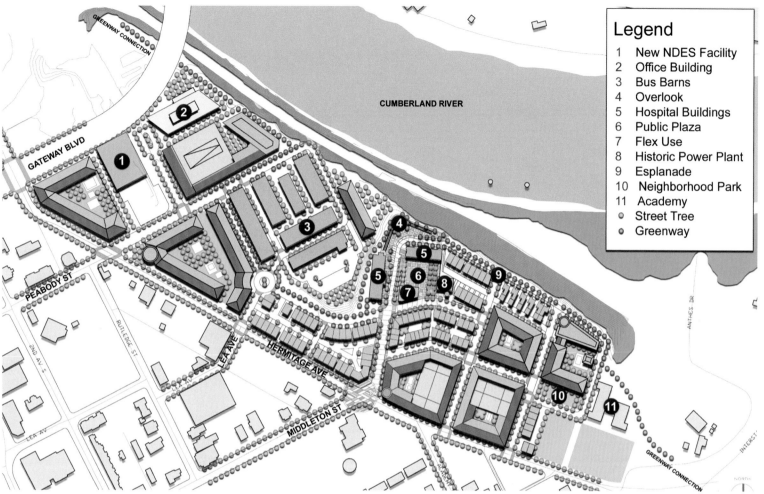

Legend

1   New NDES Facility
2   Office Building
3   Bus Barns
4   Overlook
5   Hospital Buildings
6   Public Plaza
7   Flex Use
8   Historic Power Plant
9   Esplanade
10 Neighborhood Park
11 Academy
○   Street Tree
●   Greenway

Site plan and schematic from
Rolling Mill Hill Development
Guidelines.

(Drawing, 2003: RTKL for the Metro
Development and Housing Agency)

Avenue should produce a pedestrian-friendly thoroughfare with continuous street walls of sufficient transparency at ground level to reinforce the sociability of the space. Height restrictions should preserve sightlines to downtown from the rising ground to the south.

Because of the varied topography, the treatment of building heights is an important issue for all of SoBro. The district boasts fine views of the downtown skyline as it steps up the hill to the north. Establishing limits to the scale to preserve these views from the rising land to the south and west will enhance the entire district's development potential. The Plan suggests, there-

fore, that building heights guidelines for SoBro be devised to maintain a consistent view shed for the district.

Hierarchy of Streets

While the north/south streets provide a great deal of connectivity between "NoBro" and So-Bro, the wide dimensions of Broadway form a strong boundary between the two parts of town. The perception of Broadway as borderland is enhanced by the superblocks immediately to the south. This sense of distinction need not be a negative, if the rear facades of the buildings on the south side of Broadway, as well as the

streetscape entering the district, are recognized as border elements worthy of design treatment that announces "this is where SoBro begins" rather than "this is where the nice part of downtown ends."

Principal Streets
South Boulevard
An even more obvious manmade boundary is the interstate to the south of SoBro. The elevated highway forms a barrier between neighborhoods and concentrates high volumes of traffic at the access points. Cars racing to and from downtown turn the one-way pairs of Second and

Diagram of streets and centers.
(Diagram, 2004: NCDC)

Map Key

Solid black lines: principal streets

Dashed black lines: local streets

Dashed red lines: centers

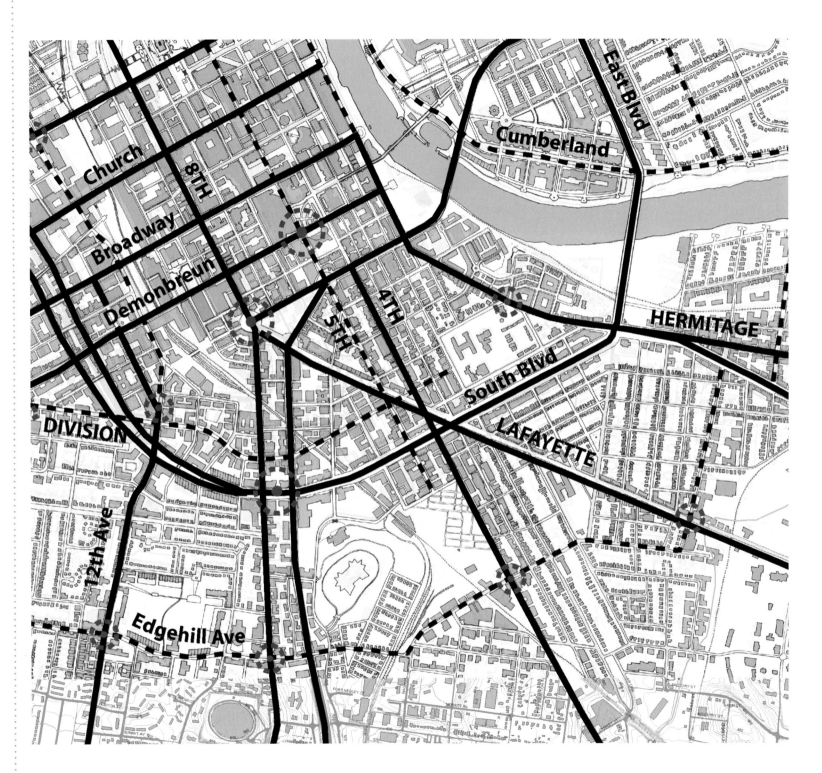

Aerial view of South Boulevard at Fourth Avenue South. The urban boulevard allows for high levels of traffic in the center lanes, and lower-speed neighborhood traffic with on-street parking in the outer lanes. Note how public transit is incorporated into the median of the boulevard.

(Digital illustration, 2004: Earl Swensson Associates, Corey Little)

Fourth Avenues into high-speed corridors that fracture the district and deter pedestrian travel. In the community workshops, citizens complained that the volume and speed of traffic, and the noise and air pollution, are detrimental to the quality of life of residents on both sides of the interstate divide

In the Plan, this south loop of the interstate is transformed into South Boulevard, a heavily landscaped surface road whose capacity is designed for large volumes of traffic at mod-erate speeds and is integrated into the existing street system. Instead of the existing five links between SoBro and the South Nashville neighborhoods, the Plan envisions thirteen, dispersing traffic to lessen its impact. Significant housing and retail of medium density can be programmed into the former interstate right-of-way. What was once a divider becomes a zipper, pulling the neighborhoods together. (For further information on the interstate transformation, see "Four-Step Program," page 77.)

Demonbreun Street has been previously considered in the Plan as a cultural axis (see "Cardo and Decumanus," pages 110–13); here the focus is on the street as a well-designed urban avenue that will link the cultural venues. Artist Jack Mackie is currently working with the Metro Arts Commission to incorporate public art into the Demonbreun streetscape, which will extend the cultural theme into the public right-of-way.

Left: Perspective view of corner block along South Boulevard. The mixed-use building type is activated at the ground level with transparent storefronts, shops, and cafes that spill onto the street. Residents in the units above also help to populate the street.

(Digital illustration, 2004: Earl Swensson Associates, Corey Little)

Center: Comparison images:

Existing conditions, with interstate cutting off access between neighborhoods.

(Map, 2002: Metro Planning Department)

The Plan for the area, with buildings addressing a fine-grained network of streets.

(Drawing, 2003: NCDC)

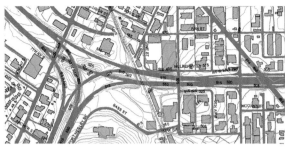

Looking south along Seventh Avenue; note the Adventure Science Center to the left, no longer isolated by the interstate. With the transformation of the interstate inside of I-440, Seventh Avenue South becomes a grand urban avenue.

(Drawing, 2003: Metro Planning Department, Jerry Fawcett)

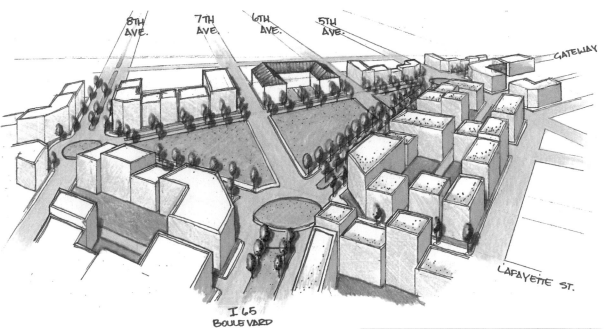

8TH AVE. 7TH AVE. 6TH AVE. 5TH AVE. GATEWAY

LAFAYETTE ST.

I 65 BOULEVARD

The three major streets cutting diagonally through the district are enhanced as grand avenues and meet at a triangular lawn. The roundabouts handle congestion and resolve the intersections of the diagonal streets with Gateway Boulevard.

(Drawing, 2003: Metro Planning Department, Jerry Fawcett and Lee Jones)

Perspective view of Gateway Boulevard. Currently under construction, Gateway Boulevard will be the "main street" and mixed-use center of the SoBro district.

(Drawing, 1997: Everton Oglesby Askew Architects, from the Subarea 9 Masterplan Update of 1997)

Right top: Demonbreun looking east. The smokestack of the Thermal Plant has since been demolished.

(Photograph, 2003: NCDC, Andrea Gaffney)

Right bottom: Demonbreun looking west.

(Photograph, 2003: NCDC, Andrea Gaffney)

Clockwise from top left:

Street section of Hermitage Avenue from the Rolling Mill Development Guidelines, which call for a small-scale, pedestrian-friendly street with a total of three travel lanes, and for the preservation of the historic stone wall that flanks the sidewalk. Because First Avenue/Hermitage Avenue has the potential to serve as the "zipper" between the Rutledge Hill and Rolling Mills Hill neighborhoods, plans to widen the thoroughfare should not be implemented.

(Digital illustration, 2003: RTKL for the Metro Development and Housing Agency)

Second Avenue South (shown here), along with Fourth Avenue, in SoBro has a much less pedestrian-friendly character than the sections of these streets north of Broadway; this is the result of their conversion to high-speed, one-way pairs to handle the large volumes of traffic fleeing and seeking the interstate. Traffic calming is best accomplished by returning all the SoBro sections of these streets to two-way traffic.

Residential street in Rolling Mill Hill, which lies between the river and Hermitage Avenue, Gateway and South Boulevards. The master plan commissioned by MDHA calls for a residentially focused neighborhood that takes advantage of the fine views of the river and downtown.

(Drawing, 1997: Dede Christopher from *The Plan for SoBro,* 1997)

Comparison of figure grounds of Rutledge and Rolling Mill Hills, 1908 (top) and 1997 (bottom), shows nine decades of changes. The building fabric has become much less intricate and complex, and is dominated instead by large building blocks.

(Drawings, 2001: NCDC, Ted Booth)

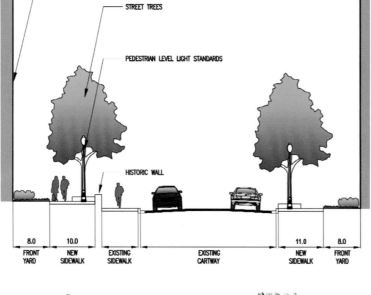

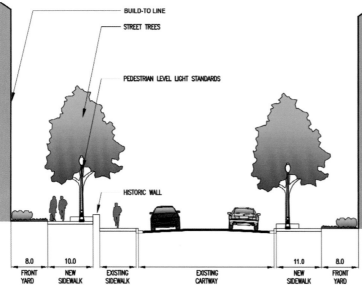

Local Streets

Fifth Avenue south of Demonbreun Street needs an infusion of urban character; the terminus of the avenue at the City Cemetery should be strengthened with a ceremonial marker or gateway.

Neighborhood Centers

Unlike the River District and Northeast and East Nashville, SoBro today presents few clues as to neighborhood centers. This is the result of dramatic changes in the pattern of buildings and use of land in the district over the last hundred years.

Parks and Civic Space

The lack of parks and civic space is a striking feature of SoBro. The Hall of Fame Park on Demonbreun Street between Fourth and Fifth Avenues is a small, prosaic space that is rarely used. The Plan strongly suggests that the original design for the park, which included a covered performance space and programming to activate the park, be implemented.

Neighborhood parks on Rutledge Hill were all but eliminated when the area ceased to be residential. In 1980, the two-acre Howell Park at Third Avenue South and Peabody Street was sold for a condominium development. At the same time, South Park shrank to little more than the size of the tennis courts that flank the building housing the Metro Planning Department, when more than ten acres of the park were sold for another condo project. Selling off park space for residential development for which park space would be an amenity seems, to say the least, to have been counterintuitive.

The Metro government campus, which occupies the former precincts of the University of Nashville, makes no pretensions to civic distinction despite the presence of the fine architecture of Lindsley Hall at its center. The placement of later buildings blocks sightlines to this

landmark, and the rest of the site is largely devoted to surface parking, some of which is surrounded by chain-link fencing topped with razor wire. Future development of this campus should consider, not merely the needs of Metro for office and parking space, but the relationship to the Rutledge Hill and Rolling Mill Hill neighborhoods.

The Plan provides new park space as part of the campus of the new elementary school proposed for a site between Fourth and Fifth Avenues South (see "Back to School" below). This open space will be shared by the students, who

The new Symphony Hall will be a focal point of the Demonbreun Neighborhood, which stretches from Broadway to the north side of Gateway Boulevard, between the river and the Gulch. This neighborhood has a central focus on the arts and entertainment, which should be strengthened by the addition of housing for the performers and artists who frequent the cultural venues.

(Quick sketch from community vision workshop, 2003)

Location for new elementary school and park in SoBro. White dashed line: school site; green: park space.

(Diagram over photograph, 2004: NCDC, Gary Gaston)

Back to School

Chattanooga's Battle Academy, built in 2003, offers an urban environment for an elementary school.
(Photograph, 2004: NCDC, Andrea Gaffney)

One potential source of civic space in SoBro is also what the greater downtown area needs to enhance its residential prospects—an elementary school. Other cities in Tennessee have realized that a school is a crucial component in urban neighborhood building. They have constructed schools in the downtown area, not to meet the needs of current residents, but to attract a new residential population more varied than the typical empty-nesters and twenty-somethings.

Memphis recently completed a new public elementary school in a developing urban village adjacent to its AAA baseball stadium and within easy walking distance of the historic Peabody Hotel. Chattanooga has gone Memphis one better, with two new public elementary schools.

The original proposal by the Department of Education of Hamilton County, which serves Chattanooga, was to build one K–5 magnet school for the approximately four hundred children who were being bused several miles out. Chattanooga's urban revivalists had a more ambitious plan. They reasoned that with only one school, it would be filled on opening day, mostly with poor children. School superintendent Jesse Register didn't want to create a "school of poverty," and urban advocates wanted growing room for subsequent residential development. The solution was two magnet schools. To supply the additional funding, the private sector kicked in eight million dollars.

To ensure a diverse student population and fill the classrooms until dwellings catch up with desks, the school system devised a special enrollment plan. Top priority for admission to the magnets goes to downtown residents, then to children of downtown workers.

Site selection was driven by the need to find land at low or no cost. One of the schools is located on city-owned property in Chattanooga's Southside, a once-blighted industrial and marginally residential area similar to SoBro. Battle Academy rests on 3.3 acres, considerably smaller than the typical eight-to-thirteen-acre campus of a Hamilton County suburban school. The tight site required building up—two stories—rather than out; recesses are staggered because of the smaller playground, which also serves after hours as a public park.

The second school, Brown Academy, stands on a still-smaller parcel: 2.5 acres owned by the University of Tennessee next to an abandoned rail corridor-turned-greenway that is part of the playground. The constricted site caused the school to rise to three stories; parking is shared after school hours with the neighborhood, mostly university student housing. Both schools provide field experience for the university's education program.

SoBro seems a logical location for an elementary school to serve downtown. The district as a whole is easily accessed from the central city to the north, offers large amounts of undeveloped and under-utilized land, and is the site of cultural institutions that could partner with the school in educational programming. Much of SoBro lies within the boundaries of Metro Development and Housing Agency redevelopment districts, giving the city the power to acquire land for a school.

The Board of Education's current guidelines for public elementary schools, however, call for a minimum lot size of five acres, with an additional acre for each one hundred students. A typical Metro elementary school has approximately six hundred students, which would mandate an eleven-acre campus. Such guidelines were developed in response to the suburban condition of cheap land available in large parcels. Enforcing these guidelines in urban conditions would make the construction of a new school all but impossible, and unwise as well. A one-story, suburban-style school on a large campus would violate the traditional street grid of SoBro as well as the scale appropriate to an urban neighborhood.

On the other hand, a school of two or three stories of good urban design, with adjacent park and playground to be shared with the neighborhood, could spur residential development and create a more diverse population in SoBro. The examples of Memphis and Chattanooga show that, with sufficient collective will, there's a way.

Christine Kreyling

Excerpted from an article that originally appeared in Planning *(July 2002).*

will use it during school hours, and residents during the hours after the children have departed. The site is centrally located between the Lafayette and Rutledge neighborhoods, and one block south of the Demonbreun neighborhood.

Housing

The most obvious issue with regard to housing in SoBro is its absence. According to the Nashville Downtown Partnership, the district currently contains only 257 residential units; of that number, 98 are rental, but many more are leased by their owners. For the district to succeed as a collection of neighborhoods, it must contain a variety of housing for diverse ages and incomes, with a sufficient percentage of owner-occupied units to support the formation of strong and active neighborhood associations. The recent location of a number of design-related and high-tech businesses in SoBro suggests that one avenue for residential development is to cater to the design professions using the existing warehouse stock for lofts and studios.

The other major housing issue lies outside the bounds of SoBro proper. During the community workshops, citizens expressed concern that the existence of the Tony Sudekum and J. C. Napier Homes south of the interstate, public housing projects which together total 923 units, is a severe deterrent to residential development in the SoBro district, and the Rutledge Hill neighborhood in particular. These housing blocks, wedged behind the barriers formed by the interstates, industry, and the wide dimensions of Lafayette Street, form a concentrated pocket of poverty that has negative impacts on nearby commercial and residential property.

Repairing this condition will require more than a federal Hope VI grant. SoBro as a whole must be programmed to disperse affordable housing for people of lower incomes throughout the entire district, which will enable the Sude-kum and Napier projects to be redeveloped along more diverse lines. This is eminently possible be-cause so much land in the district is currently vacant or underutilized.

Addressing the large homeless population of SoBro will require similar strategies of disper-sal, some of which lie outside the bounds of ur-ban design. It is understandable that people who require, not merely temporary shelter but a wide variety of social services, are more efficiently and easily provided for by centralizing shelter and services. But warehousing the homeless concen-trates the negative effects associated with their presence and deters development catering to other segments of the population. Services for the homeless are needed in SoBro—but not only in SoBro.

This pedestrian bridge is the grim rite of passage between the public housing of South Nashville and SoBro.

(Photograph, 2004: NCDC, Raven Hardison)

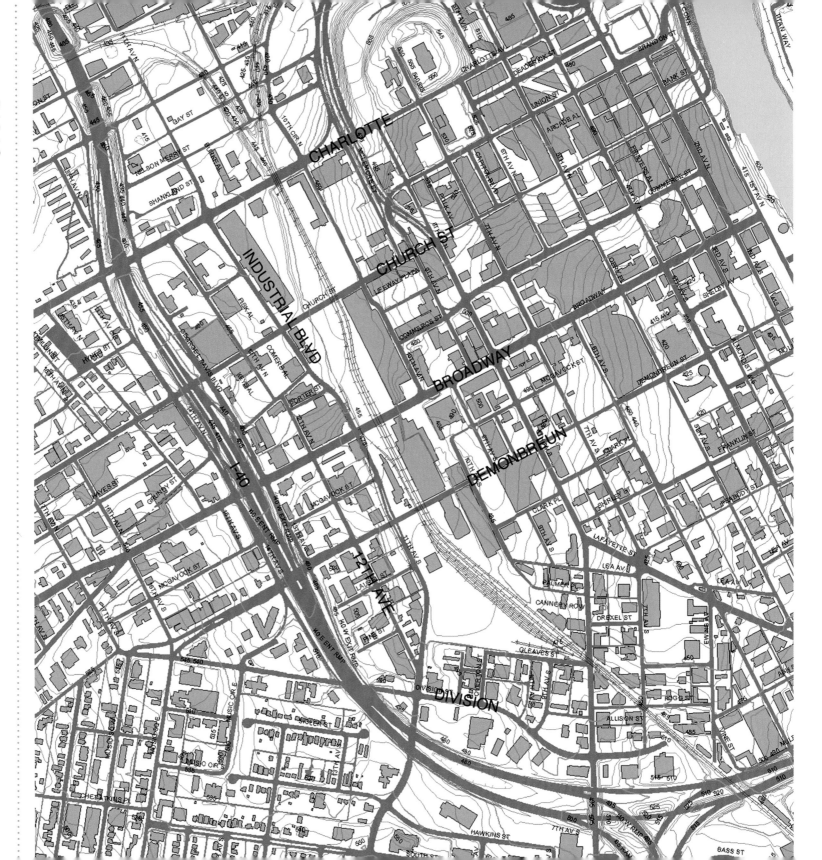

Map showing existing conditions in the Gulch District. Compare with the Plan's version of the same area on page 204.

(Map, 2002: Metro Planning Department)

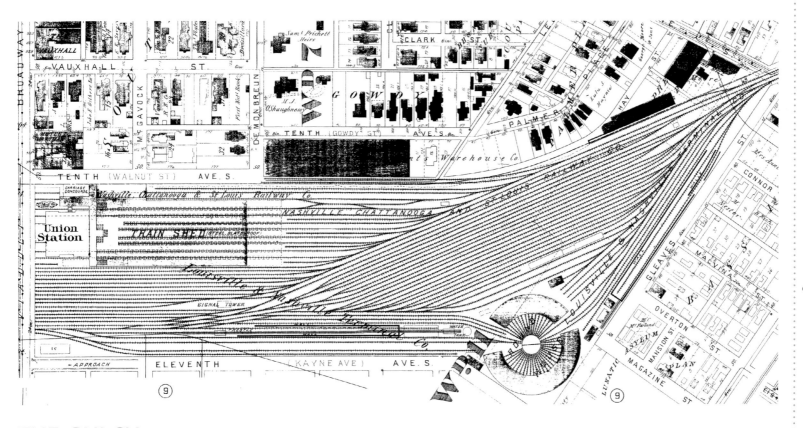

1908 map of railroad Gulch.

(Map, 1908: G.M. Hopkins Co., courtesy of Metro Historical Commission)

"Vitality shows not only in the ability to persist but in the ability to start over."

F. Scott Fitzgerald, "Note-Books," *The Crack-Up* (1945)

THE GULCH

Then and Now

The history of the Gulch is the history of the railroad in Nashville. Before the arrival of the first locomotive engine in 1850—ironically, by steamboat—the Gulch was merely a fissure in the face of Nashville that defined the western edge of town. But as railroad tracks began to eclipse the river as the predominant avenue of commerce—five lines entered the city by 1861—engineers realized that the topographical depression that was in but not of the city was a logical path for the iron horse.

During the three years of occupation by federal forces—when Nashville served as a crucial supply depot—the Louisville & Nashville

(L&N) line was especially important because it was the only major road to straddle Union and Confederacy, carrying materiel and munitions from the North and defining the path of invasion into the heart of Dixie.[23] In the postwar decades, the L&N became so dominant in the city that it was called the "octopus" after taking control of the rival line, the Nashville, Chattanooga & St. Louis, in 1880. As a gesture of public benevolence, the L&N laid plans to replace its shabby depot northwest of the city with architecture of opulence and power in the form of a new downtown terminal building. In 1896 the line developed the Gulch as an expanded railroad yard with more than three dozen tracks

and a massive roundhouse; trains unloaded under a 500-foot long shed of steel and wood and slate. At the edge of the Gulch above, Union Station opened to the public in 1900.[24]

For the next five decades the Gulch was the place where commuters and travelers arrived and "drummers" and soldiers departed. During World War II, the tracks carried more than one hundred trains a day.

After this peak of popularity, however, the Gulch quickly declined as a commercial and passenger travel hub. In 1956, the railroads discontinued their commuter service; passenger rail ceased entirely in 1979. Commercial transport shifted to the truck on the

"Let us hope that
these public
spirited men
who have put
their money in
the enterprise
will be big
enough and
broad enough
and bold enough
to come to look
upon Nashville,
not as a lemon
to be squeezed,
nor even as a
rich harvest to
be gathered, but
as a fertile field
to be cared for
and cultivated."

Mayor James M. Head,
remarks on the opening of
Union Station
(October 9, 1900)

interstate and the plane on the runway.

What to do with the Gulch became a perennial question. Developers and city officials floated schemes to build a convention center there, deck over the depression and plop office buildings on top, elevate the train shed on piers and create a "festival marketplace" beneath, put a new public library within the skeleton of the shed, make the Gulch a park. Nothing took.

In the 1980s, Union Station was renovated as a hotel; Cummins Station, the vast warehouse on the edge of the Gulch just to the south, became an office and retail complex in the 1990s. But the Gulch itself continued to languish. Because the land is literally low down, it seemed so

figuratively. A strategy to fuse an area traditionally perceived as the back door to Nashville—devoted to uses best kept out of sight—into the rest of the city was difficult to imagine.

As a gesture of faith in Nashville's mass transit future, the Clement Landport—a multimodal transit hub with parking and bus service—was constructed immediately west of Cummins Station in 1998; the facility has been little used because of the city's lack of the commuter or light rail components of mass transit. The National Landmark train shed was demolished in 2001 and the site became surface parking; the warehouses in the Gulch fell into increasing disuse and disrepair.

A group of investors and developers led by philanthropist Steve Turner formed Nashville Urban Venture, LLC, and decided to take the Gulch on its own terms. This was shrewd as well as admirable. Rather than try to make the area more like the rest of the city, they determined to exploit the Gulch's self-containedness. In 1999 the team purchased twenty-five acres south of the Broadway viaduct and created a master plan for an urban neighborhood.

The development program features an integrated mixture of land uses in structures averaging four to five stories; existing historic warehouses are renovated to capitalize on the area's industrial character. This build out will yield approximately 2.75 million square feet of office, retail, and residential space. The 1,800 dwelling units, including 20 percent affordable housing—using the standard average of 1.8 people per unit—will yield a population of 3,240. One notable lack in this master plan is central civic space; open space is placed in out-of-the-way locations, suggesting that this is not truly "public" space.

Nashville Urban Venture's projected development period is ten to twelve years. The area covered by the master plan falls within the Metro Development and Housing Agency's Arts Center Redevelopment District and is thus eligible for government financial support, primarily in the form of infrastructure improvements.

The Gulch north of the Broadway viaduct retains its gritty ambience, its proximity to downtown largely overlooked. A small collection of restaurants and clubs on Twelfth Avenue North is surrounded by the gigantic *Tennessean* plant and lots of car and truck storage. But if the area in the Gulch to the south is successful, Gulch North will undoubtedly draw the attention of developers.

The Gulch, after plan by
Nashville Urban Venture, LLC.

(Drawing, 2003: NCDC, Raven Hardison)

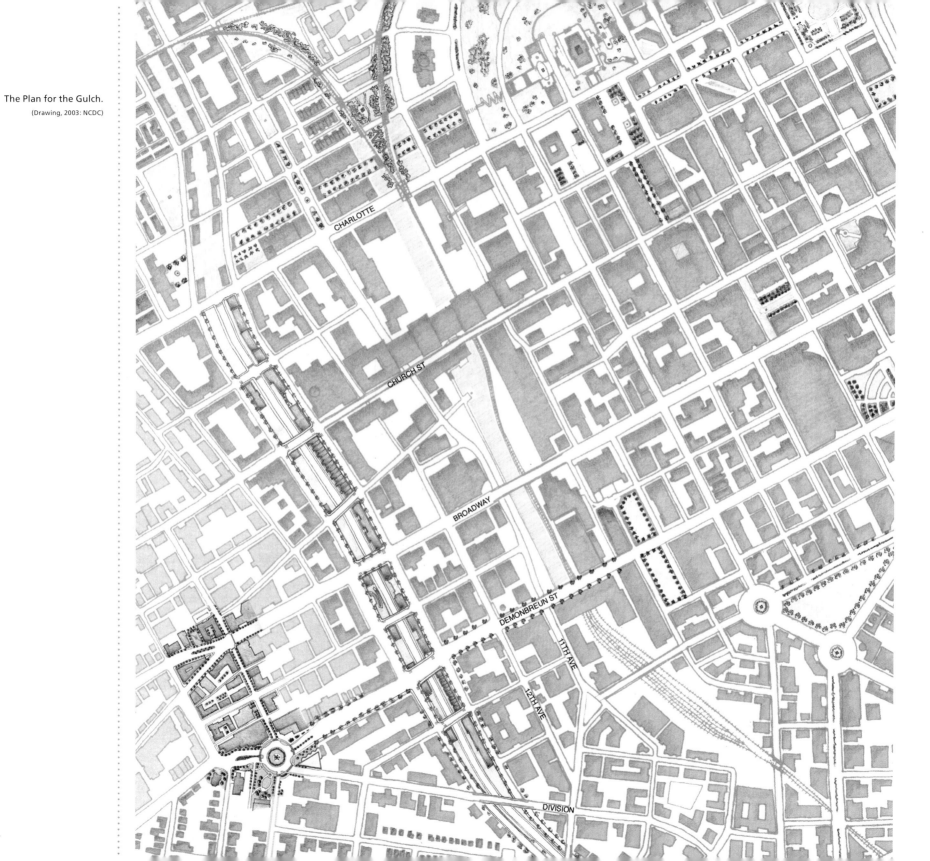

The Plan for the Gulch.
(Drawing, 2003: NCDC)

CHARLOTTE

CHURCH ST

BROADWAY

DEMONBREUN ST

11TH AVE

12TH AVE

DIVISION

The Plan

The future of the Gulch lies with acknowledging that the Industrial Revolution that rode into Nashville on rails of iron is past. It is time to start over, cultivating the district's topography while mining the district's architectural history for clues to its new character.

The key is the architectural minimalism represented by the existing industrial and warehouse buildings—the tradition of form follows function that inspired modernist design. The Plan envisions the Gulch "style" as self-consciously modern, contemporary. This is Nashville's "cutting edge" district that pushes the design envelope to the limits of basic good urban design.

The Plan for the Gulch takes the Gulch master plan for the area south of Broadway as a point of departure and extends it north almost to the Church Street viaduct. Structures are

The Twelfth and Demonbreun Building (formerly the Braid Electric Building) is a good example of the redevelopment potential of the Gulch's historic buildings.

(Photograph, 2003: courtesy of Nashville Urban Venture, LLC)

Left: Loft-style housing in the Gulch gives a contemporary edge to the industrial vocabulary.

(Photograph, 2003: courtesy of Nashville Urban Venture, LLC)

Right: View from North Gulch south to Union Station; this area has a redevelopment potential similar to the master plan for Gulch South.

(Photograph, 2004: NCDC, Gary Gaston)

RESIDENTIAL / RETAIL
LOCAL / OWNED

Natural Features

The Gulch is just that: a cleft in the topography of Nashville. The Plan recognizes the east and west edges as giving clear definition to the space; development should build *with* this unique terrain rather than attempt to regularize it. "Split-level" buildings on the western slope connect to the street fabric at both gulch and city levels, capitalizing on sightlines to the downtown skyline while providing walls to the streets above and below. Viaducts across the Gulch—visual reminders of the grade shift—should be considered design opportunities. Undersides should be lighted; replacement structures should transcend the prosaic forms of typical highway construction and aspire to the level of fine architecture that is consciously

mid-rise and mixed-use and have good transparency at street level to promote sidewalk activity. A possible site for the convention center is on the north side of the viaduct, where it would form a backdrop for the Gulch North area.

expressive of the industrial past.

The transformation of the western interstate loop into the Green Gully (see below, "Midtown" chapter, "Green Gully," pages 217–18), significantly changes the character of the Gulch's western border. Development along George L. Davis Boulevard/Thirteenth Avenue should make this an urban street rather than a car slum. Split-level buildings and arcades provide access

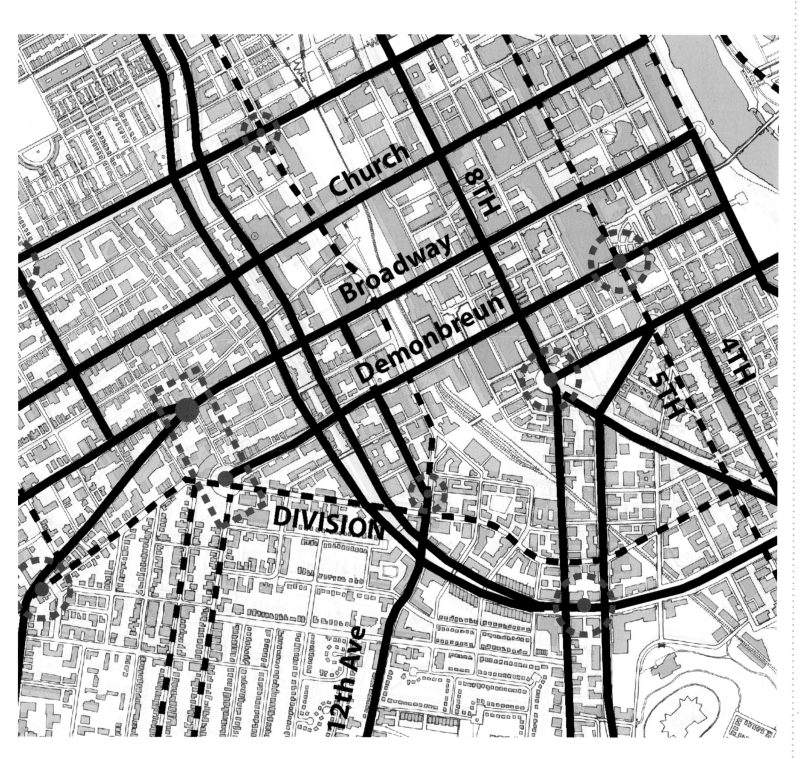

Diagram of streets and centers.
(Diagram, 2004: NCDC)

Map Key

Solid black lines: principal streets

Dashed black lines: local streets

Dashed red lines: centers

from the edge into the Gully. The historic nature of the Gulch as a distinct path around the city is exploited by a green ribbon linking north and south segments of the greenway system, following the model established in other parts of the country to transform old rail corridors for recreation and non-automotive transportation.

The Plan exploits natural and manmade features to suggest the placement of a new Nashville Convention Center to span the Gulch, flanking what is now the Church Street viaduct, between the downtown YMCA and the NES building. Railroad and automobile traffic can pass underneath the convention center. At viaduct level, the convention center can be designed in a way that engages the pedestrian, with storefront shops and spaces that open onto Church Street. Loading and unloading can be accom-

plished below, in an area that does not conflict with pedestrian or automobile traffic. (See "The Nashville Convention Center: Where To Put a New One and What To Do with the Old One," pages 126–27.)

Hierarchy of Streets

Eleventh Avenue/Industrial Boulevard is the "main street" of the Gulch. The relaxed, curving path gives it the character of a "Drive" that adjusts its course to natural features; this character should be enhanced by designing the street as a low-speed pedestrian-and-bike-friendly thoroughfare.

Twelfth Avenue defines the western edge of the Gulch south of Broadway, where it provides the occasion for "split-level" buildings discussed above. North of Broadway, the street lowers to Gulch grade. With the transformation of I-40 (see "Midtown" chapter, "Green Gully," pages 217–18), Twelfth Avenue will link the River District with the Gulch.

The Viaducts over the Gulch at Demonbreun, Church, and Broadway should feature good vertical connections to the city in the form of stairs and elevators for pedestrians. As with the design

of the bridges themselves, these vertical connectors should be examples of conscious styling.

The Demonbreun viaduct is currently closed to traffic due to its unsafe condition; the Tennessee Department of Transportation is in charge of the design of its replacement. At public meetings on the subject of the design, citizens have favored a steel—rather than concrete—viaduct, to allow light to flow through the structure, with wide sidewalks with pedestrian-scale lighting, and bike lanes as well as two lanes for cars. The Plan supports this proposal, recognizing that this viaduct presents an opportunity for a new standard of bridge design to replace that of the typical TDOT interstate-style overpass.

Neighborhood Centers

The Gulch's major focal point is where Eleventh and Twelfth Avenues intersect. This area is envisioned as a mixed-use center—including shops as well as dining and entertainment venues—topped with residential. The Plan cautions that development keep the resident in mind and not become overly geared towards tourists and visitors from other parts of the city.

Civic Space

The loss of the Union Station train shed in 2001 was a collective failure of government and citizen will and imagination. At the time of its demise, the shed was one of six of Nashville's National Landmarks and the longest single-span, gable-roofed structure in the country. Its basilican profile was a reminder that to the nineteenth century, a "cathedral of commerce" was not hype but a visible symbol of a belief system, with the gospel of Jesus and the gospel of progress as complementary theologies. But as a New World engineering marvel rather than the high-style Old World revivalism of the Union Station passenger terminal, the shed's magnificent architecture never got the respect it deserved—until it was gone.

Citizens in the Plan's community workshops lamented the giant gap the demolition of the train shed has left in the Gulch. And the Gulch master plan lacks a civic focal point, an architectural special event to serve as the community's monument. The Plan proposes, therefore, a modern reinterpretation of the shed in the form of a mixed-use complex combining transit hub (see information on Nashville's future transit system, pages 87–91), decked parking, retail space, and hotel meeting rooms.

Twelfth Avenue South looking towards Mercury View Lofts with proposed development. Compare to photo of this view at left.

(Drawing, 2002: courtesy of Nashville Urban Venture, LLC)

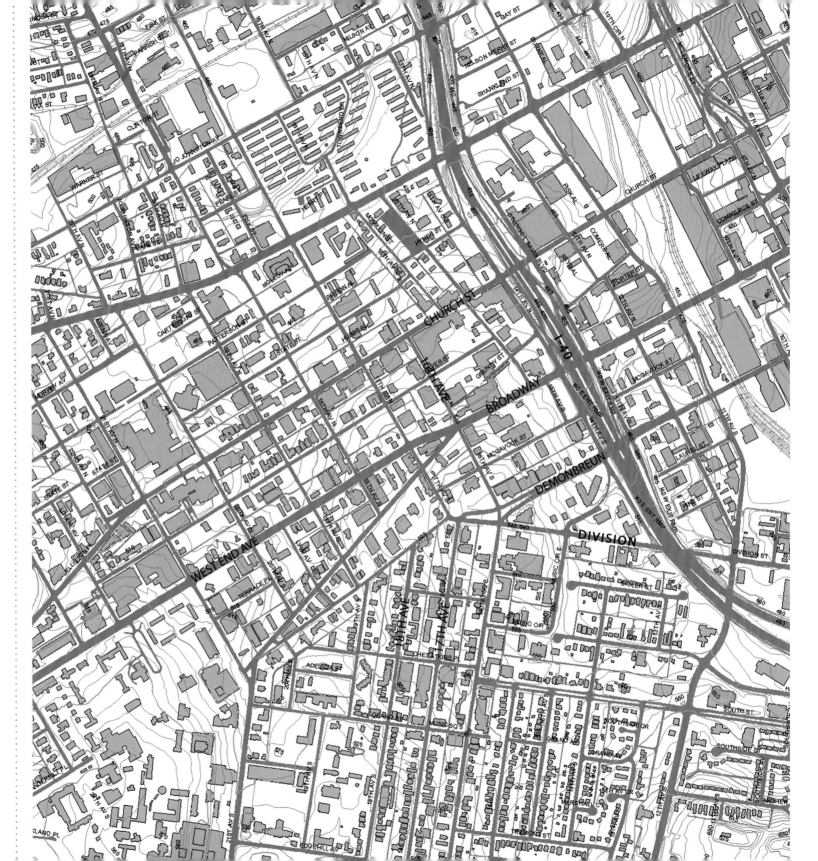

Map showing existing conditions of the Midtown District. Compare with the Plan's version of the same area on page 214.

(Map, 2002: Metro Planning Department)

MIDTOWN

Then and Now

The topographical depression that gave the Gulch its name was also responsible for limiting Nashville's westward expansion until the 1880s. The mule-drawn trolley cars that carried Nashville's early suburbanites north and south and east had great difficulty descending and ascending the steep slopes. The construction of wooden viaducts over the railroad tracks at Broadway and Church Street in 1880, and the appearance of faster electric trolleys in 1888—the first "juiced" line ran out Broadway to Vanderbilt University—opened up the area west of the Gulch for development.

Several factors made what was largely farm land attractive to those scouting avenues of escape from the central city. Land prices were cheaper than those in other suburbs such as East Nashville. Industry whose noise and filth and poor laborers had encroached on earlier suburbs was largely absent. The prevailing west-east winds enabled the district to evade the smells and soot of the city center and surrounding industrial belt. The foundation of Vanderbilt University in 1873 established nearby land as a good investment.

Consolidation of the small, neighborhood trolley lines was compelled by the costly steam-driven generating plants. This consolidation brought about economies of scale—increasing passenger volume by lower fares and reduction or elimination of transfer fees—that stimulated trolley line extensions. "The expansion of a centralized trolley system," according to historian Don Doyle, "was integrally connected to the promotion of suburban real estate; the two frequently involved the same entrepreneurs…The major thrust of suburban expansion in the electric trolley car era was to the west."[25]

Historic view of West End Avenue looking east from Vanderbilt towards the tower of West End Methodist Church, a magnificent structure that once stood near the Broadway/West End split. (See page 38.)
(Photograph, 1900s: Metro Archives)

> "We want integrated live-work culture, no more drive-by culture."
> Kaaren Hirschowitz Engel, community workshop participant

Same view along West End Avenue with cars; note that the split is now punctuated by a billboard and most of the historic mansions have been razed.
(Photograph, 1950s: Metro Archives)

Public parks were the third side of the trolley–real estate triangle. Many transit lines originally ended at a park developed and maintained by trolley and suburban land companies to entice town dwellers to hop on board. Families seeking the natural beauty of wooded lands paid the five-cent fare for weekend outings that carried them right by park-like building lots that just happened to be for sale. The grounds of the Tennessee Centennial had been a popular destination since 1897. In 1902, the Nashville Railway and Light Company gave Centennial Park to the city. The park acted, Doyle says, "as a powerful magnet pulling the suburban frontier to the west and beyond."

East of Hillsboro Pike, Roger Williams University was established in 1874 for the education of African Americans on the site later partially occupied by Peabody College. What Belmont-Hillsboro historian Eugene TeSelle describes as a "suspicious fire" destroyed the main administration building in 1905, after unsuccessful "attempts to buy the land, since the 'Belmont area' was becoming attractive for residential development." The school relocated to White's Creek Pike, and the abandoned campus was deed restricted to prohibit any part of the property from being "conveyed to anyone 'of African descent,' although allowing them to live there 'in the capacity of servants.'"[26]

By the early 1900s the midtown district was essentially built out. Residential development patterns were similar to earlier suburbs: a grid of streets lined with narrow lots, on which stood homes with minimal setbacks and alleys to the rear. In the area immediately west of the Gulch and north of West End was "Little Ireland," home to many Irish-Americans who found work with the railroads. St. Joseph's Catholic Church, dedicated in 1886, and its adjoining school were the focal point of this neighborhood and stood on ample grounds on what is now the site of the NES building. More stately mansions flowed out West End, as wealthy families abandoned their town homes for this newly fashionable avenue.

The first incursion of a medical facility into the area between Church Street and Charlotte Pike occurred in 1898 with the purchase of the Jacob Dickinson estate on Hayes Street by the Catholic Diocese for the construction of St. Thomas Hospital. This medical campus was regularly expanded until St. Thomas moved to new quarters to the west in the 1970s. In 1918 the Protestant Hospital opened on Church Street on the site of what would become the sprawling Baptist Hospital complex.

As the trolleys' grasp reached far past the city limits to Harding Pike, however, and country estates, most notably Belle Meade plantation, were subdivided into large building lots, Midtown was eclipsed as a residential neighborhood.

Cars replaced trolleys as the vehicle of choice for personal travel, and traffic increased on the roads leading west. In the 1950s, the music industry began to relocate from downtown to Sixteenth and Seventeenth Avenues South, which would become Music Row. Country music evolved into a tourist attraction, and souvenir stands blossomed on the upper reaches of Demonbreun Street, magnetized by the Country Music Hall of Fame, which opened in 1967. I-40 cut a broad corridor through the area immediately west of the Gulch. Commercial zoning took over West End Avenue and the mansions were bulldozed. The campuses of hospitals and educational institutions expanded into the surrounding neighborhoods.

The most controversial campus amplification was that of Vanderbilt University as part of the

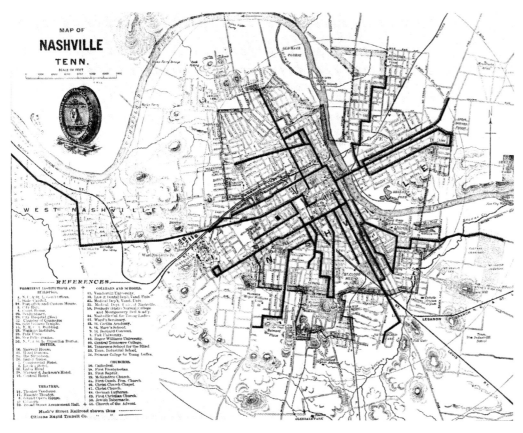

MAP OF
NASHVILLE
TENN.

REFERENCES

Church, the historic architecture of the Vanderbilt campus, the Peabody College campus, the Scarritt-Bennett Center, the Disciples of Christ Historical Society, and the Murphy School near Charlotte Pike.

Today Midtown is growing in density, due to pricey land values and good office occupancy

rates. High-rise—by Nashville standards—buildings march out West End Avenue. Other new office construction, especially for medical-related businesses, is gradually obliterating the residential relics remaining north of West End. The area between Vanderbilt and Music Row is experiencing new hotel construction and proposals for high-rise residential. Mid-rise commercial construction is beginning to encircle the Demonbreun roundabout. The street network in Midtown retains its good connectivity, but the major avenues need significant traffic calming to enhance the linkages for pedestrians.

The Plan

The Midtown district boundaries are the Gulch, Charlotte Pike, Vanderbilt University/Centennial Park and Music Square East. The Plan for Midtown—recognizing that the area has good urban bones, but some missing teeth—focuses on strengthening the network by establishing consistent street walls. Density is increased along the principal streets, such as West End Avenue and the western portions of Church

University Center urban renewal plan approved by the Metro Council in 1967. "Vanderbilt University's need for expansion room," TeSelle says, "coincided with the Metropolitan Government's need for matching funds to receive Federal urban renewal grants."[27] The Nashville Housing Authority declared a neighborhood to the south of the campus as "blighted." The university acquired the property and Metro paid to construct new streets and utility lines. Massive opposition to the loss of their neighborhood by residents of the area led to a lawsuit that went all the way to the Tennessee Supreme Court, without success.

Another part of the University Center plan was Mayor Beverly Briley's proposal to build a six-lane road through the middle of Music Row—from 21st Avenue to Demonbreun Street—to speed commuters from the southwest on their way. Briley's Boulevard was to be lined

with high-rise towers, to give the music industry a stronger physical presence—and a swanky address—in the city. Right-of-way acquisition proved to be too expensive, and only the strip that is Magnolia Boulevard was completed. The alternative adopted was turning Sixteenth and Seventeenth Avenues into a pair of one-way high speed corridors.

The result of this fundamental shift to commercial and institutional uses was the loss of much of Midtown's residential fabric—in particular the governor's mansion that was replaced by a fried chicken emporium (now the site of the Caterpillar office building). Father Ryan High School abandoned its campus on Elliston Place and followed the outward migration. Fine architecture still remaining includes the Cathedral of the Incarnation, the Corinthian Masonic Lodge No. 414 F&AM, West End United Methodist

Historic streetcar lines. The presence of multiple routes made Midtown easily accessible.

(Map, 1897: Don Doyle, *Nashville in the New South: 1880–1920*)

Governor's Mansion, once located at 2118 West End Avenue, was demolished in 1979 to build a fast food restaurant.

(Photograph, 1970s: The Nashville Room, Nashville Public Library)

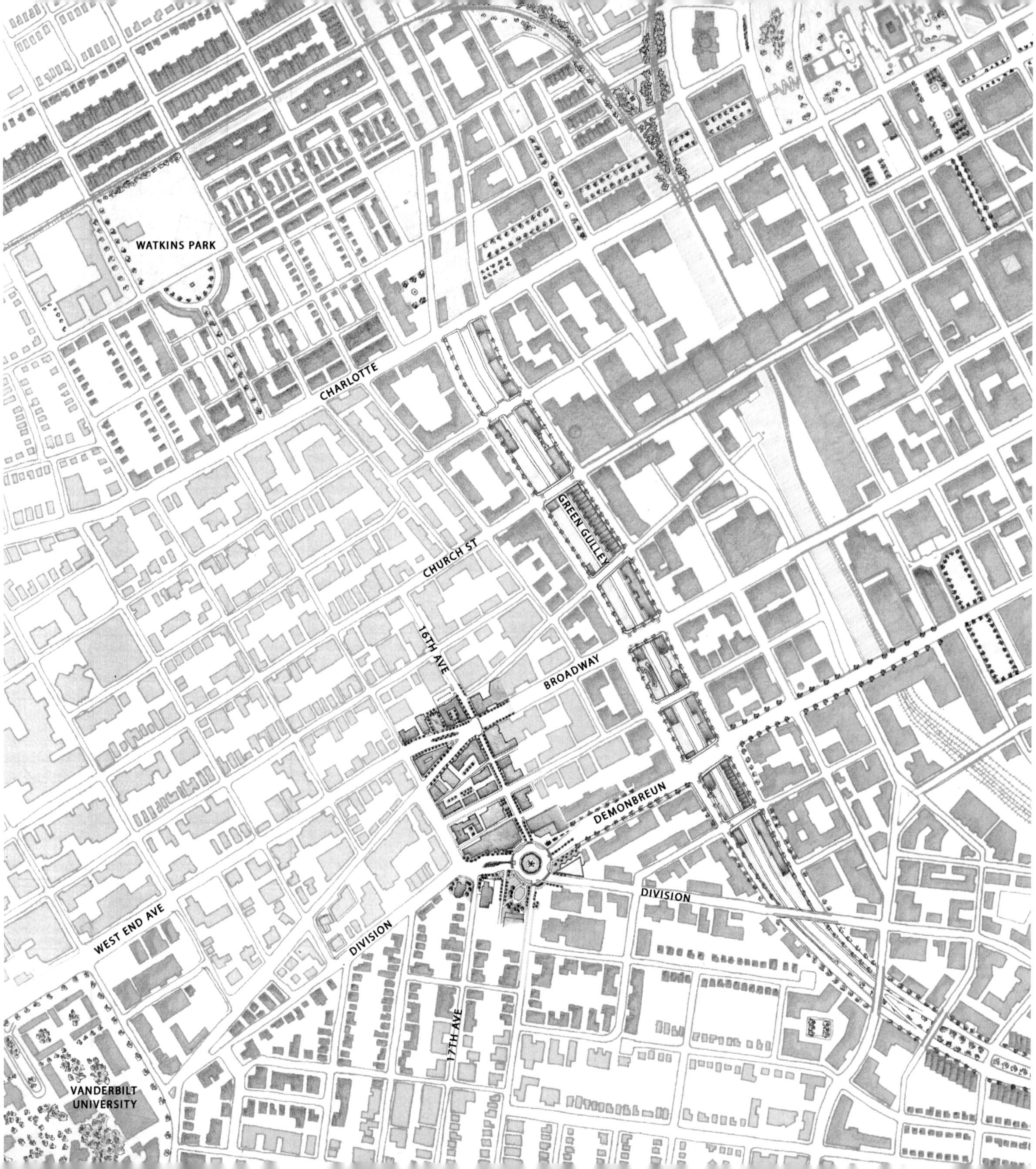

Map showing the proposed
changes in the Plan of Nashville.

(Drawing, 2003: NCDC)

WATKINS PARK

CHARLOTTE

GREEN GULLEY

CHURCH ST

16TH AVE

BROADWAY

DEMONBREUN

DIVISION

DIVISION

WEST END AVE

17TH AVE

VANDERBILT
UNIVERSITY

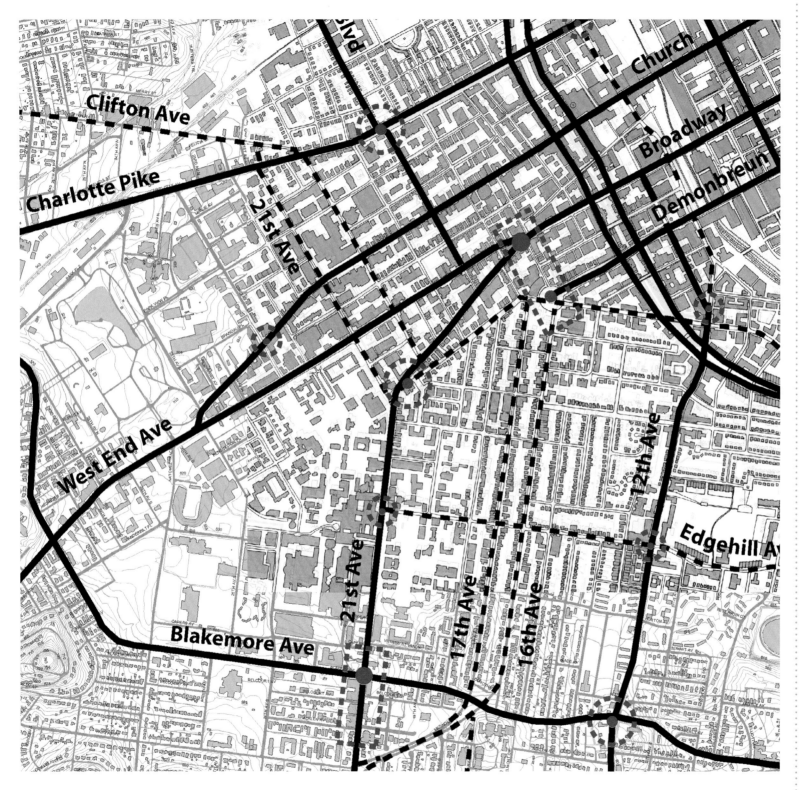

Diagram of streets and centers.
(Diagram, 2004: NCDC)

Map Key

Solid black lines: principal streets

Dashed black lines: local streets

Dashed red lines: centers

Street; more housing is needed, especially between these streets. The traditional neighborhood character of Music Row should be maintained by preserving existing building fabric and preventing its replacement with larger, office park–style buildings.

Natural Features

The edge formed by the Gulch on the east is reinforced by its manmade cousin, the interstate gully, a few blocks farther west. While the amount of traffic entering and exiting the interstate makes this a dangerous boundary for pedestrians and bicyclists to negotiate, it is fortunate that much of the street connectivity was maintained by placing the interstate in a trench and extensively bridging across it. As the land rises beyond the Gulch to the west, and then undulates out West End Avenue, fine sightlines provide design opportunities currently unrealized.

Hierarchy of Streets

West End Avenue was selected by 67 percent of the participants in the Plan of Nashville "Building a Consensus" survey, in response to the question: What major street should be developed as our "signature street" or "miracle mile"? The avenue's width and heavy traffic define it as the "main street" of the west, but its visual quality and degraded pedestrian environment are hardly miraculous.

West End Avenue is flanked by a mismatched collection of gas stations, fast food franchises, new and used car lots, mid-rise and high-rise offices, strip shops, and hotels. Sidewalks are fragmented by many curb cuts. Further reinforcing the eclectic nature of the streetscape, the historic profile of Vanderbilt University's Kirkland Hall gives way to prosaic high-rise dormitories and the part-strip-mall/part-high-rise at 2525 West End.

For West End Avenue to become the

"miracle mile," a streetscape master plan is needed to establish consistent build-to lines to form street walls at the pedestrian level, as well as standard sidewalk widths, landscaping, and lighting. One block of West End, for example, currently features five different styles of lighting fixtures. Pedestrians should be protected from the rush of traffic by more pronounced crosswalks signalized to provide adequate time to cross seven lanes, sidewalks buffered by planting strips, and on-street parking that extends through peak hours, and the elimination of curb cuts. These features—and design guidelines for the West End streetscape—should be incorporated into the update of the community plan for Midtown, which is scheduled for late 2004 by the Metro Planning Department.

The Green Gully replaces the interstate with two layers of thoroughfares, made possible by the large grade shift. In the lower level, the interstate roadbed is replaced by a linear park and a low-speed, pedestrian-and-bike-friendly two-lane drive with broad sidewalks and carefully delineated crosswalks. The upper level—

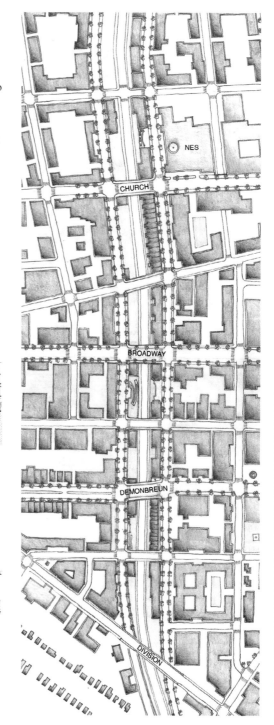

Quick sketch done during community vision workshop.
(Sketch, 2003)

Center: Street section and detail of plan of the Green Gully.
(Drawing, 2004: NCDC, Jason Hill)

Right: Plan of the Green Gully.
(Drawing, 2003: NCDC)

which includes the rights-of-way now used by the broad entrance and exit ramps as well as the surface streets flanking the interstate trench—becomes a pair of one-way avenues, four lanes each, designed for high volumes and moderate speeds. Vehicular access to the gully is limited to Charlotte Pike on the north, and from the new South Boulevard as it curves out of SoBro.

Mixed-use buildings—restaurants, shops, and residential—are located on the eastern side of the former right-of-way; structures on the west would block sunlight from reaching the gully floor. These buildings would be accessed at both gully and avenue levels. Vertical pedestrian access to the park—stairs and elevators—is provided at the viaducts: Demonbreun, Broadway, and Church.

Demonbreun Street's recent redevelopment has been spurred by what was originally perceived as a major misfortune for the commerce of the street: the relocation of the Country Music Hall of Fame and Museum from the edge of Music Row to SoBro. When the move was announced in the mid '90s, merchants and property owners in the upper Demonbreun reaches realized that they were losing their tourist anchor and facing economic upheaval. The Metro Development and Housing Agency stepped in with funds for a planning study, incorporated the area into its Arts Center Redevelopment District, and committed $3.5 million for infrastructure improvements. The Metro Planning Department responded by establishing an urban design overlay for the area and commissioning design guidelines to shape the redevelopment.

The most dramatic infrastructure change is the Demonbreun roundabout, a traffic calming device for what had been the hellish intersection of Demonbreun Street, Division Street, and Music Square East and West. Other improvements to Demonbreun include more on-street parking, broad sidewalks, crosswalks, landscaping, and new lighting. The goal has been to

remake a place where pedestrians feared for their lives into an avenue where people want to stroll.

The roundabout has attracted a large mid-rise office building that curves around the northern segment. Restaurants and bars have opened on the northern side of Demonbreun Street, several with outdoor terraced seating, a Nashville rarity. The southern side of the street, however, is occupied by a surface parking lot. This should be developed with similar urban characteristics, but by buildings of larger scale with residential above.

Church Street leaves the downtown at the interstate trench, where the street's character changes to a sequence of low- and mid-rise buildings, many of which have decent street presence—tight to the sidewalk, ground-level transparency—not fully exploited by current occupants. Despite the gaps formed by suburban-style infill, Church Street, therefore, has great potential.

One land use obviously missing—especially at night, when the street goes dead—is housing. The ongoing redevelopment of the downtown portions of Church Street to include a major residential component should be extended to the Midtown segment as well. One step in this direction would be to rehab the upper floors of existing warehouses and light-industry buildings for living quarters.

Neighborhood Centers

The Broadway/West End Avenue split is the center of Midtown. This focal point is currently occupied by a car repair shop and used car lot and a gigantic billboard—clearly not highest and best uses. The Plan exploits the signature nature of this site with a "Flatiron-type" building, flanked by other structures that define the street edge. Traffic calming is accomplished through broad sidewalks with extensions or "bulbs" to shield

on-street parking. Landscaping enhances the pedestrian experience.

The Demonbreun Roundabout is in the process of significant development. This success should not obscure, however, the importance of good urban design to Seventeenth Avenue, the link between the roundabout and the West End/ Broadway split. A tree-lined, pedestrian-friendly street, primarily residential in nature, will enable

Perspective view of the split; drive-by culture becomes live/work culture.

(Drawing, 2003: Ben Johnson)

the mutual reinforcement of these two centers and stimulate the redevelopment of the intervening blocks.

Broadway Gate is the triangular intersection of Broadway, Division Street, and Twenty-first Avenue identified as the Scarritt-Peabody neighborhood focal point in the *Vanderbilt University Land Use and Development Plan* of 2001.[28] This area has many restaurants and shops and, therefore, strong pedestrian usage, particularly from the nearby university and medical complex. The lack of consistent street walls and clearly defined crosswalks, however, degrades the pedestrian experience. Curing these conditions would make the area more attractive, not only to the Vanderbilt community, but to the community at large.

Vanderbilt University is quite obviously a major resource for the surrounding community. The institution provides cultural, educational, recreational, and entertainment opportunities, not only for those officially affiliated with the university, but for many who live in adjacent neighborhoods. Its campus is a green oasis for a district lacking—with the exception of Centennial Park—this amenity.

The *Vanderbilt University Land Use and Development Plan* contains several principles that deal with the physical relationship between town and gown. The plan states that "future growth should be concentrated within campus boundaries as much as possible to maintain the compactness and tightly-knit civic structure of the campus. Development at campus edges will be focused on sites that can enhance the quality of the land use relationship between the University and the community." The implementation of such principles will make the campus edge a permeable membrane and Vanderbilt a part of its neighborhood.

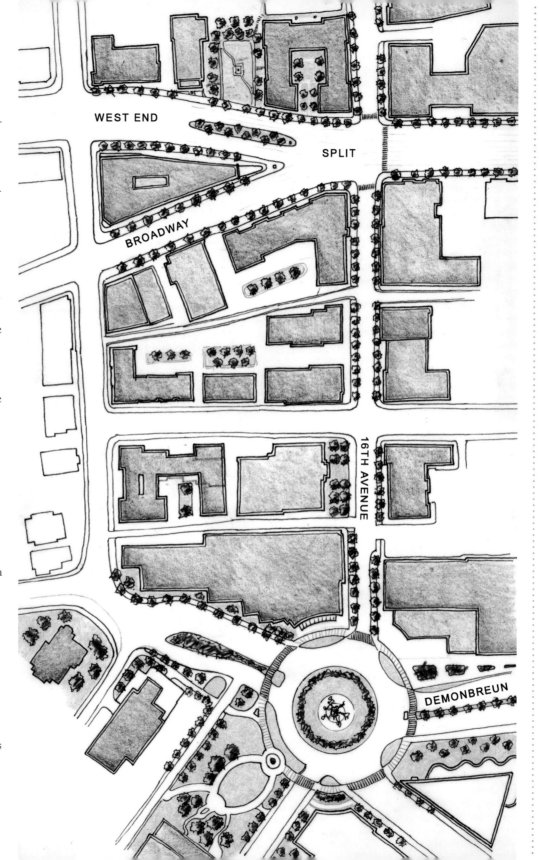

The plan of the split and roundabout. Note the beautification of Sixteenth Avenue as the connection between the split and roundabout.

(Drawing, 2004: NCDC, Gary Gaston)

Left top: Owen Bradley Park, at the roundabout.

(Photograph, 2004: NCDC, Gary Gaston)

Left bottom: The triangular site at Broadway and Division Street is an underutilized focal point.

(Photograph, 2004: NCDC, Gary Gaston)

Center top: DuPont Circle in Washington, D.C., sets a good example for dealing with triangular sites.

(Photograph, 2003: James Manning Jr.)

Center bottom: Image of Lake Watauga, in Centennial Park.

(Photograph, 2003: NCDC, Gary Gaston)

A pedestrian-friendly section of Twenty-first Avenue South, one edge to the Vanderbilt campus.

(Photograph, 2004: NCDC, Gary Gaston)

Medium-density row housing on Eighteenth Avenue South suits the Midtown District.
(Photograph, 2004: NCDC, Gary Gaston)

Parks and Civic Space

Unlike the River District and East Nashville, Midtown lacks small-scale, internal "neighborhood" parks. Midtown's evolution as a commercial, educational, and health care center left little room for residents, and therefore little demand for such parks. The majority of current residents are students for whom the campus serves as park and civic space.

What Midtown does have is Centennial Park. Like Shelby Park and Bottoms in East Nashville and Fort Negley/City Cemetery just outside of SoBro, Centennial Park lies at the edge of the district and serves as green space for the residents of Midtown as well as an attraction for the city at large. This pattern of first-ring districts with large green space at the periphery is an urban design motif that the Plan of Nashville seeks to strengthen with the addition of Buena Vista Bottoms to the River District and Cumberland Northeast Park to Northeast Nashville.

Housing

Recent housing initiatives in Midtown are multifamily; few single-family homes remain. The compact residential character should be encouraged, particularly in the Elliston neighborhood between West End and Charlotte Pike. Providing living opportunities for people employed in the medical complexes could reduce the peak-hours traffic congestion in this neighborhood and stimulate a more mixed-use environment.

Midtown lacks the large blocks of public housing that deter reinvestment in other first-ring districts. High-rise dwellings should be permitted only if compatible with their immediate context and if they define a strong street wall and include retail offerings at the pedestrian level.

Building the Affordable Neighborhood, One Block at a Time

It is an axiom of the Plan of Nashville that the neighborhood is the building block of the city. In the Plan, the ideal neighborhood has a variety of housing for a broad range of ages and incomes: rental and owner-occupied, single and multi-family. Included in that range must be various types of affordable housing.

To fully grasp the challenge of housing affordability, it is crucial to understand it, not as an end unto itself, but as a means for achieving sustainable communities. By definition, such communities are, among other things, economically, ethnically, and architecturally diverse—and therefore interesting and desirable places to live.

Over the last twenty-five years, the importance of housing affordability in the life of cities, large and small, has been extensively researched. This research has concluded that, all along the economic ladder, when housing conditions are safe and secure, families are more stable and children perform better in school. Consequently, there is less strain on a community's social services, public health facilities, and law enforcement system.

It is also generally accepted that the lack of affordable housing options drives families farther away from the city to areas where land and development costs are less and housing prices are therefore lower. This out-migration or "sprawl" erodes a city's property tax base, limiting the effectiveness of basic services and diminishing revenues that support the quality of neighborhood life, such as parks and schools. Because those who choose to migrate tend to be middle-income families, the economic disparity between the so-called "haves" and "have-nots" who remain in the city is exacerbated. Sprawl also contributes significantly to traffic congestion.

A common dilemma is how to ensure affordability as a matter of public policy. In many cities, mixed-income development, which designates affordable units for sale or rent in an otherwise market-rate development, has gained favor as a compromise that enables a city to meet its affordable housing needs without public resistance. Mixed-income development can assuage the fears of residents who fear the impact on property values of housing that is clearly identifiable as lower income.

Another benefit of the mixed income approach is that it reverses a historical trend by dispersing rather than concentrating populations in need of affordable housing. In a new subdivision or apartment building, for example, a number of units might be set aside as "affordable," thereby creating a mix of market-rate and lower cost units. The economics of the project are adjusted through the use of incentives such as density bonuses, which grant a developer increased units beyond the normally allowed maximum for a project. This increase enables the developer to realize the return anticipated for a fully market-rate project.

The mixed-income approach can also work well in an older neighborhood that has a high incidence of low-cost housing. In this context, higher priced homes or apartments are developed in conjunction with affordable units to help increase property values and foster economic stability. This is usually referred to as "leading the market" and is a common neighborhood revitalization tool.

Such was the case leading to the development of the Row 8.9n townhomes between Eighth and Ninth Avenues in the Hope Gardens community of North Nashville, which were completed in 2003. The Hope Gardens community revitalization initiative had been underway since 1997. A number of new single-family homes had been constructed and property values had increased, but the revitalization effort was attracting exclusively lower income families and individuals to an area that was already one of Nashville's lowest income census tracts. To stabilize and enhance the community's economic base, Row 8.9n was conceived as housing with superior design features that would appeal to the pent-up market for homes located close to downtown. The project's intent was to lead the market by offering a more "high end" housing option than had previously been available in the area. It also sought to capitalize upon the successful revitalization of the nearby Germantown neighborhood and take full advantage of two urban amenities: the Farmers Market and the Bicentennial Mall.

Row 8.9n is a model for mixed-income development that could be replicated in other first-ring Nashville neighborhoods. Sales of eleven of the twenty-nine units were subsidized for households at or below 80 percent of the city's median income—

Row 8.9n, Ninth Avenue facades. This project, which combines affordable and market-rate units, is a prime example of the Hope Garden neighborhood's revitalization.

(Photograph, 2004: Gary Gaston)

$34,500 for a single person. The remaining units were sold on the open market at prices well above the area average. The resulting economic mix of residents benefited the community as well as the nearby Jefferson Street commercial district. Row 8.9n sold out before completion of construction and led to a similarly successful project on nearby Ireland Street: ireland28.

Both Row 8.9n and ireland28 relied heavily on government funding that had been previously allocated to help revitalize the Hope Gardens community. Significant government investment, which is critical to successful affordable housing and community development, is, however, increasingly difficult to come by. Local and state governments have constrained budgets and the federal government is reducing its support for housing and community development. Without government support or an alternative funding source, developers are hesitant to take the risks inherent in the production of affordable housing and the redevelopment of first-ring neighborhoods.

Furthermore, sustainable communities must be supported by planning and regulatory agencies that recognize and share common goals, operate efficiently, and have enough flexibility to respond to the differing needs of emerging communities. Local governments typically use a "one size fits all" approach to development and redevelopment. Such an approach ignores the uniqueness that is inherent to each development and is counter to cost-effective production.

It is important to recognize the gradual nature of achieving sustainable growth and ensuring affordability. By their nature, large-scale initiatives are difficult to mount and maintain. Incremental adjustments to public policy and resource allocation have the added benefit of lessening the impact on existing policies and programs. Following is a summary of some incremental strategies—typical of other cities—that have been part of Nashville's public discourse regarding affordable housing. None is, in and of itself, a solution. Taken together over time, they could be of significant benefit.

Increase Resources

A dedicated source of revenue for housing has been discussed locally for some time. Typically this would take the form of a housing trust fund. Capital for the fund would derive from an identified source such as a real estate transaction fee. After a sufficient capitalization period, fund revenues are used to supplement or leverage government and private resources.

Nashville relies heavily on federal funds to meet its housing needs, particularly for lower income households. Even though government and housing are inextricably attached, it is unwise to rely so heavily on federal support. A reliable source of revenue would ease the pressure on federal funds and enable higher allocations to programs that serve low- and no-income populations.

Gain Community Acceptance

A community's willingness to look beyond individual self-interest and to effect policies that serve the greater good is a measure of its maturity. Community resistance, however, is a key obstacle to sustained affordability, whether it is based on opposition to increased housing density, negative stereotypes about ethnic or racial diversity, or concerns over property depreciation. It is typically cited among the top five national issues inhibiting the development of workforce housing. While the Plan of Nashville is not a handbook for behavior modification, it is incumbent on any plan to acknowledge an impediment and encourage the public at large to think and act in the interest of the common good. It is also important to recognize that diverse neighborhoods are strong neighborhoods and that families should have some measure of choice when deciding where to live.

Reduce Development Costs

As previously discussed, mitigating financial risk for the developer is essential to attracting investment for emerging communities and is critical for the production of affordable housing. It is common for infrastructure and utility costs to be borne by project developers and then passed on to the home buyer or renter. Most cities, Nashville included, are struggling to update an aging infrastructure and to comply with new environmental and accessibility mandates.

Developers of affordable housing are less able to pass extra costs along to their customers in the form of higher rents or home prices. A strategy to help non-profit and other providers of affordable housing offset infrastructure and utility costs would greatly enhance productivity and reduce overall housing costs.

Eliminate Regulatory Impediments

The 2003 Mayor's Housing Summit highlighted the need to address local regulatory barriers that cause delays and increase housing production costs. Participants noted that planning approvals generally take in excess of one year, and that the Metro review process is unnecessarily decentralized and duplicative, often resulting in jurisdictional conflict and confusion. They recommended a "one-stop shop" for development approvals and suggested that the city more adequately reward developers for including affordable units in new projects.

Housing affordability is a key component of community sustainability. It is fundamental to broad planning archetypes such as New Urbanism, which seeks to recast the way communities are created. It is equally fundamental to the Hope VI program, which seeks to undo our warehouse approach to public housing. Clearly, a supply of decent, safe, and affordable housing is a large consideration for the future of all cities. For Nashville, affordability through sustainability should be the ultimate goal.

Steve Neighbors
President, The Home Company of
Middle Tennessee

CONCLUSION

IDEAS INTO REALITY

It is IMPORTANT to understand what urban planning is—and isn't—when considering avenues to the realization of the Plan of Nashville. In 1914, New York City's Committee on the City Plan gave this explanation:

City planning does not mean the invention of new schemes of public expenditure. It means getting the most out of the expenditures that are bound to be made and the saving of future expense in replanning and reconstruction. With or without a comprehensive city plan, the City will probably spend hundreds of millions of dollars on public improvements during the next thirty years. In addition, during this same period property owners will spend some billions of dollars in the improvement of their holdings. To lay down the lines of city development so that these expenditures when made will in the greatest possible measure contribute to the solid and permanent upbuilding of a great and ever greater city—strong commercially, industrially, and in the comfort and health of its people—furnishes the opportunity and inspiration for city planning.[1]

With the Plan of Nashville, we have a similar intersection of inspiration and opportunity.

The Plan "lays down lines of city development" that are to be used as the litmus test for Nashville's urban future, the measure by which proposals for individual initiatives are evaluated.

The publication of the Plan is, therefore, not an end point, but a point of departure. The Plan must now be tested against the realities of Nashville. Those realities include some government policies that run counter to basic principles of urban design, tight government budgets, and vested interests that would prefer "business as usual"—the development patterns we've practiced for the last fifty years.

The converse reality is the citizens who came together to make this vision. Transforming ideas into facts will depend on the collective will of this same public, as well as political representatives and government officials, neighborhood and corporate leaders, developers and educators, architects and planners—and the degree to which they can and will cooperate.

This will only happen with strong education and action programs that establish broad awareness of the Plan and position the vision in the forefront of Nashville development.

"Our lives are not totally random. We make commitments, we cause things to happen."

Wendy Wasserstein,
"The Messiah,"
Bachelor Girls
(1990)

> "No town plan can be adequately described in terms of its two-dimensional pattern; for it is only in the third dimension, through movement in space, and in the fourth dimension, through transformation in time, that the functional and esthetic relationships come to life."
>
> Lewis Mumford,
> *The City in History*
> (1961)

Education is the first step. The Nashville Civic Design Center will develop a program that includes:

- A speakers' bureau to present the Plan to civic groups, professional and neighborhood organizations, politicians, Metro Council members, government officials, senior citizen and parents' groups, etc.;
- The publication of articles about the Plan in local, state, and national media;
- The incorporation of the Plan into the continuing education program at the Nashville Civic Design Center;
- The development of a simplified version of the Plan that can be used in Nashville's public and private schools.

The intention of the Plan is to steer development and redevelopment, as they occur, into channels of good urban design. One of the crucial tasks in implementation, therefore, is the modification of existing public policies that would obstruct the Plan and the establishment of new ones that would further Plan goals.

Such policies exist at two levels: the daily operational methods and design standards of government agencies and quasi-government agencies such as the public utilities, and the planning documents and building codes that guide growth and establish construction standards. Metro policies are spelled out in the *General Plan,* the *Major Thoroughfare Plan,* and the Community (Subarea) Plans, as well as the Capital Improvements Budget, which establishes funding priorities. The Metro Board of Education defines its construction standards and building program in *Educational Specifications, Specification Guidelines* and *Metro Nashville Public Schools: Facilities Master Plan.* The Tennessee Department of Transportation is also formulating its Long Range Transportation Plan that will have a major impact on patterns of growth and development. The modification of these documents and policies to accommodate the principles and goals of the Plan is, therefore, a top priority.

Other implementation strategies include specific initiatives recommended in the Plan: design guidelines for selected areas, master plans for downtown parking and civic space, traffic calming of streets that need it, the integration of affordable housing into new residential development, and the incorporation of public art in individual civic and private development projects.

Politicking the Plan

The Plan of Chicago is a model of the effective comprehensive plan, serving as a reference point for development for several generations. The Chicago plan's success was in part because of its "persuasive diagnosis" of the city's problems and its "convincing proposals" for solving them, according to Alexander Garvin in *The American City.*[2] Once the plan was published in 1909, the City Council established a 328-member City Plan Commission, published and distributed 165,000 copies of a 93-page booklet summarizing the plan, and in 1911 formally adopted the plan as city policy. Within a decade of the plan's publication, the city had spent $327 million in public improvements and acquired 14,254 acres of forest preserve. More important, the City Plan Commission proved to be not a money-spender but a money-maker, "generating increased property values and city revenues in the areas immediately adjacent to these improvements."

"The most important reason that so much of the *Plan of Chicago* was implemented, however, was effective politicking by its supporters," Garvin writes. "In the ten years after the plan's publication, slide shows illustrating it were presented to more than 175,000 citizens. During 1912 alone, the Plan Commission placed articles that appeared in 575 magazines, periodicals, and trade publications." Champions of the plan "even persuaded the Board of Education to produce 70,000 copies of a simplified version of the Plan that became the eighth-grade civics textbook in the city's public schools."[3]

The Plan of Nashville could become a similar action agenda, or—like so many previous Nashville plans—be filed away as a dust catcher on a shelf, ultimately devolving into a mere historical curiosity. The fate of the Plan will depend on the willingness of the public to embrace it, and on the Metro government bureaucracy's readiness to respond. Our work has just begun.

Community assessment workshop.
(Photograph, 2002: NCDC, Mark Schimmenti)

PROCESS

CITIZEN PLANNERS: DOCUMENTING THE PROCESS

IN 1995, SEVERAL NASHVILLIANS, fearing the negative effects of Metro government's plan for a six-lane highway called the Demonbreun, later Franklin, Corridor through the area of downtown south of Broadway (So-Bro), organized the Nashville Urban Design Forum to bring public debate to the shaping of the city. Education was the initial aim of the forum; the long-term goal was the creation of an urban design center as an independent entity to chart a future for the city's built environment. To advance community education, forum members approached the dean of the University of Tennessee's College of Architecture, Marleen Davis, with the request for a faculty member to teach a class in Nashville on urban design.

The college sent Professor Mark Schimmenti. His first class gave more than fifty interested Nashvillians a basic understanding of urban design principles. Perhaps even more important, the class provided a common language with which to discuss planning and design issues facing Nashville.

The next step was to establish a positive vision for SoBro as an alternative to Metro's "corridor fixation." In January 1997, the *Nashville Scene* newspaper sponsored the "SoBro Charrette," a three-day planning workshop led by Schimmenti with eighteen other design professionals drawn

from across the nation, and attended by more than a hundred Nashvillians. The result was published by the *Scene* as *The Plan for SoBro*. One of the most significant aspects of this document was that the citizens of Nashville—rather than a government department or a small group of property or business owners—had instigated a plan for their city.

In consequence of these initiatives, urban design activists became a political force in the city. In his campaign for mayor, forum-member Bill Purcell made urban design issues and the founding of an urban design center part of his platform. After his election in 1999, Purcell appointed a task force to explore the form the center should take. In December 2000, the mayor announced the establishment of the Nashville Civic Design Center (NCDC).

The term "Plan of Nashville" as applied to the present project was first used publicly at a lunch meeting of the Nashville Downtown Partnership in early 2001. After a presentation about the then-fledgling civic design center by Mark Schimmenti, Partnership members asked the design director what was the center's major goal. Schimmenti's answer: to produce a plan similar to the *Plan of Chicago*, a 1909 vision for that city which guided

> "What is the city but the people?"
>
> William Shakespeare,
> *Coriolanus* 3.1.199

development for half a century. In the spring of 2002, after the mission and operation of the center were clearly established, the center's board gave the green light to the Plan of Nashville.

NCDC staff conceived a procedure that addressed three objectives. First, the community would determine the issues, goals, and principles. Second, local architects, landscape architects, planners, preservationists, and those closely aligned with the Urban Design Forum—the people who had already committed themselves to enhancing the quality of Nashville's built environment—would shape the urban design principles and physical guidelines to turn the community vision into a plan. Third, the study would be closely tied to Nashville's unique history, culture, and physical circumstances.

Who

The Plan of Nashville was orchestrated by the staff of the Nashville Civic Design Center. Staff members organized and assigned the tasks, staged the community workshops and panels, and compiled the resulting information, maps, and diagrams.

Design Center staff:

Stacy Battles, *Administrative Director (2003–present)*
Lara Brewton, *Administrative Director (2001–2002)*
T. K. Davis, *Design Director (2004–present)*
Andrea Gaffney, *Design Intern (2002–2003)*

Gary Gaston, *Associate Design Director (2002–present)*
Raven Hardison, *Design Intern (2003–2004)*
John Houghton, *Executive Director (2002–2003)*
Kate Monaghan, *Executive Director (2004–present)*
Mark Schimmenti, *Design Director (2001–2004)*

Metro staff assigned to the Plan of Nashville:

Randy Hutcheson, *Metro Planning Department (2001–2004)*
David Koellein, *Metro Development and Housing Agency (2002–present)*
Judy Steele, *Metro Development and Housing Agency (2001–2003)*

Early on in the preparation, the staff determined that they would need advice, hands-on expertise, and critical review. To get these, they formed two committees.

Steering Committee

The Steering Committee provided oversight for the process and reviewed each stage of the development of the Plan. This committee gave advice on matters political, logistical, and promotional.

Rick Bernhardt, *Executive Director, Metro Planning Department*
Ed Cole, *Chief of Environment and Planning, Tennessee Department of Transportation*
Mike Fitts, *Architect of the State of Tennessee*
Steve Gibson, *Interim Executive Director, Nashville Downtown Partnership*
Kim Hawkins, *Hawkins Partners Landscape Architects*
Christine Kreyling, *writer and architectural historian*
Mark McNeely, *McNeely, Pigott & Fox, public relations*

Left: Design Center staff from left to right: Lara Brewton, Gary Gaston, Stacy Battles, Mark Schimmenti, Judy Steele, Kate Monaghan.

Right: Steering Committee and Team Leaders from left to right: Frank Orr, Phil Walker, Keith Covington, Mark McNeely, Kim Hawkins, Gary Hawkins, Blythe Semmer, Debbie Frank, David Minnigan, David Coode, Gary Everton, Cyril Stewart, Seab Tuck.

Jeff Ockerman, *attorney, Stites and Harbison, PLLC*

Doug Perkins, *Associate Professor, Human and Organizational Development, Peabody College, Vanderbilt University*

Phil Ryan, *Executive Director, Metropolitan Development and Housing Agency*

Ralph Schulz, *President and CEO, Adventure Science Center*

Butch Spyridon, *Executive Director, Nashville Convention & Tourism Commission*

Seab Tuck, *Tuck Hinton Architects*

Tom Turner, *Executive Director, Nashville Downtown Partnership*

Design Committee

The Design Committee provided design expertise for the development of the Plan. The committee was composed of nine teams; each team had two leaders or captains. To ensure a diversity of expertise, no team had leaders from the same profession. The leaders recruited the additional members of their teams. Each team was responsible for a section of the Plan's study area. To ensure that the Plan was truly community-based, the teams did not begin designing until after the completion of all the community workshops.

The Design Committee also met regularly with the Steering Committee to report on progress and engage in a collective critique of the work.

Team Leaders:

Study Area A
Keith Covington, *Urban Designer, Metro Planning Department*
David Minnigan, *Earl Swensson Associates Architects*

Study Area B
Ben Crenshaw, *Ben Crenshaw Group*
Kem Hinton, *Tuck Hinton Architects*

Study Area C
David Coode, *Lose and Associates Landscape Architects*
Gary Everton, *Everton Ogelsby Architects*

Study Area D
Gary Gaston, *Associate Design Director, NCDC*
Andrea Gaffney, *Design Intern, NCDC*

Study Area E
Hunter Gee, *Looney Ricks Kiss Architects*
Cyril Stewart, *Director, Space and Facilities Planning, Vanderbilt University Medical Center*

Study Area F
Joe Hodgson, *Hodgson Douglas Landscape Architects*
Gillian Fischbach, *Fischbach Transportation Group*

Study Area G
Gary Hawkins, *Hawkins Partners Landscape Architects*
Bert Mathews, *The Mathews Company*

Study Area H
Jerry Fawcett, *City Planner, Metro Planning Department*
Blythe Semmer, *Preservation Planner, Metro Historical Commission*

Study Area I
Debbie Frank, *Executive Director, North Nashville Community Development Corporation*
NCDC Staff

Study Area J
Frank Orr, *Hart Freeland Roberts Architects*
Phil Walker, *The Walker Collaborative*

"Begin at the beginning," the King said gravely, "and go till you come to the end; then stop."

Lewis Carroll,
Alice's Adventures in Wonderland
(1865)

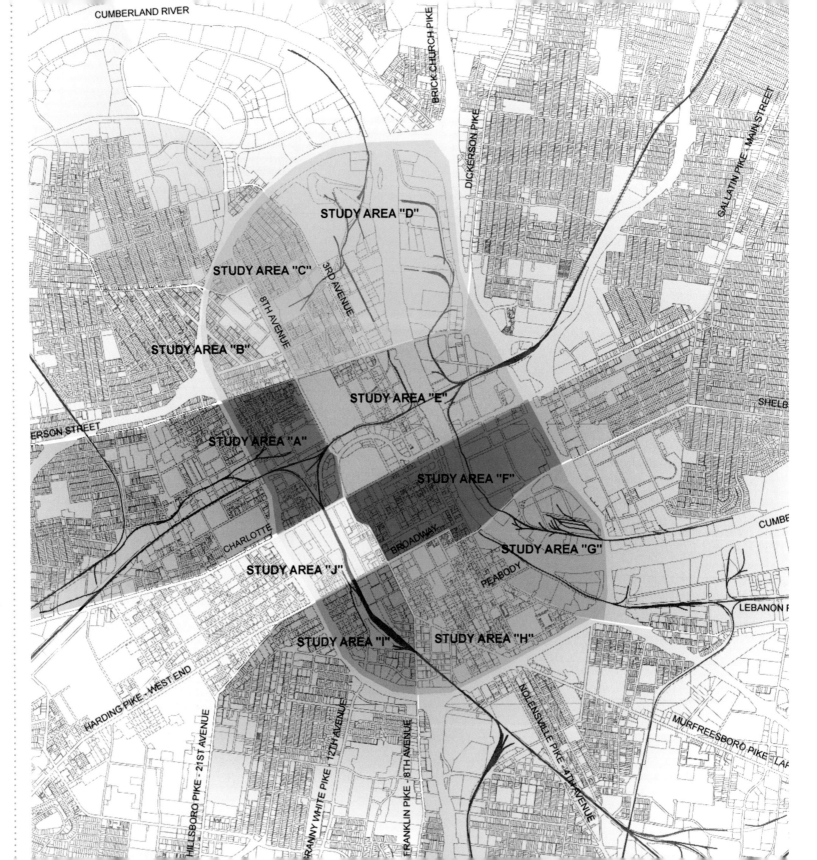

Study area, divided into sections. The solid colors indicate the prime area of focus of each design team; sections in lighter colors are those that the teams considered necessary to establish additional context for the Plan. Note that the river is never the edge of a section.

(Map, 2002: NCDC)

"We can chart our future clearly and wisely only when we know the path that has led to the present."

Adlai Stevenson, speech, Richmond, Virginia (September 20, 1952)

Design Center's John Houghton places a comment from a citizen onto the Nashville timeline during a community meeting.
(Photograph, 2002: NCDC)

What

The Plan of Nashville process had three aims:

- Establish, through community participation, a long-term vision and core set of design principles to guide current and future development in Nashville.
- Increase public awareness and understanding of the physical environment through community participation in historical research and design workshops.
- Produce a book that serves to record and illustrate the vision plan, design principles, and the process that established them.

Where

The original concept for the Plan's area of study was inside the inner loop of the interstate. But after discussion among NCDC staff and the committees, two considerations emerged that caused the scope of the Plan to expand to include the surrounding first-ring neighborhoods. First, the study, while focusing on the downtown, should examine the organic boundaries of the city rather than the artificial ones created by the interstates. Second, the river should not be treated as an edge but always studied as a center of focus, as a point of connection rather than division.

The next step was to divide this study area into smaller, more manageable chunks. Each design team needed a section of focus that was cohesive, included whole neighborhoods, and was of a manageable scale. The historic pikes were used to delineate each team's section, because the pikes were the traditional divisions between neighborhoods. The exception to this was Jefferson Street; although not strictly speaking a pike, this street's historic importance made it the edge of four sections. Because the river was not to be treated as an edge, relevant sections included both east and west banks.

The pairs of team leaders were then assigned a section, with two cautions: that the boundaries were to be considered as soft to allow for overlapping and combination when issues warranted, and that eventually the sections would have to be reassembled for consideration as a whole.

The high degree of participation by first-ring neighborhood residents and business owners in the subsequent community workshops validated the decision to expand the study area to consider the relationship between downtown and the surrounding neighborhoods.

The Process of the Plan

The Plan process was structured in five overlapping stages: research, community input on history and existing conditions, community vision development, synthesis, and production.[1]

Research

The first step toward a plan was looking backwards. In June 2002, the Design Committee team leaders formed ten study groups to investigate Nashville history and current conditions. Each group was assigned a particular topic: natural history and topography, cultural history, economic history, social and political history, history of urban form, history of urban proposals and plans, Nashville as downtown of the region, existing conditions and land use, transportation (local and regional systems), and contemporary case studies comparing Nashville with other mid-sized American cities.

The purpose of the research was to expand the consciousness of the design professionals who would be shaping the citizens' vision, thus ensuring that the Plan would be grounded in its historical context. In September 2002, the research culminated in a preliminary draft of the Nashville timeline, an edited version of which appears in "Nashville Past and Present" (see pages 5–38).

Listening to the Community

The community collaboration phase in the Plan process occupied roughly six months. The backbone of this phase was the community workshops, attended by more than eight hundred citizens. These workshops were augmented by panel discussions and presentations by experts in particular fields needing a focused critique: public art, transportation infrastructure,

> "To listen acutely is to be powerless, even if you sit on a throne."
> Cynthia Ozick,
> "Italo Calvino: Bringing Stories to Their Senses,"
> *Metaphor & Memory*
> (1989)

Community assessment
workshops.
(Photographs, 2002: NCDC)

and regional issues. All sessions were open to the public and advertised on the NCDC Web site, the Urban Design Forum and neighborhood e-mail mailing lists, media community calendars, and at meetings of neighborhood organizations. Each community meeting was held at a location within the study area section familiar to residents and business owners, such as a church hall, branch library, or school.

After research into numerous methodologies for community-based design charrettes and workshops by Randy Hutcheson, NCDC staff selected the organization and sample worksheets presented in *Planning for the Future: A Handbook on Community Visioning,* Center for Rural Pennsylvania Model, produced by the Hubert H. Humphrey Institute of Public Affairs (second edition, 2000).

Plan of Nashville: Avenues to a Great City *(Urban Design Forum, Nashville Public Library, September 19, 2002)*

NCDC staff presented the concept of the Plan and explained how the process would be organized.

Community Organization Meetings *(October–November 2002)*

The design teams introduced themselves to the community, explained the scope and process of the Plan of Nashville, and ascertained the best time, day of the week, and location for future meetings. The team captains also asked those attending to identify the names of community activists, historians, and special interest groups who should be recruited for participation.

Building a City *(panel discussion, Nashville Civic Design Center, October 24, 2002)*

While the design team leaders were organizing the community volunteers for each section, NCDC presented a panel discussion to address urban theory and practice from diverse perspectives. The idea was to establish a "big picture" ground on which to build the Plan. Experts representing the disciplines of architecture and planning, urban geography, environmental psychology, and community development banking were asked to define what is a city and then consider what makes a city "great," before answering questions from the audience.

Among topics the panelists discussed were the need for greater population density in the central city, how to build wealth and sustain human contact in cities, the

---

Should all future riverfront development require public access to the river?

Yes	83%
No	17%

From the "Building Consensus" Workshop

To what degree do you value historic buildings and the effort to preserve them?

Very important	94%
Somewhat important	6%
Somewhat unimportant	0%
Unimportant	0%

From the "Building Consensus" Workshop

relationship between transportation and settlement patterns, and what distinguishes urban from suburban form.

Panelists:

Jon Coddington, *Head of the Graduate Program in Architecture, University of Tennessee*

Ron Foresta, *Department of Geography, College of Arts and Sciences, University of Tennessee*

Susan Saegert, *The Center for Human Environments, City University of New York Graduate Center*

Steven Weiss, *South Shore Bank of Chicago*

Moderator: Betty Nixon, *Director of Community, Neighborhood, and Government Relations, Vanderbilt University*

Community Assessment Workshops *(November 2002–January 2003)*
The focus of this workshop series was on history and present conditions in each section of the study area. The design team presented data derived during the research phase and then formed breakout groups of no more than ten community members. Each group had a design team member as a lead, a notetaker, and a sketch artist.

During a series of exercises, group leaders asked participants to:
- Identify significant or defining events in your community in the past few years/decades.
- Describe your community (physical, social, communal) as though talking to a stranger.
- List three places you avoid taking out-of-town visitors.
- Name three or more sites that you consider public places where people can meet to discuss community issues.

- Name at least three natural and manmade features that make your community special and unique.
- Share any other reflections on the past or lessons learned.

Responses were simultaneously recorded in written notes and graphic sketches as well as on large maps. At the conclusion, all groups were brought back together and each presented its findings. NCDC staff subsequently compiled all the information into one list of issues and onto one map for each section of the study area.

Participants were also asked to review the draft of the Nashville timeline and add dates and events significant to their community.

History Caucus *(Nashville Civic Design Center, January 24, 2003)*
Nashville historians received copies of the timeline draft in advance of the caucus for critical review. They then gathered to suggest changes and additions to the timeline, and answer questions about local history from the audience.

Panelists:

Jeff Coker, *Department of History, Belmont University*

Don Doyle, *Department of History, Vanderbilt University*

John Egerton, *author of several books on Nashville history*

Douglas Henry, *State Senator*

Jim Hoobler, *Curator of Art, Tennessee State Museum*

Carol Kaplan, *Librarian of The Nashville Room, Nashville Public Library*

Christine Kreyling, *writer and architectural historian*

Should neighborhoods adjacent to the river incorporate it as part of their identity?

Yes	93%
No	7%

From the "Building Consensus" Workshop

Does Nashville need design guidelines for new development and civic space?

Yes	89%
No	5%
Not sure	6%

From the "Building Consensus" Workshop

Community vision workshops.

(Photographs, 2003: NCDC)

Bobby Lovett, *Department of History, Geography, and Political Science, Tennessee State University*

Reavis Mitchell, *Department of History, Fisk University*

Annette Ratkin, *Archives Director, The Jewish Federation of Nashville*

Ann Roberts, *Executive Director, Metro Historical Commission*

W. Ridley Wills II, *author of several books on Nashville history*

George Zepp, *"Learn Nashville" columnist,* The Tennessean

Moderator: Mark Schimmenti, *design director, Nashville Civic Design Center*

Community Vision Workshops *(February 2003)*

This workshop series asked the community to consider what they wanted to see in the Nashville of the future. At the suggestion of the participants in the community assessment workshops, sections of the study area were combined for the vision workshops to produce a broader consensus. These combined sections were ultimately used to define the treatment of the first-ring neighborhoods (see "Nashville and Its Neighborhoods: Fanning the Flames of Place," pages 139–224).

Each session began with team leaders presenting a summary of the Plan process to date, the data derived from the previous assessment workshop, and a list of potential major projects on the civic agenda—a convention center, baseball stadium, federal courthouse, civic square in East Nashville, etc.—so that the citizens could consider possible developments when addressing their respective sections of the study area.

Then breakout groups were formed. Each group had a design team member as a lead, a notetaker, and a sketch artist. The group was led through a series of questions about their dreams and aspirations for their neighborhood:

- If you could have three or more attractions in your community to take out-of-town visitors to, what would they be? (Examples: restaurants, parks, museums, stores, churches, public art, or a great street.)
- Name three or more sites that could be public places.
- Name three or more natural and manmade features that could make your community special and unique.
- Name three or more streets, paths (i.e., greenway or trail), and edges (i.e., river) that could make your community better.
- What areas of your community do you want to change (and what kind of change do you want to see) and what areas do you want to keep the same?

- What ten things would bring the biggest improvements to the city in the future?

As with the previous community workshops, responses were simultaneously recorded in written notes and graphic sketches as well as on large maps. At the conclusion, all groups were brought back together and each presented its proposals. Team leaders subsequently compiled all the information into one list of issues and onto one map for each section of the study area.

How to Create an Urban Renaissance *(Urban Design Forum, Nashville Civic Design Center, February 20, 2003)* Presentation by Nancy Graham, developer and former mayor of West Palm Beach, Florida. Graham discussed strategies for revitalizing a downtown.

Contemporary Issues in Urban Design *(Urban Design Forum, Nashville Civic Design Center, March 26, 2003)* Presentation by Victor Dover, urban designer with Dover Kohl firm of Coral Gables, Florida. Dover discussed planning techniques to supply urban character in the redevelopment of underutilized and abandoned sites in a city.

The Mayor as Urban Designer *(Urban Design Forum, Nashville Civic Design Center, April 9, 2003)* Presentation by Joseph P. Riley, Mayor of Charleston, South Carolina. Riley discussed how local public policies focused on good urban design can restore historic building fabric, create new infill, add affordable housing, and in general revitalize a city.

Building Consensus Workshop *(Nashville Convention Center, April 12, 2003)* This second vision workshop, which considered all sections of the study area as a whole for the first time, was designed to develop agreement on the principles of the Plan and consolidate the vision for Nashville. More than 250 people attended the Saturday morning session. The agenda included a kick-off speech by Mayor Purcell, an introduction on basic principles of urban design, a

---

If there was a convenient, extensive public transit system located within five blocks of your house, would you use it instead of your car to commute to work?

Yes	77%
No	23%

From the "Building Consensus" Workshop

Should future public/ affordable housing be dispersed throughout the community?

Yes	96%
No	7%

From the "Building Consensus" Workshop

Should a plan be created and financed to place overhead utilities underground?

Yes	93%
No	7%

From the "Building Consensus" Workshop

Should a downtown elementary school be built for people who live and work downtown?

Yes	90%
No	10%

From the "Building Consensus" Workshop

Sample of the maps produced
in each vision workshop.

(Drawings over map, 2003:
vision workshop participants)

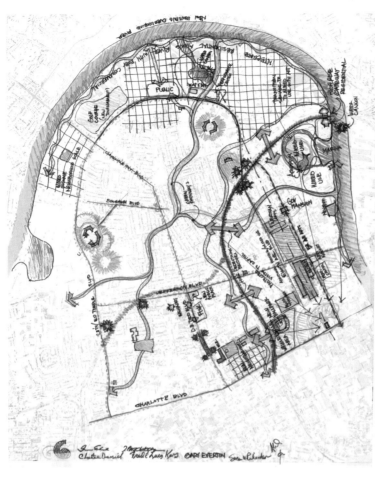

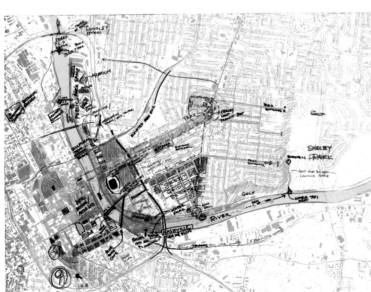

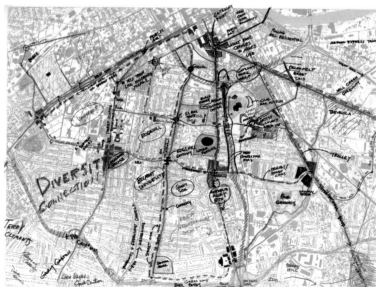

presentation on the previous vision workshop results from a citizen representing each of the sections, followed by an extensive electronic survey.

The survey was developed in consultation with Betina Finley, President of TurnKey Video and New Media in Seattle. The eighty-two questions in ten categories established the demographics of the participants and then asked their opinions on issues relating to the Cumberland River, cultural attractions, the natural and built environment, neighborhoods, transportation infrastructure, economic development, housing, urban design, and education.

This initial survey was then augmented by an online survey to which an additional three hundred citizens responded. The information derived from the survey was used by NCDC staff and design team leaders to finalize the Plan's goals and principles, which were in turn used to produce the design of the Plan. The workshop concluded with an inspirational speech entitled "Painting a Canvas" by the Reverend Ed Sanders.

Envisioning Public Art in the Plan of Nashville *(Nashville Civic Design Center and Shelby Bridge, April 26, 2003)*
Workshop conducted by Jack Mackie, public artist, Seattle, Washington. The Metro Nashville Arts Commission teamed with the Design Center to sponsor two workshops that explored the numerous ways that public art can serve as a tool of urban design and identified the most favorable locations for Nashville's initial public art projects.

The first workshop began with a slide presentation by Jack Mackie that examined how artists are currently working in public art, followed by a discussion of the Plan of Nashville's principles and goals. Participants formed teams, then studied maps and evaluated locations suggested as public art sites during the Plan's community meetings. Photographs plus historical and cultural notes helped the teams choose areas where public art could be a tool for accomplishing the Plan's goals. At the close of the workshop, the teams gathered and voted for the top three locations. The Shelby Street Bridge area was identified as the favorite site for an initial project within Nashville's public art program.

In a second workshop, participants explored and evaluated the breadth of public art opportunities on the Shelby Street Bridge and in the surrounding area. Participants heard presentations about the site—its history and ecology, function and symbolism—and then walked the bridge. From this removed-from-the-city yet surrounded-by-the-city point of view, participants now saw the Plan of Nashville and the Nashville Public Art Program as merged or complementary methodologies to produce good urban design and unique icons for one of the city's best public places.

The Role of Public Space in the American City *(Urban Design Forum, Nashville Civic Design Center, May 15, 2003)*
Presentation by Fred Kent of the Project for Public Spaces. Kent discussed how to create successful public places and critiqued the urban design values and open space in Nashville's downtown.

Synthesis and Production
By late April, NCDC staff had completed draft versions of the Plan's principles and presented them to the Steering Committee. The staff and interns then began the task of pulling the results of the vision workshops and the work of the design teams into a unified vision. Maps of the complete study area were derived by using multiple overlays of maps and diagrams generated by the workshops and refined by the design teams. Eventually the completed maps were transferred to the computer and diagrammatic information was extracted for analysis of the emerging Plan.

NCDC staff then coordinated a series of meetings with the team leaders to resolve issues that transcended sections, such as interstate transformation and the treatment of the Cumberland River banks. The result was a vision map for the entire study area.

"Sprawl is the common enemy of the farmer and the downtown merchant, but they're not working together."

Steve Gibson, Nashville Downtown Partnership, at "Downtown and the Region" forum

Design Center staff working on the Plan.
(Photograph, 2003: NCDC)

Putting the Plan Together *(Urban Design Forum, Nashville Civic Design Center, June 19, 2003)*
NCDC staff presented the vision map and analytical composite diagrams that summarized the results of the community vision workshops for feedback and discussion.

The Plan of Nashville: Cultural Policy at the Grassroots *(Curb Center for Art, Enterprise, and Public Policy, Vanderbilt University, July 10-11, 2003)*
This symposium focused on how public policy affects Nashville's cultural life. A series of paired presentations—the Nashville perspective and the national perspective—addressed topics such as arts education, cultural tourism, affordable housing, and artist venues, concluding with a group discussion on the role of arts organizations in the Plan of Nashville.

National consultants:
Vincent Marron, *Executive Director, North Carolina A+ Schools Program*
Jane Polin, *philanthropic adviser, New York City*
Barbara Steinfeld, *Director of Cultural Tourism, Portland Oregon Visitors Association*
Laura Weathered, *Executive Director, Near NorthWest Arts Council, Chicago*

Facilitators:
Bill Ivey, *Director, Curb Center for Art, Enterprise, and Public Policy at Vanderbilt*
Ellen McCulloch-Lovell, *President and CEO, Center for Arts and Culture*

Transportation: Walter Kulash *(Urban Design Forum, Nashville Civic Design Center, July 17, 2003)*
Nationally known traffic engineer Walter Kulash made a presentation on new theories of transportation infrastructure and responded to questions about how they might apply to Nashville. He also worked with the design committee and NCDC staff specifically to address issues about the interstate system that had arisen during the Plan process.

In his talk, Kulash said he thought it feasible to explore dissolving Nashville's interstate inner loop, and that the political challenges of interstate reform outweighed the engineering challenges. He advised that to build a case for change, Nashvillians should study the value and amount of land that could be reclaimed—especially around interchanges—and establish comparisons with peer cities on the number of lane-miles of inner-city interstates.

Downtown and the Region *(panel discussion, Urban Design Forum, Nashville Civic Design Center, August 21, 2003)*
This panel was presented to bring added consideration to regional issues in the Plan, such as the health of the Cumberland River watershed, the lack of appropriate limits to development in floodplains and on steep slopes, declining air quality, greenways as wildlife habitat not merely recreational space, Nashville as the hub of the region's transportation infrastructure, the city's role as a jobs center, and the absence of state planning to guide development in ways that balance economic and environmental needs.

Panel:
Ed Cole, *Chief of Environment and Planning, Tennessee Department of Transportation*
Mark DeKay, *College of Architecture, University of Tennessee*
Margo Farnsworth, *Executive Director, Cumberland River Compact*
Mike Fitts, *Tennessee State Architect*
Bridget Jones Kelly, *Executive Director, Cumberland Region Tomorrow*
Trip Pollard, *Senior Attorney, Southern Environmental Law Center*
Wendy Smith, *Environmentalist, World Wildlife Fund*
Kathleen Williams, *President and Executive Director, Tennessee Greenways*

Moderator: Christine Kreyling

Visions for Nashville *(Urban Design Forum, Nashville Civic Design Center, September 18, 2003)*
During the summer, design team leaders had worked to bring specific plans and highlights within their sections, such as the Ellington Parkway terminus and the Governor Green, to a high level of design resolution. At the September forum, each pair of team leaders presented the plan for their section within the context of the entire study area.

This forum was thus the culmination of the Plan of Nashville process, and marked the conclusion of the year spent in developing the Plan. At this point the teams turned over all their designs to NCDC staff, and the staff began to prepare final illustrations and develop rationales in preparation for the publication of the Plan.

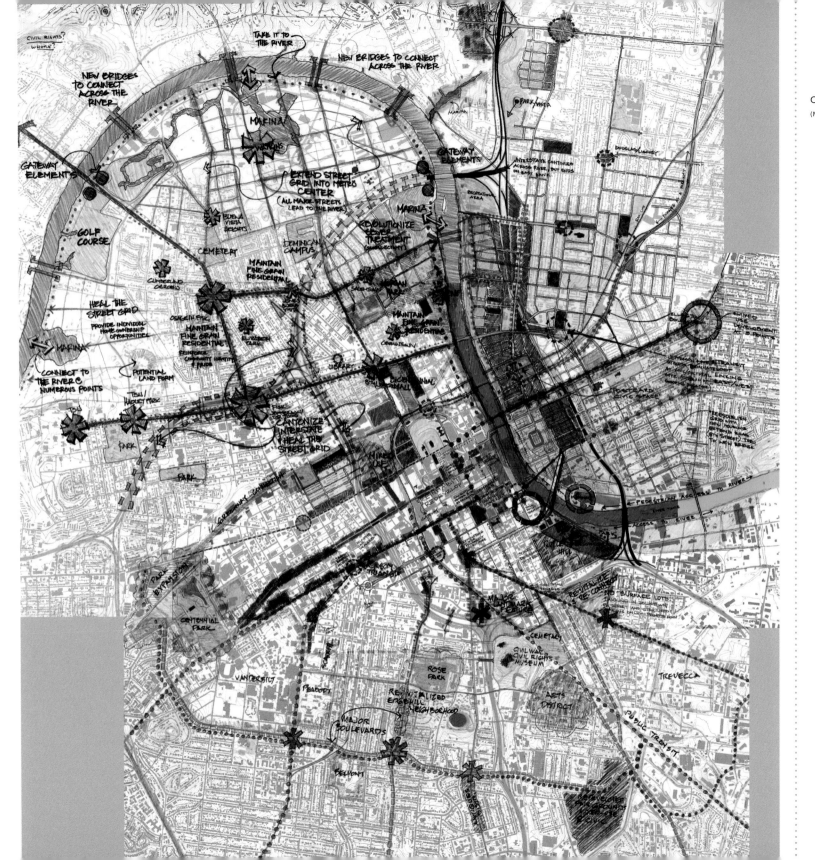

Compiled vision map.
(Map, 2003: NCDC)

241

The Challenges of Citizen Participation

The process of residents getting together with architects and planners to decide how they want their city to develop represents a relatively new orientation. Decisions about urban planning and development in the United States have traditionally been limited to the financially and politically powerful, and the professionals they hire. In fact, most of the developments that characterize Nashville—such as urban renewal and transportation infrastructure—were not based on any sort of public consensus, but were the result of decisions made from the top.

The Nashville Civic Design Center—like other organizations employing innovative methodologies in urban design—has used its resources to push for an expanded role for people of diverse backgrounds in the planning of their city. The Plan of Nashville process is an example of the incorporation of citizen participation in the determination of a city's future. The staff and volunteers of the Design Center went out to the neighborhoods and asked questions, attempted to build consensus, then shaped the preferences and ideas with their own expertise.

Working for deeper democracy in an entrenched system of power, though, is never easy. Processes like this raise interesting questions. For instance, who were these residents who came to the meetings when the decisions were made? What was the nature of their experience? What about the people who didn't or couldn't show up? Were they aware of the meetings? Were some important viewpoints excluded from the process? What about disagreements? How is it possible to tell when residents have truly reached consensus, and when only the opinions of a particular demographic or vested interest are being captured?

The questions will multiply as this book is published and Nashville continues to grow and develop. Will the residents that contributed their efforts to the process recognize this new vision, which has been adapted by architects and designers? Will neighborhoods use the Plan to advocate for development that fits this vision? Will they stand up against those who do not develop according to the vision? Will they be successful in efforts to influence the city's development process? How closely will the Nashville of the future resemble this collective vision of what it could be?

As a step toward being able to effectively answer these questions, the Design Center has collaborated with us, community development researchers, in designing a survey for the Plan's participants. The survey will be made available shortly after the release of this book. The analysis of these data will contribute to the growing body of knowledge on participatory planning and design. Our hope is that our study of the Plan of Nashville process will contribute to the enhancement of the practice of participatory urban design, both in Nashville and in other cities. We hope that this shift toward more egalitarian community development processes will continue, and we believe that the end result will be more interesting, beautiful, and livable cities.

The vision put forward by this book reflects the use of state-of-the-art methodology, but the challenges of achieving genuine citizen participation in civic design and development are far from met. We look forward to being able to capture the experiences, characteristics, and opinions of the participants in the Plan, and to sharing our analyses of those data with those who wish to continue with this type of work.

Brian Christens and Daniel Cooper
Ph.D. students in Community Research and Action, Department of Human and Organizational Development, Peabody College, Vanderbilt University

Notes

Introduction

1. Robert Campbell, quoting landscape architect Warren Byrd, *Architectural Record* 191 (June 7, 2003): 62.

Nashville Past and Present

1. Early economic history from Anita Shafer Goodstein, *Nashville 1780–1860: From Frontier to City* (Gainesville: University of Florida Press, 1989), xi.

2. The grid and its historical application from Spiro Kostof, *The City Shaped: Urban Patterns and Meaning Through History* (Boston: Bulfinch Press, Little, Brown and Co., 1991), 95–157.

3. Goodstein, *Nashville 1780–1860*, 4.

4. John Egerton, *Nashville: The Faces of Two Centuries, 1780–1980* (Nashville, Tenn: PlusMedia Inc., 1979), 37.

5. Kostof, *City Shaped*, 121.

6. Kostof, *City Shaped*, 232.

7. Goodstein, *Nashville 1780–1860*, 23–24.

8. Goodstein, *Nashville 1780–1860*, 106.

9. History of water supply from Wilbur Foster Creighton, *Building of Nashville* (Nashville, Tenn.: privately printed, 1969), 44–47.

10. Civil War history from Egerton, *Nashville: The Faces of Two Centuries*, 117–26, and Don Doyle, *New Men, New Cities, New South: Atlanta, Nashville, Charleston, Mobile, 1860–1910* (Chapel Hill: University of North Carolina Press, 1990), 24–31.

11. Doyle, *New Men, New Cities, New South*, 27–28.

12. Noble L. Prentis, in *Southern Letters*, 1881, quoted in Egerton, *Nashville: The Faces of Two Centuries*, 144.

13. Information on commerce and living conditions in Nashville during this period from Doyle, *New Men, New Cities, New South*, 39–108.

14. Don Doyle, *Nashville in the New South: 1880–1930* (Knoxville: University of Tennessee Press, 1985), 83.

15. History of Nashville's suburban expansion from Doyle, *Nashville in the New South*, 87–120.

16. Parks history from Leland R. Johnson, *The Parks of Nashville: A History of the Board of Parks and Recreation* (Nashville, Tenn.: Metropolitan Nashville and Davidson County Board of Parks and Recreation, 1986), 33–50.

17. Information on Nashville in the 1920s from Doyle, *Nashville in the New South*, 183–234.

18. *Tennessean*, 18 January 1925; quoted in Doyle, *Nashville in the New South*, 200.

19. Doyle, *Nashville in the New South*, 199-201.

20. Information on the rise of the public sector from Robert G. Spinney, *World War II in Nashville: Transformation of the Homefront* (Knoxville: University of Tennessee Press, 1998), 1–16.

21. Douglas Smith, *New Deal in the Urban South*, quoted in Spinney, *World War II in Nashville*, 8.

22. The evolution of zoning in Nashville from Lester M. Salamon and Gary L. Wamsley, "The Politics of Urban Land Policy: Zoning and Urban Development in Nashville," in *Growing Metropolis: Aspects of Development in Nashville*, ed. James F. Blumstein and Benjamin Walter (Nashville, Tenn.: Vanderbilt University Press, 1975), 141–90.

23. Planning history from Randal L. Hutcheson, "A History of Planning in Nashville, Tennessee," Nashville Civic Design Center, 2004.

24. History of postwar Nashville from Don Doyle, *Nashville Since the 1920s* (Knoxville: University of Tennessee Press, 1985), 108–42.

25. History of public housing policy in Nashville from Margaret Martin Holleman, "Federal Housing Policy," Nashville Civic Design Center, 2003.

26. Doyle, *Nashville Since the 1920s*, 97–98.

27. History of Capitol Hill and downtown renewal from Doyle, *Nashville Since the 1920s*, 121–42.

28. History of urban renewal in Nashville from Holleman, "Federal Housing Policy," and Robert James Parks, "Grasping at the Coattails of Progress: City Planning in Nashville, Tennessee, 1932–1962" (master's thesis, Vanderbilt University, 1971).

29. The coming of Metro government from Doyle, *Nashville Since the 1920s*, 179–221, and Parks, "Grasping at the Coattails of Progress," 190–234.

30. Insights on the impacts of Metro on the old city from Jerry Fawcett, interview with author, Nashville, Tenn., 2 August 2004.

31. Desegregation in Nashville from Doyle, *Nashville Since the 1920s*, 222–60.

32. Country Music Hall of Fame and Museum, *Night Train to Nashville: Music City Rhythm & Blues, 1945–1970* (Nashville, Tenn.: Country Music Foundation Press, 2004) 4–5, 62.

33. Preservation in Nashville from Ann Roberts and Blythe Semmer, "Preservation of the Built Environment," Metro Historical Commission, 2004.

34. Joel Kotkin, quoted by Martin C. Pedersen in "Cities in the Digital Age," *Metropolis*, January 2004, *http://www.metropolismag.com/html/content_0104/ob/ob01_0104.html* (January 2004).

The Plan: Nashville and Its Region

1. Federal Writers' Project, Tennessee, *The WPA Guide to Tennessee* (1939; reprint, Knoxville: University of Tennessee Press, 1986), 372–74.

2. Kristen Schaffer, introduction to *Plan of Chicago*, by Daniel H. Burnham and Edward H. Bennett (1909; reprint, New York: Princeton Architectural Press, 1993), v.

3. Gillian L. Fishbach and P. Suzanne Jackson, "The Origin and Advancement of Nashville's Transportation System," *ITE Journal* (March 2000): 27.

4. U. S. Public Interest Research Group, "More Highways, More Pollution: Road-Building and Air Pollution in America's Cities," U. S. PIRG Reports, 9 March 2004. *http://www.uspirg.org* (March 2004).

The Plan: Nashville and Its Downtown

1. Jane Jacobs, *The Death and Life of Great American Cities* (New York: Random House, 1961; reprint, New York: Vintage Books, 1992), 165.

2. This and following citations from Kostof, *City Shaped*; this citation pp. 215–18.

3. Kem Hinton, *A Long Path* (Franklin, Tenn.: Hillsboro Press, 1997), 26.

4. Pam Neary, "OutLANDish TAXes?" *The New Rules*, Summer 1999, *http://www.newrules.org/resources/outland* (July 2004).

5. Lewis Mumford, *The City in History* (New York: Harcourt, Brace and Co., 1961, reprint 1989), 304.

6. Jacobs, *Death and Life of Great American Cities*, 349–50.

The Plan: Nashville and Its Neighborhoods

1. Colin Powell with Joseph E. Persico, *My American Journey* (New York: Random House, 1995; reprint, New York: Ballantine Books, 1996), 10–11.

2. The composition of the ideal neighborhood is from *Charter of the New Urbanism*, ed. Michael Leccese and Kathleen McCormick (New York: McGraw-Hill, 2000), 79-86.

3. Mumford, *City in History*, 304.

4. Kulash citations from Leccese and McCormick, *Charter*, 83–86.

5. Peirce F. Lewis, *New Orleans: The Making of an Urban Landscape*, 2nd ed. (Santa Fe, N.Mex., and Harrisonburg, Va.: Center for American Places in association with the University of Virginia Press, 2003), 4.

6. Historical information from Historical Commission of Metropolitan Nashville–Davidson County, *Nashville: Conserving a Heritage* (Nashville, Tenn.: Historical Commission of Metropolitan Nashville–Davidson County, 1977), 35–36, 53–55.

7. Bobby L. Lovett, *The African-American History of Nashville, Tennessee, 1780–1930* (Fayetteville: University of Arkansas Press, 1999), 55.

8. Parks history from Leland R. Johnson, *The Parks of Nashville: A History of the Board of Parks and Recreation* (Nashville, Tenn.: Metropolitan Nashville and Davidson County Board of Parks and Recreation, 1986), 242–43, 258.

9. Historical information from Historical Commission, *Nashville: Conserving a Heritage*, 55-57.

10. Lovett, African-American *History of Nashville*, 76.

11. Parks history from Johnson, *Parks of Nashville*, 236, 245–46.

12. E. Michael Fleenor, *Images of America: East Nashville* (Charleston, S.C.: Arcadia Publishing, 1998), 7.

13. History unless otherwise indicated from Historical Commission, *Nashville: Conserving a Heritage*, 27–28.

14. Doyle, *Nashville in the New South*, 87–92.

15. American Institute of Architects, *R/UDAT: A Plan for East Nashville* (1999).

16. Nashville Civic Design Center, *East Bank of the Cumberland River: Findings and Recommendations* (2002).

17. Lovett, *African American History of Nashville*, 73–74.

18. Doyle, *Nashville in the New South*, 80–82.

19. Doyle, *Nashville in the New South*, 45.

20. Rutledge Hill history from Historical Commission, *Nashville: Conserving a Heritage*, 32–33.

21. Benjamin Walter, "Ethnicity and Racial Succession in Nashville, 1850–1920," in Blumstein and Walter, *Growing Metropolis*, 28–30.

22. Everton Oglesby Architects for the Metro Development and Housing Agency, *Subarea 9 Master Plan Update* (December 1997).

23. Doyle, *New Men, New Cities, New South*, 23–24.

24. Egerton, *Nashville: The Faces of Two Centuries*, 163–71.

25. Doyle, *Nashville in the New South*, 89-95.

26. Eugene TeSelle, *Hillsboro Village: Yesterday, Today and Tomorrow* (Nashville, Tenn.: Belmont-Hillsboro Neighbors, Inc. and Vanderbilt University, 1993), 1.

27. TeSelle, *Hillsboro Village*, 4.

28. Sasaki Associates, Inc., *Vanderbilt University Campus Land Use and Development Plan* (November 2001).

The Plan: Ideas into Reality

1. Committee on the City Plan, *Development and Present Status of City Planning in New York City* (New York: City of New York, Board of Estimate and Apportionment, Committee on the City Plan, 1914), 12, quoted in Alexander Garvin, *The American City: What Works, What Doesn't* (New York: McGraw-Hill, 1996), 428.

2. Garvin, *American City*, 437.

3. Garvin, *American City*, 437.

Process

1. A complete documentation of the Plan of Nashville process is available in the archives of the Nashville Civic Design Center and in the Special Collections division of the Nashville Public Library.

Bibliography

American Institute of Architects. *R/UDAT: A Plan for East Nashville*. 1999.

Bel Geddes, Norman. *Magic Motorways*. New York: Random House, 1940.

Benevolo, Leonardo. *The History of the City*. Cambridge: MIT Press, 1980.

Burnham, Daniel and Edward H. Bennett. *Plan of Chicago*. 1909. Reprint, New York: Princeton Architectural Press, 1993.

Calthorpe, Peter. *The Next American Metropolis: Ecology, Community, and the American Dream*. New York: Princeton Architectural Press, 1993.

Clarke and Rapuano. *Central Loop: General Neighborhood Renewal Plan*. Nashville, Tenn.: Nashville Housing Authority, December 1963.

Country Music Hall of Fame and Museum. *Night Train to Nashville: Music City Rhythm & Blues, 1945–1970*. Nashville, Tenn.: Country Music Foundation Press, 2004.

Crabb, Alfred Leland. *Nashville: Personality of a City*. Indianapolis: Bobbs-Merrill, 1960.

Creighton, Wilbur Foster. *Building of Nashville*. Nashville, Tenn.: privately printed, 1969.

Crouch, Dora P., Daniel J. Garr, and Axel I. Mundigo. *Spanish City Planning in North America*. Cambridge: MIT Press, 1982.

Downs, Anthony. *New Visions for Metropolitan America*. Washington, D.C.: Brookings Institution and Lincoln Institute of Land Policy, 1994.

Doyle, Don H. *Nashville in the New South: 1880–1920*. Knoxville: University of Tennessee Press, 1985.

Doyle, Don H. *Nashville Since the 1920s*. Knoxville: University of Tennessee Press, 1985.

Doyle, Don H. *New Men, New Cities, New South: Atlanta, Nashville, Charleston, Mobile, 1860–1910*. Chapel Hill: University of North Carolina Press, 1990.

Duany, Andres and Elizabeth Plater-Zyberk. *Towns and Townmaking Principles*. New York: Rizzoli, 1991.

Duany, Andres, Elizabeth Plater-Zyberk, and Robert Alminana. *The New Civic Art: Elements of Town Planning*. New York: Princeton Architectural Press, 2003.

Durham, Walter T. *Reluctant Partners: Nashville and the Union, July 1, 1863, to June 30, 1865*. Nashville, Tenn.: Tennessee Historical Society, 1987.

Egerton, John. *Nashville: The Faces of Two Centuries*. Nashville, Tenn.: PlusMedia Inc., 1979.

Egerton, John and E. Thomas Wood, eds. *Nashville: An American Self-Portrait*. Nashville, Tenn.: Beaten Biscuit Press, 2001.

Everton Oglesby Architects for the Metro Development and Housing Agency. *Subarea 9 Master Plan Update*. December 1997.

Faragher, Scott. *Nashville in Vintage Postcards*. Charleston, S.C.: Arcadia Publishing, 1999.

Federal Writers' Project, Tennessee. *The WPA Guide to Tennessee*. 1939. Reprint, Knoxville: University of Tennessee Press, 1986.

Fishbach, Gillian L. and P. Suzanne Jackson. "The Origin and Advancement of Nashville's Transportation System." *ITE Journal* (March 2000): 24–33.

Fleenor, E. Michael. *Images of America: East Nashville*. Charleston, S.C.: Arcadia Publishing, 1998.

Garvin, Alexander. *The American City: What Works, What Doesn't*. New York: McGraw-Hill, 1996.

Goodstein, Anita Shafer. *Nashville 1780–1860: From Frontier to City*. Gainesville: University of Florida Press, 1989.

Graham, Eleanor. *Nashville: A Short History and Selected Buildings*. Nashville, Tenn.: Historical Commission of Metropolitan Nashville–Davidson County, 1974.

Gratz, Roberta Brandes and Norman Mintz. *Cities Back from the Edge: New Life for Downtown*. New York: John Wiley and Sons, 1998.

Hegemann, Werner and Elbert Peets. *The American Vitruvius: An Architects' Handbook of Civic Art*. 1922. Reprint, New York: Princeton Architectural Press, 1988.

Hinton, Kem. *A Long Path*. Franklin, Tenn.: Hillsboro Press, 1997.

Historical Commission of Metropolitan Nashville–Davidson County. *Nashville: Conserving a Heritage*. Nashville, Tenn.: Historical Commission of Metropolitan Nashville–Davidson County, 1977.

Hoobler, James. *Images of America: Nashville from the Collection of Carl and Otto Giers*. Charleston, S.C.: Arcadia Publishing, 1999.

Hylton, Thomas. *Save Our Land, Save Our Towns: A Plan for Pennsylvania*. Harrisburg, Penn.: RB Books, 1995.

Jackson, Kenneth T. *Crabgrass Frontier: The Suburbanization of the United States*. New York: Oxford University Press, 1987.

Jacobs, Allan B. *Great Streets*. Cambridge: MIT Press, 1993.

Jacobs, Allan, Elizabeth Macdonald, and Yodan Rof. *The Boulevard Book: History, Evolution, Design of Multiway Boulevards*. Cambridge: MIT Press, 2002.

Jacobs, Jane. *Cities and the Wealth of Nations: Principles of Economic Life*. New York: Random House, 1984.

Jacobs, Jane. *The Death and Life of Great American Cities*. New York: Random House, 1961; reprint, New York: Vintage Books, 1992.

Johnson, Leland R. *The Parks of Nashville: A History of the Board of Parks and Recreation*. Nashville, Tenn.: Metropolitan Nashville and Davidson County Board of Parks and Recreation, 1986.

Katz, Peter. *The New Urbanism: Toward an Architecture of Community*. New York: McGraw-Hill, 1994.

Kelbaugh, Douglas. *Common Place: Toward Neighborhood and Regional Design*. Seattle: University of Washington Press, 1997.

Kelbaugh, Douglas, ed. *The Pedestrian Pocket Book: A New Suburban Design Strategy*. New York: Princeton Architectural Press, 1989.

Kostof, Spiro. *The City Shaped: Urban Patterns and Meanings Through History*. Boston: Bulfinch Press, Little, Brown and Co., 1991.

Kreyling, Christine, Wesley Paine, Charles W. Warterfield, Jr., and Susan Ford Wiltshire. *Classical Nashville: Athens of the South*. Nashville, Tenn: Vanderbilt University Press, 1996.

Krier, Léon. *Houses, Palaces, Cities.* New York: St. Martin's Press, 1984.

Kulash, Walter. Essay 12 in *Charter of the New Urbanism*, edited by Michael Leccese and Kathleen McCormick, 83–86. New York: McGraw-Hill, 2000.

Kunstler, James Howard. *Home from Nowhere: Remaking our Everyday World for the Twenty-first Century.* New York: Simon and Schuster, 1996.

Kunstler, James Howard. *The Geography of Nowhere: The Rise and Decline of America's Man-Made Landscape.* New York: Simon and Schuster, 1993.

Langdon, Philip. *A Better Place to Live: Reshaping the American Suburb.* Amherst: University of Massachusetts Press, 1994; New York: Harper Perennial, 1995.

Leccese, Michael, and Kathleen McCormick, eds. *Charter of the New Urbanism.* New York: McGraw-Hill, 2000.

Lejeune, Jean-Francois, ed. *The New City.* Vol. 3, *Modern Cities.* New York: Princeton Architectural Press, 1996.

Lewis, Peirce F. *New Orleans: The Making of an Urban Landscape.* 2nd ed. Santa Fe, N.Mex., and Harrisonburg, Va.: Center for American Places in association with the University of Virginia Press, 2003.

Lovett, Bobby L. *The African-American History of Nashville, Tennessee, 1780–1930.* Fayetteville: University of Arkansas Press, 1999.

MacKaye, Benton. *The New Exploration: A Philosophy of Regional Planning.* 1928. Reprint, Champaign: University of Illinois Press, 1994.

Mumford, Lewis. *The City in History.* New York: Harcourt, Brace and Co., 1961, reprint 1989.

Nashville Civic Design Center. *East Bank of the Cumberland River: Findings and Recommendations.* 2002.

Nashville Housing Authority. *Capitol Hill Redevelopment Project.* April 1952.

Neary, Pam. "OutLANDish TAXes?" *The New Rules*, Summer 1999. *http://www.newrules.org/resources/outland* (July 2004).

Norman, Jack, Sr. *The Nashville I Knew.* Nashville, Tenn.: Rutledge Hill Press, 1984.

Pedersen, Martin C. "Cities in the Digital Age." *Metropolis*, January 2004. *http://www.metropolismag.com/html/content_0104/ob/ob01_0104.html* (January 2004).

Planning Commission, Metropolitan Government of Nashville and Davidson County. *History and Physical Setting, Nashville and Davidson County.* Nashville, Tenn., February 1965.

Plater-Zyberk, Elizabeth. Essay 11 in *Charter of the New Urbanism*, edited by Michael Leccese and Kathleen McCormick, 79–82. New York: McGraw-Hill, 2000.

Polyzoides, Stefanos, et al. *Courtyard Housing in Los Angeles: A Typological Analysis.* 2nd ed. New York: Princeton Architectural Press, 1992.

Powell, Colin with Joseph E. Persico. *My American Journey.* New York: Random House, 1995. Reprint, New York: Ballantine Books, 1996.

Reps, John. *The Making of Urban America: A History of City Planning in the United States.* Princeton: Princeton University Press, 1965, reprint 1992.

Rybczynski, Witold. *City Life: Urban Expectations in a New World.* New York: Scribner, 1995.

Salamon, Lester M. and Gary L. Wamsley. "The Politics of Urban Land Policy: Zoning and Urban Development in Nashville." In *Growing Metropolis: Aspects of Development in Nashville*, edited by James F. Blumstein and Benjamin Walter. Nashville, Tenn.: Vanderbilt University Press, 1975.

Sasaki Associates, Inc. *Vanderbilt University Campus Land Use and Development Plan.* November 2001.

Schaffer, Kristen. Introduction to *Plan of Chicago*, by Daniel H. Burnham and Edward H. Bennett. 1909. Reprint, New York: Princeton Architectural Press, 1993.

Sennett, Richard. *The Fall of Public Man.* Cambridge: Cambridge University Press, 1977. Reprint, New York: W. W. Norton, 1992.

Sherman, Joe. *A Thousand Voices: The Story of Nashville's Union Station.* Nashville, Tenn.: Rutledge Hill Press, 1987.

Sitte, Camillo. *City Planning According to Artistic Principles.* Translated by George R. Collins and Christiane Crasemann Collins. First published Vienna, 1889. New York: Random House, 1965.

Spinney, Robert G. *World War II in Nashville: Transformation of the Homefront.* Knoxville: University of Tennessee Press, 1998.

TeSelle, Eugene. *Hillsboro Village: Yesterday, Today and Tomorrow.* Nashville, Tenn.: Belmont-Hillsboro Neighbors, Inc. and Vanderbilt University, 1993.

Unwin, Raymond. *Town Planning in Practice: An Introduction to the Art of Designing Cities and Suburbs.* New York: Princeton Architectural Press, 1994.

U. S. Public Interest Research Group. "More Highways, More Pollution: Road-Building and Air Pollution in America's Cities." U. S. PIRG Reports, 9 March 2004. *http://www.uspirg.org* (March 2004).

van Pelt, Robert Jan and Carroll William Westfall. *Architectural Principles in the Age of Historicism.* New Haven: Yale University Press, 1991.

Van West, Carroll, ed. *Tennessee's New Deal Landscapes: A Guidebook.* Knoxville: University of Tennessee Press, 2001.

Venturi, Robert, Denise Scott Brown, and Steven Izenour. *Learning from Las Vegas.* Cambridge: MIT Press, 1972.

Waller, William. *Nashville in the 1890's.* Nashville, Tenn.: Vanderbilt University Press, 1970.

Waller, William. *Nashville, 1900–1910.* Nashville, Tenn.: Vanderbilt University Press, 1972.

Walter, Benjamin. "Ethnicity and Racial Succession in Nashville, 1850–1920." In *Growing Metropolis: Aspects of Development in Nashville*, edited by James F. Blumstein and Benjamin Walter. Nashville, Tenn.: Vanderbilt University Press, 1975.

Index

(Note: Names of individual volunteers and members of the Nashville Civic Design Center staff, as they are listed in the section of The Plan of Nashville titled "Citizen Planners: Documenting the Process" are not included in the index; they can be found in the text, pages 230–31.)

Lisa Abell • John Abernathy • Angie Adams • Lisa Akbari • John Albert • Sam Albert • Joanne Alexander • Shatavia Alexander • David Allard • Jeffrie D. Allen • Jerry Allen • Robert G. Allen • Linda Anderson • Jane Andrews • Yin Aphinyana • Nerissa Aquino • Carol Ashworth • Garry Askew • Patrick Avice Du Buisson • Blythe Bailey • Clara Bailey • Cresa Bailey • David Bailey • Lindsey Bailey • David Baird • Mary Baker • Chris Barbour • Loretta Bard • Alice Ann Barge • Bill Barker • Joe Barker • Bill Barkley • Bill Barnes • Zach Barnes • Dorsey Barnett • Janice Barron • Peter B. Batarseh • Monte Batey • Stacy Dawn Battles • Jeff Baxter • Matt Baxter • John P. Beach • Fabian Bedne • Eileen Beehan • Jodie A. Bell • Paul E. Bell • Deb Belue • Mike Beneini • Rick Bernhardt • Gil Berry • Susan Besser • David Best • William Beucini • Eric Beyer • Shawn Bible • Scott Billingsby • Pete Bird • Glendyn Bishop • Cynthia Black • Tonya Blades • Brian Bobel • Craig Boerner • Lindsay Bohannon • Victoria Boone • Alexa Bosse • Peter Botarseh • Michelle Bowen • Paula Bowers-Hotvedt • Uuan Bowles • Hamilton Bowman • John Boyle • E. J. Boyson • Jane Braddock • Christine Bradley • Grace Brady • Alex Brandau • Ed Branding • Barry Brechak • Lara Brewton • John Bridges • Fenecia Briggane • David Briley • Greer Broemel • Kim Brooks • Anne Brown • Betty Brown • Robert Bruce • David Brush • Theodore Bryson • Bob Buchanan • J. Mark Buck • Victoria Buckner • John Calhoun • Isabel Call • Berdelle Campbell • Ernest Campbell • Steve Cardamone • Charlie Cardwell • Caroline Carlisle • Hannah Cassidy • Harriet Cates • Kevin Caudle • Jack Cawthon • Scott Chambers • Cynthia Chatman • Barbara Chazen • Robert Cheatham • Won Choi • Brian David Christens • Betsy Clapsaddle • Hal Clark • Henry Clark • Nancy Clements • Terry Clements • Janet Clough • Jon Coddington • Catherine Coke • Jeff Coker • Ed Cole • William Collins • Toby Compton • Mindy Conley • Heather Connelly • Sally Connelly • Rick Conner • David Coode • Dan Cooper • Michael Cooper • Scot Copeland • Mary Coplen • Don Corlew • M. Coston • Catherine Cove • Keith Covington • Christy Craig • Donna Crawford • Laurel Creech • Ben Crenshaw • Jeanette Crosswhite • David Currey • Elizabeth Dachowski • Cloee Daniel • Alma Dans • Jamie Dans • Tony Darsinos • Victor Davidson • Alma J. Davis • Betty D. Davis • Harold Davis • Janice Davis • Jonathan Davis • Julie Davis • Kirby Davis • Marleen Davis • Melissa A. Davis • T. K. Davis • Ray Dayal • Bernadette Deal • Sheila deBettencourt • Allen DeCuyper • Kristen Deitrick • Mark DeKay • Doug Delaney • Ann Deol • Kathryn Dettwiller • Mark Deutschmann • Sheila Dial • Ellen Dill • Jack Diller • Allison Dillon • Ruthie Diroff • Charlie Doggett • Marc Donovan • Jeremy Doochin • Sarah Dotterweich • Victor Douer • Michael Douglas • Tina Douglas • Colleen Dowd • Tyrone Dowell • Don Doyle • Adam Dread • Nick Dryden • Mary Dubose • Emma Duesterhaus • Anneita C. Dunbar • Sandra Duncan • Sharon Durham • R. Lane Easterly • Irma Ecksel • John Egerton • March Egerton • R. Eisler • Kaaren Hirschowitz Engel • Adam Epstein • Kysa Estes • Gary Everton • Lindsay Fairbanks • Sarah Farley • Margo Farnsworth • Jerry Fawcett • Russ Faxon • Bill Feehely • Buddy Ferguson • Whitney Ferre • Billy Fields • Jillian Fincher • Will Fischer • Gillian Fischbach • Irwin Fisher • Mike Fitts • Jack Fleischer • Gayle Fleming • Richard Fletcher • Judy Floyd • Mike Floyd • Rachel Fontenot • Tracey Ford • Ron Foresta • Dane Forlines • Fay Forlines • Leroy Forlines • Bettye Jeane Forrester • Vali Forrister • Shellie Fossick • Richard Allen Foster • George Fournier • Mitchell Fox • Debbie Frank • Rebecca Frary • Craig Freeman • Kathryn Fuller • Enoch Fuzz • Sunina Gaddipati • Andrea Gaffney • Sheila Gaffney • Chuck Gannaway • Lanie Gannon • Pedro Garcia • Pam Binkley Garrett • Gary Gaston • Sandra Gaston • Cooper Gee • Hunter Gee • Kara Gee • Adam Gelter • Tony Giarratana • Jason Gibson • Steve Gibson • Ellen Gilbert • Lelia Gilchrist • Casey D. Gill • Melvin Gill • Ben Gilliam • Leah Gilliam • Terri L. Givens • Ron Gobbell • Jeff Goff • Minnie Goodman • Christopher Goods • Curtis W. Goodwin • Brian Gordon • Daniel Gordon • Jane Gordon • Jayne Gordon • Meg Gordon • John Gore • Nancy Graham • Anetha Grant • Omar Greane • Deleda C. Green • J. Todd Greene • Lorraine Greene • Omari Greene • Rusti Greene • Ronnie Greer • Matt Gregg • Steven Greil • Batey Gresham • Sabrina Gresham • Chippey Grier • Debra Grimes • Tom Grooms • Grete Gryzwana • Maritza Gualy • Katie Guenther • Kevin Guenther • John Gupton • Johan Hagaman • Beth Haley • Audrey Hall • Nellie Carter Hall • Susan Hall • Lawrence Hall, Jr. • Mary Kay Hamel • Hope Hamilton • Deborah Hampton • Carrie Hanlin • Robert Hannon • Tom Hardin • Raven Cofer Hardison • Jamye Hardy • Frank Hargrove • David Harper • Thelma Harper • Elizabeth Harris • Robert Harrison • Tom Harvey • Tricia Hassenfeld • Jeanie Hastings • Jim Hastings • William Hastings • Doug Hausken • Ginger Hausser • Gary Hawkins • Keller Hawkins • Kim Hawkins • Parker Hawkins • Diane Hayes • Michael Haynes • Christina Heidel • Hank Helton • Ken Henley • Douglas Henry • Laura Henry • Shawn Henry • Ray Hensler • Cecil Herrell • Bob Hickman • Jason Hill • Jean H. Hill • Sharon Hill • Wade Hill • Edward S. Hill, Jr. • Kem Hinton • Mike Hodge • Joe Hodgson • Karen Holder • King M. Hollands • Nick Hollomon • Bartlomiej Hominski • Jim Hoobler • Meredith Hoos • Terry Horgan • John Horton • Teresa Horton • John Houghton • Joe P. Howard • Samuel H. Howard • Bill Howell • Matt Howlett • Geneva Howse • Rowland Huddleston • Brian Hudson • Keel Hunt • Brian Hunter • Sherri Hunter • Patrick Hurt • Randal Hutcheson • Andrea Hutchinson • Ismael Ismael • Bill Ivey • Mary Ivy • William Jackson • Beverly Jacobs • Lynette Jacobs • Mike Jameson • Kuba Janyst • Dorothy Jenkins • James Jenkins • Billy N. Jennings • Michal Jezierski • Ericke Johannes • Anne Laurence Johnson • Bobby J. Johnson • Carlyle Johnson • Christine Johnson • Jim Johnson • Linda Johnson • Patricia Johnson • Paul Johnson • Diana Jones • Greg Jones • Lee Jones • Mercedes Jones • Tonya Jones • Joyce Jordan • Ruchi Kapadia • Carol Kaplan • Marshall Karr • Bridget Jones Kelly • James Kennon • Anderson Kenny • Del Ketcham • Fred Kewt • Anna Ruth Kimbrough • Blaine Kimbrough • Michael King • Tim King • Don Kintner • D. T. Kiser • Mike Klamann • Don Klein • Genna Knab • Lydia Knab • Maggie Knab • David Knudtson • David Koellein • Bridgette Kohnhorst • Anna Kowalczuk • Margaret Krakowiak • Christine Kreyling • Michael Kreyling • Page Krugman • Walter Kulash • James Kunstler • Barbara Kurland • Fred Kurz • Lucy Kurz • Gordon Kutil • Chris Laidlaw • Katie Lamb • Julia Landstreet • Pat Lane • Margaret J. Lanius • Randall Lantz • Eddie Latimer • Ryan Latimer • Maggie Law • Jeff Lawrence